CHIPPEWA MUSIC

SMITHSONIAN INSTITUTION
BUREAU OF AMERICAN ETHNOLOGY
BULLETIN 45

CHIPPEWA MUSIC

BY

FRANCES DENSMORE

TWO VOLUMES IN ONE

Ross & Haines, Inc.
Minneapolis, Minnesota 55408
1973

Library of Congress No. 73-91925
ISBN O-87018-067-3

Originally printed
WASHINGTON
GOVERNMENT PRINTING OFFICE
1910 and 1913

INTRODUCTION for Frances Densmore's *Chippewa Music*

Two years prior to the publication of *Chippewa Music* (1910), William H. Holmes, then Chief of the Bureau of American Ethnology, announced in his Administrative Report that, "During the year [1907-1908] for the first time the study of native Indian music was seriously taken up by the Bureau (Holmes 1916:19)." His reference was to Frances Densmore's fieldwork among the Chippewa (Ojibwa), and particularly to her already "extensive" collection of recordings. He concluded by surmising that, "the investigation promises results of exceptional interest and scientific value."

The results of Densmore's study were subsequently published by the Bureau as two of its Bulletins: *Chippewa Music* (Bulletin 45) in 1910, and its companion volume, *Chippewa Music—II* (Bulletin 53), in 1913. The two volumes comprise a single work, which is a landmark in the study of American Indian music. Densmore's fieldwork produced what is still the largest collection of recorded music from a single North American tribe, and her study, based on the recordings, is one of the most comprehensive in the early literature of ethnomusicology.[1] Little has been published on Chippewa music since.

Holmes's description of Densmore's work as "serious" and "scientific" is significant. Music was one of the last facets of American Indian culture to be investigated in any depth by ethnographers (cultural anthropologists). One reason Indian music was so neglected prior to 1900 was that most ethnographers had found it unappealing. What little attention they did devote to the subject was limited to subjective reactions — mostly negative. Because such reports also contain musical terminology which is used imprecisely, they reflect the musical illiteracy of their authors and are of little value to us today. Furthermore, the most accurate, i.e., "scientific," means of collecting American Indian music for study was field recording equipment, which was not generally in use until about 1890.

The serious study of any body of music requires some permanent record of it for analysis, in either musical notation, or recordings, and preferably both. The American Indian lacked any written tradition for his music. Instead, he preserved his songs in his memory and transmitted them orally to succeeding generations. To study such "unwritten" music, the ethnographer had first to obtain some record of the music, permanent enough to permit repeated observation. This, as Densmore notes in her Foreward to *Chippewa Music* (1910), was only possible with recording equipment.[2]

Densmore's first assignment for the Bureau was on the White Earth Reservation (Minnesota) to study the music of the traditional Chippewa religious fraternity — the Grand Medicine Society, or Mide'wiwin. Apparently the Bureau desired a "scientific" follow-up to the researches of an earlier ethnographer, Walter J. Hoffman, who had done fieldwork from 1887-1889, also at White Earth. Hoffman and Garrick Mallery had travelled to northern Minnesota as pictographic specialists for the Bureau. Their main purpose was to investigate Henry R. Schoolcraft's earlier assertion (1851:116) that the Chippewa used color in their pictography. (Their suspicions to the contrary were confirmed.) Hoffman's research during this assignment led to his lengthy and important study of Grand Medicine, which the Bureau published in 1891.

Although Hoffman's monograph included transcriptions for 27 Grand Medicine songs, it is evident that he considered the music of the Society only peripheral to his study. Characterizing many of the nearly 300 songs he collected as little more than "monotonous repetition[s] of four or five notes in a minor key (1891:192)," Hoffman did not bother to include transcriptions for them in the published study.

Instead, he provided only their pictographs and texts.

Because his fieldwork antedated the earliest known recordings of Indian music, the songs which Hoffman did transcribe must have been taken down by ear. The 27 transcriptions in his monograph contain a number of notational inconsistencies and peculiarities which are suspect in light of what we know of Mide' music. Without recordings to verify them, their accuracy cannot be assumed. Twenty years later, Densmore, using recording equipment, was in a position to improve by scientific means on the musical aspects of Hoffman's study, as well as to preserve a song literature which would soon be extinct.

Her success at White Earth and the Bureau's support of her work encouraged Densmore to broaden her investigations and, ultimately, to publish her findings in the Bureau's Bulletins. The rather uneven format of her first few studies reflects Densmore's early methods of collecting Indian music and reporting on it. She submitted the results of her fieldwork to the Bureau each year in the form of preliminary reports. When a sufficient number of such reports had been compiled to warrant a publication, the Bureau Chief submitted the manuscripts together as a "paper," or "memoir," to the Secretary of the Smithsonian Institution, recommending that they be published as one of the Bulletins. This accounts for the format of *Chippewa Music:* rather than being a cohesive study of the music in a single volume, it is more a collection of separate and loosely related chapters, published in two installments and arranged in what appears to be an arbitrary fashion. However, the order of the chapters does reflect somewhat the chronology of Densmore's collecting.

Even before she had completed the manuscript of *Chippewa Music—II*, Densmore's fieldwork had increased so greatly that the study of one tribe's music began to overlap with the study of another's. One of her Chippewa singers, Mec'kawiga'bau, performed Sioux songs from the Drum-presentation Ceremony for her, and this prompted her to begin fieldwork in Sisseton, South Dakota, in 1911. In that year she submitted to the Bureau two papers on Chippewa music and one on the Sioux Sun Dance. Before *Chippewa Music—II* had gone to press, she had completed three additional studies on Sioux music, was preparing a fourth, and had begun fieldwork among the Mandan and Hidatsa at Ft. Berthold in North Dakota.

In collecting Chippewa music, Densmore faced a number of problems. The serious study of musical cultures outside of Western European art-music was only in its beginnings. There was little published material available to guide her in eliciting information from singers or in recording them. Furthermore, the Chippewa tribe is widely dispersed. It consists of a number of separate bands, each with its own history and customs. Densmore had therefore to study several musical styles and repertoires. At first she was unable to anticipate the kind of material she would find and had to rely on leads wherever she found them. The experience gained in preparing *Chippewa Music* (1910) facilitated collecting for the second volume. The discovery of the various song genres in the Chippewa repertoire for Bulletin 45 ennabled her to request similar material from singers for the completion of the study.

Although *Chippewa Music* includes transcriptions for only 363 songs, the study was based on about 500 songs Densmore collected from that tribe. Her goal had been a systematic analysis of that number of songs, according to Frederick W. Hodge, Ethnologist in Charge of the Bureau. Such a sizeable sample was, in his opinion, "a safe basis for what might be termed a scientific study of primitive song (Hodge 1918:20)."[3]

The nature of her recording equipment prevented Densmore from collecting songs within their usual context. It would have been impossible, for instance, to have recorded successfully during the course of a Grand Medicine initiation. The phonograph at that time was simply too heavy and bulky to be moved quickly from one part of the long medicine lodge to another as the ceremony progressed, or to be carried behind Mĭde'priests in their circuits of the lodge to collect their processional songs. Also, the machine demanded constant attention: it needed to be wound often to maintain an even tension on the springs; the cylinders had to be changed frequently, since they accommodated only a small amount of music; and the recording horn required proper positioning in front of the singer.

These circumstances meant that Densmore had to record in some improvised studio. Once the singer was seated in front of the phonograph, she could better follow some orderly recording procedures. To be systematic, she recorded the singer's name and the number of his song onto most of the cylinders. To play the cylinder back at the proper speed, she preceded the performance of most songs by sounding a C on the pitch pipe as part of the recording.

Studio conditions also permitted Densmore, through interpreters, to pose important questions to singers about their songs and to gain knowledge of their musical beliefs. The improvised studio also afforded the isolation necessary for the experiments she devised. For example, such privacy once allowed her to sing one of Maiñ'gans's songs back to him to see if it were "correct." (On this occasion Maiñ'gans stated that the melody was correct, but that Densmore lacked the "Indian throat" — the ability to produce pulsations on sustained tones distinctly, using only the muscles of the throat, but without the aid of syllables [Densmore 1953:213].) These experiments yielded invaluable information about traditional Chippewa attitudes toward music and its performance.

In the studio, too, Densmore could more easily exercise some control in the selection of songs by requesting specific material from a singer. Frequently, however, the singer simply followed his whims and performed songs at random. E'niwûb'e, for example, recorded in succession a Dream song, a Woman's Dance song, a Hand Game song, two Moccasin Game songs, a Deer Hunting song, two Buffalo songs, two Love songs, another Deer song, and so on. Such a variety of material meant that Densmore had to impose some order on the songs in preparing them for publication, and to restore what she understood to be their proper context in writing about them.

The material for *Chippewa Music* was organized in one of two ways. Because one purpose of Densmore's study was to determine whether there was some connection between the use of a song and its stylistic features, she classified the majority of songs according to reservation and grouped them by genre for analysis. Such classification necessarily disturbed the order in which singers had been recorded as well as their ordering of songs, but she was thus able to examine the general characteristics of each genre she collected and to compare, for example, the Chippewa War songs as a group to the Moccasin Game songs.

Densmore's other method of organizing her material produced a more engaging text for the reader. Wherever possible, she reconstructed a real-life context for the songs. She reported the chronology either of some event she had witnessed, such as the Fourth of July celebration at Red Lake in 1908 (1910:166-173), or of one which had been described to her, such as the Mĭde' Initiation Ceremony of th First Degree (1910:24-51).

To enrich the context of these reconstructions, Densmore included a wealth of ethnographic data, much of it collected from a large number of Chippewa on widely scattered reservations. Events in the lives of singers, histories of individual songs, descriptions of herbal preparations, photographs of religious ceremonies, and speeches delivered during their course — these all are interspersed between the song analyses and transcriptions. When she lacked firsthand knowledge, Densmore consulted authorities in many fields. Her text was documented with citations from William W. Warren's history of the Chippewa tribe (Warren 1957), or articles from the Bureau's *Annual Reports* and scholarly journals, such as the *American Anthropologist*. The birds and herbs mentioned in connection with the songs are identified by their proper Latin names, which she obtained from ornithologists and pharmacologists.

Many of the plates are unique in showing details of Chippewa costumes and artifacts that were used at the turn of the century. In an attempt to give an air of verisimilitude to her text, Densmore requested the singers to pose in costume for some of the plates. Thus we have the poignant portrait of Odjib'we, blind at the time, but in the posture of a scout searching for the enemy (1913:Plate 11); a picture of Ma'djigi'jig recounting his scalping adventures (1913:Plate 14); and one of A'kiwĕn'zi the former warrior, who donned his roach, skunkskin anklets, fur necklace, and war-paint to be photographed, but neglected to remove his starched white collar and necktie (1913:Plate 15). (Densmore's interest in the general ethnology of the tribe inspired her later publication, *Chippewa Customs*, Bulletin 86)

The recording of so many of the songs was Densmore's principal achievement as a student of Chippewa music. We are particularly indebted to her for collecting the *oldest* songs of the tribe, thereby rescuing them from certain oblivion. It is remarkable that she was able to record as much of the sacred repertoire as she did. The Chippewa singers were as reluctant as those of other tribes to give up their music to the white man's recording devices, despite assurances that their voices would be forever preserved "in the building in Washington that would not burn down." In recording the old songs, Densmore met the sort of problems faced by George Catlin a century earlier in painting Indians' portraits, and later by Edward S. Curtis, the photographer, in capturing their images on glass plates. The singer Main'gans was ostracized from the Mide' lodge for performing for non-members that Society's sacred songs, and his wife's death shortly after this happened was attributed to his disclosure of religious secrets (Densmore 1942:529). Odjib'we had a premonition of his own death following the recording of his dream song for Densmore, for he had given up "his most sacred possession (Densmore 1913:67)."

The field recordings — unique for their time in number, variety, and excellence of recording quality — are Densmore's greatest contribution. Despite her predecessors' detailed reports in all other matters concerning Chippewa ethnology, they lacked the actual sounds which accompanied the events they described. Densmore's recordings are a necessary complement to Hoffman's work on the Mide'wiwin (1891), and to Barrett's on the Drum Dance (1911).

Realizing the inadequacies of transcriptions and verbal descriptions of Indian songs, Densmore always stressed the importance of *hearing* the recordings she so laboriously collected, for to her mind, "nothing is lost so irrevocably as the sound of a song (1945:639)." To promote such listening, towards the end of her life she selected a number of her cylinders from many tribes for a series of recordings released by the Library of Congress. The first of the series, "Songs of the Chippewa" (Archives of American Folk Song L22 [1950]), is truly a representative sampling of 30 songs, sung by sixteen different singers from several localities, and includes examples of most genres she encountered. It is a convenient and essential adjunct to her two books on Chippewa music.[4]

In addition to its merits as a study of Indian culture, *Chippewa Music* reveals much about Frances Densmore herself. Here was a serious Western musician in a new role, facing new challenges. Although there had been other pioneers before her — Baker, Fletcher, Curtis and Burton, for example — Indian music was still a largely unexplored field. The inadvertent distortions in Densmore's work that stemmed from her Western bias show the difficulties she faced in comprehending and evaluating a totally foreign musical culture.

Densmore's training and early musical activities had been confined to the art-music tradition of Western Europe and had included the study of harmony at the Oberlin Conservatory (1884-1886), piano in Boston and counterpoint at Harvard (1889-1890). The education had been, in her words, "Spartan in its severity."

Before becoming committed to Indian music, she had lectured on the operas of Richard Wagner, published an article on the childhood of Felix Mendelssohn (Densmore 1901), and served as church organist and music teacher in the small town of Red Wing in southern Minnesota, her lifelong home. The turn to the music of Native Americans marked a significant change in Densmore's career, demanding a virtually new musical education.

Her first exposure to Indian music was as a child, when she could hear the nighttime sounds of a dance from a Sioux camp near Red Wing. This early "call of the Indian drum," she later reflected, had predestined her to study Indian music: "I have heard it in strange places, in the dawn and at midnight, with its mysterious throb (Hoffman 1968:1)."

Stimulated in 1893 by reading Alice C. Fletcher's reports on Omaha music, and through personal acquaintance with John C. Fillmore, who had transcribed and analyzed the music for Fletcher's book, Densmore, then 26 years old, began the study of Indian music seriously. With Fletcher's permission and encouragement, in 1895 she added Omaha music to her lecture topics, accompanying the songs on the piano. Shortly thereafter, Native American percussion instruments served in place of the piano to accompany her lecture-demonstrations of the songs.

Collecting on her own began in about 1901, when, for the first time, she took down by ear an Indian melody from a Sioux woman near Red Wing. Three years later, she wrote down a melody which the famous Apache warrior Geronimo was humming as he whittled arrows. (Geronimo, who was on exhibition at the St. Louis Exposition, had balked at Densmore's earlier request for him to sing, so she simply "slipped into ambush behind him" to collect the song.) The first Chippewa music she wrote down was in 1905, when Little Spruce, upon request, performed a Grand Medicine song near Grand Portage, Minnesota.

These early, sporadic exposures to Indian music failed to divest Densmore of the idea that, however fascinating it might be, the music of the Indian was still an art in its infancy. The first of many articles she published on the subject (Densmore 1905) reveals a strongly ethnocentric bias. There are, for instance, numerous references to the childlike aspects of Indian song and dance. Relegating these arts to the levels of development typical of white children, Densmore implies they have a long way to progress: the songs contain few words, "like the broken sentences of a little child;" Indian dancing, she thinks, resembles the attempts of a white three-year-old; and the scalp dance she likens to a "ring-around-a-rosy."

By 1910, however, such depreciatory views had been abandoned. Through fieldwork in preparation for the writing of *Chippewa Music,* Densmore clearly had gained a new respect for the complexities of Indian music. The first volume of her study reveals an enlightened Densmore, one who had discovered that the musical culture of the Chippewa was far from "primitive" or "childlike." The songs contained unusual metrical patterns and revealed underlying isorhythmic structures (her "rhythmic units"). Western notation was found to be quite inadequate for representing the Indian's tonal nuances, so she adopted "special signs" for the transcriptions (see 1910:xix, 5-6, for the signs and her explanation of their use). Because there was still much to be learned about the music, the system of song classification devised for *Chippewa Music,* she warned, "must be recognized as broad in outline and somewhat tentative."

Despite her new insight and avowed effort to approach Indian music without a Western cultural bias, Densmore falters in several respects. Many of the ideas expressed in *Chippewa Music* are clearly ethnocentric and simply untenable. For example, she states that, "the interest of a Chippewa song frequently diminishes as the song proceeds, and in some instances the closing measures contain characterless phrases, repeated indefinitely (1913:8)." Here she probably refers to the final phrases in Chippewa songs, which tend to "flatten out," i.e., as the melody descends, near its end the intervals become smaller, until the final tone is sustained or repeated a number of times. In describing this decrease in melodic motion as "characterless," Densmore is applying Western musical standards. From the Indian's standpoint, these final phrases may have just as much character and interest as phrases containing more tonal motion. In fact, even by Western standards, the Chippewa performance of sustained tones in final phrases is usually quite subtle in its rhythmic organization. (Such subtlety may have escaped Densmore, as it is missing from her transcriptions.)

Two aspects of Densmore's song analyses in particular illustrate her difficulty in divorcing herself completely from 19th century Western music. First, there is the determination to find programmatic content in Indian music. One of the most important precepts during Densmore's early training was that music is capable of expressing thoughts and feelings — either explicitly, through such devices as word painting, or implicitly, through such means as Berlioz's *idée fixe,* or the *leitmotif,* as used by Wagner or Richard Strauss.

Densmore admonishes the reader to disassociate Indian music from Western music. She tells us that, in Chippewa music, "a correspondence between the idea of a song and its melody or its rhythm cannot be taken too literally or pushed too far (1910:131)." Nevertheless, her own approach to the music is characterized by a constant search for some relationship between the text of an Indian song and its musical setting. The possibility that music for the Indian might simply be an indifferent carrier of the words probably did not occur to her. Throughout *Chippewa Music,* whenever even the vaguest programmatic content in a song suggests itself, she draws attention to it in her analysis. Where a specific example, such as word painting, cannot be cited, she implies that the character or mood of the song somehow reflects the meaning of the text.

In some instances the analyses resemble brief program notes, describing the songs almost as though they were miniature Symphonic Poems. For example, the melody of Niski'gwûn's "Song of Help in the Fight (1913:112)" is not particularly inspiring in Densmore's opinion. But, she finds, "there is something in it deeper and stronger than enthusiasm; there are steadiness and control. Strongest of all is the idea of the words — the picture of the prairie, calm in its consciousness of power (1913:113)."

Consistent with this programmatic approach is Densmore's belief that Indian songs contain incipient word painting, specifically, songs whose texts convey the idea of movement. In the continuous outlining of the single minor seventh chord at the beginning of "As the Hawk Soars (1910:130)," she sees an expression of "the close attention with which one follows moving objects." The rhythm of the Song of Thanks for a Pony (1910:202) suggests, "though somewhat remotely, the galloping of an Indian pony." The descending seventh appears frequently in songs of pursuit; in a Menominee hunting song, possibly the descent is meant to suggest "the shooting and fall of the deer (1932:64)."

Densmore became convinced that rhythm, above all, expresses the meaning of a song text. For instance, one of Odjib'we's song texts (1913:117) she finds divided between two contrasting musical settings within one song. Each setting appropriately expresses its portion of the text: the irregular rhythms of the first part of the song show "the effect of perturbation" (the singer's text: "alas, I cannot travel"); the more regular rhythms of the second part of the song parallel his resolution of the dilemma ("but I will borrow that by means of which I can arrive"). In Henry Selkirk's "I Am Afraid of the Owl (1910:135)," which he had composed as a child, Densmore perceives the principal rhythmic unit, a quarter-note followed by two 8th-notes (   ), as "a subdivision of a double measure which suggests fear." Later, she even assigned a title to this rhythmic motif — "Rhythm of Childish Fear (1920:63)."

Where contrasting rhythms are used for texts of similar content, Densmore simply ignores the inconsistency. In discussing two "derisive" songs (1913:120), she reads the same emotion into near opposites. One of these songs describes the cowardice of a man who had refused to join a war-party. Here the derision is said to be "subtle and tantalizing and the rhythmic swing is long, without a clearly defined unit." In the other song, in which the singer wonders if the Sioux woman whom he has decapitated feels herself humiliated, "the derisive idea is more direct, the taunting more keen, finding expression in a short, crisp rhythm."

A second significant influence of 19th century thought lies in Densmore's belief that the Indian had an innate sense of harmony. This view reflects a cultural misconception which was prevalent in her early years and unfortunately has persisted somewhat to the present time.

One non-scientific outgrowth of Darwinian theory was the widely-held belief that the arts in Western Europe had evolved, in logical fashion, to their highest cultural levels. The arts in more "primitive" societies were thought to have reached various stages of lower development in the evolutionary scheme. Eventually, they too would pursue the same course as Western culture and attain the same results.

The elaborate system of Western tonal harmony, based on the diatonic scale, was pointed to as one manifestation of the high level achieved by Western art-music. Upon first exposure to the music of the American Indians, many non-Indians were disturbed by the complete absence of harmony and mistook it as an indication of the "primitive" level of Indian musical culture. Often, the Western musician "set" the Indian melodies, using traditional Western chords, and then played them back on a piano or reed-organ to the Indians for their reactions. Fletcher played harmonizations of their melodies for the Omaha in this way, as did Frederick Burton for the Eastern Ojibwa. Their reports describe the Indians as pleased with the improved versions of their songs (see Fletcher 1911:375, 387 and Burton 1909:119).

Densmore's early lectures on Indian music reflect Fillmore's belief that tonal harmony, being universal, was latent in Native American music. She speaks of Fletcher's experiments with confidence: "[The Omaha] knew absolutely nothing about harmony, they had never made an attempt to produce it, but when they heard it they recognized it at once (Hofmann 1968:4)." Furthermore, the Indian could distinguish between "proper" and "faulty" harmony: "the chords which satisfied them were usually chords we would call musically correct." That she believes all races to share the same musical impulses is illustrated by her assertion that, "the Navajo Indian howls his song to the war god on the chord of C major, and Beethoven makes the first theme of his Eroica Symphony of precisely the same [sic] material." (Beethoven's Third Symphony, as well as its first theme, are in E-flat major, not C major.)

The harmonic approach to *Chippewa Music* is evident in several aspects of Densmore's analyses. Melodies are designated as "harmonic" in structure if their accented tones outline Western triads, seventh chords, or their inversions. The melodic tones of some songs are arranged vertically into chords and then bracketed to imply harmonic relationships (e.g., see her analysis of Song No. 125 [1910:140]).

Densmore's harmonic interest leads her to investigate what she terms "the psychology of Indian song" — i.e., the relationship between a song's content (meaning) and its "tonality." Believing that "tonality" exists in Chippewa music, Densmore tries to demonstrate how it functions in fixed relationships between emotions and their musical expression. Three examples will illustrate the point:

First, the minor tonality for Densmore expresses, among other things, uncertainty. Since two-thirds of the Moccasin Game songs are found to be in this tonality, the minor may reflect the "uncertainty" of the game's outcome.

Second, in "As the Hawk Soars (1910:130)," Densmore finds that the minor chord, outlined in the melody, may somehow "resolve" by moving to a major triad on the tonic, and thus the music parallels the imagery suggested by the text. After the singer has spent some time observing the hawk in the sky (the first 17 measures of her transcription), he arrives at a "satisfying resultant chord [the major triad on the tonic]." The arrival at this chord and "the free melody with its even rhythm suggests the return of the singer's attention to his song and to his more immediate surroundings."

Third, change in tonality, as Densmore perceives it in a Divorce Song (1913:162), may reflect a change in emotions (presumably she means that one married partner desires to break off the relationship).

Densmore's beliefs to the contrary, all Chippewa music is purely melodic and has no basis in tonal harmony whatsoever. Therefore her application of Western aesthetics to the music is inappropriate, and her interpretations of the songs' meanings must remain purely speculative.

Although *Chippewa Music* contains much useful information, the reader should be forewarned about certain aspects of Densmore's transcriptions and some of the ethnographic details included in the study. *All* transcriptions of Indian music must be approached with caution, for they are at best only skeletal representations of musical performances. No matter how detailed a transcription may be, it can never capture totally every dimension of the music it seeks to describe. Densmore's transcriptions give only the most general account of the songs. Furthermore, because they contain errors and omissions, their accuracy cannot be accepted at face value.

The serious student of Indian music should consult the Library of Congress recordings to determine for himself to what degree Densmore's transcriptions are useful. When compared with the actual performances on the cylinders, the transcriptions reveal that Densmore omits such salient features of Chippewa vocal style as attack tones and portamentos. Also, her notation is frequently a vastly oversimplified version of the performance. For example, many Chippewa singers Densmore recorded and most of them today conclude each melodic phrase by sustaining its final tone for two or three beats. In doing so, they almost invariably subdivide this sustained tone into syncopated patterns, using one of a number of standard rhythmic/vocable formulae. Densmore's transcriptions often disguise the rhythmic complexity of these formulae by representing the patterns simply with a half-note or dotted half-note. Thus the recordings reveal that her half-note (♩) in reality is usually performed as follows: ♫♩ ♫♩

Because Densmore's tabulated analyses are based on her transcriptions, they must also be carefully assessed. The transcriptions are often inaccurate in showing the melodic range, or compass, of a song. Chippewa songs are noted for some of the widest ranges in all of American Indian music, and frequently the range of a song exceeds the limits of the singer's natural voice. As the melody descends beyond his lower limit, the singer often finds it difficult to perform the final phrases with much volume at all. Today's playback equipment reveals some of the songs to contain low tones in their final phrases which must have been simply inaudible to Densmore, as they are missing from her transcriptions. Odjib'we's performance of The Song of De'kûm (1913:121), according to Densmore's transcription, has low C as the final note, giving the melody the range of a 10th. In the final phrase, however, Odjib'we descends a minor third below C to A, albeit nearly inaudibly on the cylinder recording. Thus the correct range of the song is a 12th, and its misrepresentation as a 10th negates the accuracy of the figures in several of Densmore's tables.

The reader should also take into account the size of Densmore's sample in relation to the tabulated percentage figures. Table 15, for instance, shows that 53% of the Mide'songs begin on the unaccented part of a measure. However, when this figure was computed, nearly half of the Mide'sample was excluded — the 42 songs which were "transcribed in outline." (Densmore came to realize the insignificance of many of the tables in *Chippewa Music* and gradually reduced their number in later monographs.)

Many of the transcriptional omissions and errors can be attributed to the recording equipment available in Densmore's early years of collecting. In fairness, it should be pointed out that she recognized the limitations such equipment imposed on the study of Indian music and looked forward to improved methods to facilitate collecting and transcribing (Densmore 1945:637).5

The fragility of wax cylinders was a problem for every collector in the field. Some of Densmore's cylinders appear to have been damaged in transit before the recordings could be transcribed. The poor quality of sound reproduction on others precludes accurate transcriptions of the music; the near inaudibility of the songs of Deda'bica' and Gegwe'djiwe'binûñ, probably accounts for Densmore's providing only their texts. To prevent further damage and deterioration to the cylinders, and to permit their duplication for research, the recordings were ultimately moved to the Library of Congress and transferred to acetate discs.

The translations for the song texts in *Chippewa Music* are generally good, when compared with those given by Hoffman or the literary versions given by Schoolcraft. They were provided by a number of bilingual interpreters, often in consultation with each other to give Densmore the closest English equivalents of the Chippewa. However, in their published form, the vertical alignment of the English opposite the Chippewa can be misleading, since the translation is occasionally out of sequence with the original. (Compare, for instance, the correct ordering of the translation for Song No. 31 with the incorrect ordering for Song No. 30 [1910:65].)

Some of the plates appear to have been reversed in the printing; as a result, they suggest practices exactly the opposite of what was photographed. Plate 6 (1910) shows Maiñ'gans holding the rattle in his right hand, while Densmore's text describes it to be in his left hand. In Plate 44 (1913), while some of the war-dancers appear to dance in place facing the drum, the majority circle the drum in a *counter*clockwise direction, which is the reverse of the customary practice. (See Plate 12[1910] for the standard clockwise direction.)

Occasionally it is also unclear whether Densmore presents the Chippewa interpretation or her own. A case in point is the explanation for the pictograph of "Chief Woman (1910:17)." Here the singer has drawn a figure with a line leading from her neck to a circle on her breast, which line Densmore identifies as a pearl necklace holding a locket. Wherever else this symbol is used in Chippewa pictography, it commonly represents the heart (cf., the pictographs for Songs No. 36, 59, 71, 72, 73, 103 in [1910]; also, Hoffman 1891:222).

Despite its minor limitations, *Chippewa Music* can serve as an excellent introduction to Native American music. This is what Densmore would wish, for her intention was always that her work would stimulate further study. That desire is clear in the typically modest statement concluding her summary of nearly 50 years involvement with Indian music: "throughout this study the objective has been to record the structure of the Indian songs under observation, with my interpretation. Other students, scanning the material, may reach other conclusions. My work has been to preserve the past, record observations in the present, and open the way for the work of others in the future (Densmore 1942:550)."

Today, 60 years after the completion of Densmore's study, Chippewa music is still very much alive. Although acculturation has had drastic effects on all other areas of tribal life, the music has remained relatively intact. What changes have occurred reflect the effects of acculturation in general: as the number of Chippewa who speak their own language has diminished, so has the proportion of texted songs. As the traditional source of spiritual power — the boy's vision quest — was abandonned, so vanished most of the dream songs.

Many of the song genres which Densmore recorded are nearly extinct or have disappeared entirely. Pipe Dance songs and Begging Dance songs are now part of the historical past. Love songs are remembered by only a handful of the oldest generation. Moccasin Game songs, once considered sacred, had already become secular at the time Densmore collected them. When the Government prohibited gambling on some Chippewa reservations in the early 1920s, the action hastened the game songs decline. By mid-century the songs had been forgotten, although a drum still accompanied the game in the few places where it was played.

Despite such changes, the substance of Chippewa music has not been radically affected and continues to be virtually uninfluenced by Western music. Singers use many of the same vocal techniques, tonal patterns, and song forms that one hears on Densmore's cylinders, and they still observe the distinction between the drum-beat patterns for the War Dance songs and the Woman's Dance songs. The melodies of many songs in *Chippewa Music* have survived in variant versions.

Chippewa song and dance today serve as focal points of renewed pride in the tribe's cultural heritage. More members of the tribe, particularly from the younger generations, each year attend the annual summer powwows at Red Lake and Leech Lake. On those reservations where songs had been forgotten, tribal councils now bring in singers from other Chippewa communities to stimulate a renaissance of their former musical tradition.

The future of Chippewa music as a stylistic identity is uncertain. Distinctions between tribal styles are increasingly blurred, due primarily to increased mobility and the advent of inexpensive recording equipment. The "powwow circuit" each summer takes Chippewa singers by car to the celebrations of the Winnebago, Sioux, and Sauk and Fox. There, in addition to performing, they collect songs from the other tribal groups, using cassette tape recorders. The tapes are brought home and the new songs learned and taught to others. As tribal repertoires merge in this way, Chippewa music may lose some of its former identity. But it is certain that the sound of the drum which prompted Frances Densmore's career will long be heard "in the land of pine trees, lakes and hills."

LaPointe, Wisconsin   Thomas Vennum, Jr.
August, 1973

Acknowledgement: I wish to express my gratitude to William Bineshi Baker, Sr., of Lac Court Oreilles Reservation, Wisconsin, who first introduced me to the music of his people. Bineshi's songs most certainly would have been found among Densmore's pages, had her study been carried out a generation later and included his reservation.

NOTES

1. Ethnomusicology is that branch of musical research devoted to the study of tribal, folk, and popular music. It is distinguished from musicology, which restricts its investigations to the art-music tradition of Western Europe. Because much of ethnomusicological research involves studying a music in its cultural context, the approach of this discipline is often anthropological as well as musical. To the reader wishing to pursue the subject, I would recommend two books: Curt Sachs, *The Wellsprings of Music* (1961), ed. Jaap Kunst (the 1965 paperback edition was published by McGraw-Hill, Inc., New York); and *Readings in Ethnomusicology* (1971), ed. David P. McAllester (published by Johnson Reprint Corporation, New York).

2. A few early collectors of Indian music — Natalie Curtis in particular — possessed such extraordinary ears for the music that they could take down accurately by dictation the melodies they heard in the field without resorting to recordings of them. Most ethnographers, however, were not so gifted.

3. Densmore's "List of Songs" in *Chippewa Music—II* indicates that she assigned catalogue numbers to at least 469 songs collected from the Chippewa. Many of her cylinders, however, contain more than one song, and in those instances some of the additional songs appear not to have been catalogued. Because many of her original cylinders are missing from the Library of Congress collection, the exact number of Chippewa songs she collected is unknown.

4. The long-playing recording (AAFS L22), including Densmore's descriptive pamphlet on the music, may be ordered only through the Recorded Sound Section, Music Division, Library of Congress, Washington, D.C. 20540. (A check or money order for $4.95 should be made payable to the Music Division, Library of Congress.) The listener who wishes to follow Densmore's notations of the music may find convenient the following collation of the album's selections with her transcriptions for each song:

A 1 1913:271	A11 1913:287	B 7 1910:103
A 2 1913:256	A12 1913:285 (top)	B 8 1910:97
A 3 1913:260 (top)	A13 1910:158 (bottom)	B 9 1913:298
A 4 1910:127	A14 1913:291	B10 1913:218
A 5 1910:129	B 1 1913:264	B11 1913:293
A 6 1910:128	B 2 1910:122	B12 1913:220 (bottom)
A 7 1910:143	B 3 1913:262	B13 1913:300
A 8 1910:144	B 4 1910:30	B14 1910:149 (top)
A 9 1913:192 (top)	B 5 1910:31	B15 1910:149 (bottom)
A10 1913:191	B 6 1910:43	B16 1910:183 (bottom)

5. Densmore began her recording in 1907 with an Edison Home phonograph ("the best recording equipment available at that time"), which the Bureau replaced in 1908 with a Columbia graphophone. Although during her lifetime she experimented with a variety of recording devices, including the dictaphone and aluminum disc recorder, she was never willing to give up completely the cylinder machine and used it as late as 1940, when she recorded Zuñi songs.

REFERENCES CITED AND SUGGESTED FURTHER READING

Baker, Theodore
1882   Über die Musik der nordamerikanischen Wilden. Leipzig: Breitkopf und Härtel.
Baraga, Frederic
1966   A dictionary of the Otchipwe language [2nd ed. (1878-80)]. Minneapolis: Ross and Haines.
Barrett, Samuel A.
1911   "The dream dance of the Chippewa and Menominee Indians of northern Wisconsin," *Bulletin of the Public Museum of the City of Milwaukee*, i, 251-406.
Burton, Frederick R.
1909   American primitive music with special attention to the songs of the Ojibways. New York: Moffat, Yard and Company.
Curtis, Natalie
1968   The Indians' book [2nd ed. (1923)]. New York: Dover Publications, Inc.
Densmore, Frances
1901   "The boyhood of Mendelssohn," *Musician*, vi, 197.
1905   "The music of the American Indians." *Overland Monthly*, xlv, 230-234.
1910   Chippewa music. Washington: U.S. Government Printing Office, (Smithsonian Institution, Bureau of American Ethnology [hereinafter: BAE], Bulletin 45).
1913   Chippewa music—II. (BAE, Bulletin 53).
1918   Teton Sioux music. (BAE, Bulletin 61).
1920   "The rhythm of Sioux and Chippewa music," *Art and Archaeology*, ix, 59-67.
1932   Menominee music. (BAE, Bulletin 102).
1942   "The study of Indian music," *in* Annual Report of the Smithsonian Institution for the Year Ended June 30, 1941.
1945   "The importance of recordings of Indian songs," *American Anthropologist*, xlvii, 637-639.
1953   "Technique in the music of the American Indians," *Anthropological papers. No. 37*, (BAE, Bulletin 151), 211-216.
1970   Chippewa customs [1929]. Minneapolis: Ross and Haines, (BAE, Bulletin 86).
Fletcher, Alice C., and La Flesche, Francis
1893   A study of Omaha Indian music. Cambridge, Mass.: Peabody Museum, Harvard University, (Archaeological and Ethnological Papers, I/5).
1911   "The Omaha tribe," *in* Twenty-Seventh Annual Report of the BAE (1905-1906).
Hickerson, Harold
1970   The Chippewa and their neighbors: a study in ethno-history. New York: Holt, Rinehart and Winston, Inc.
Hodge, Frederick W.
1918   "Administrative report," *in* Thirty-First Annual Report of the BAE (1909-1910).
Hoffman, Walter J.
1891   "The Midéwiwin; or, 'Grand Medicine Society' of the Ojibwa Indians," *in* Seventh Annual Report of the BAE (1885-1886).
Hofmann, Charles, ed.
1968   Frances Densmore and American Indian music: a memorial volume. New York: Museum of the American Indian, Heye Foundation.
Holmes, William H.
1916   "Administrative report," *in* Twenty-Ninth Annual Report of the BAE (1907-1908).
Landes, Ruth
1968   Ojibwa religion and the Midéwiwin. Madison: University of Wisconsin Press.
Schoolcraft, Henry R.
1851   Information respecting the history, condition and prospects of the Indian tribes of the United States. Volume I. Philadelphia: Lippincott, Grambo.
Warren, William W.
1957   History of the Ojibway nation [1885]. Minneapolis: Ross and Haines.

LETTER OF TRANSMITTAL

SMITHSONIAN INSTITUTION,
BUREAU OF AMERICAN ETHNOLOGY,
Washington, D. C., July 8, 1909.

SIR: For the greater part of the last two years Miss Frances Densmore has been engaged, under the auspices of this Bureau, in making a study of Indian music. The results of her labors are embodied in part in the paper which I have the honor to present herewith—"Chippewa Music." I suggest the publication of this material as Bulletin 45 of the Bureau's series.

Yours very respectfully,

(Signed)   W. H. HOLMES, *Chief.*

The SECRETARY OF THE SMITHSONIAN INSTITUTION,
Washington, D. C.

FOREWORD

The purpose of the present work is to determine what constitutes the music of the Chippewa Indians, and to record results in such a manner that they will be available for reference. By means of the phonograph it is possible to obtain an accurate record of Indian song, which, though permanent, is of necessity limited in scope. To the phonograph record and its analysis must therefore be added abundant field notes, giving the results of observations of the musical performances, together with descriptions of circumstances and surroundings. These three—phonograph record, analysis, and field notes—are the necessary data of this branch of research.

The study of Indian music is more than the collection of Indian songs. It includes a consideration of the vocal expression of a mental concept; therefore incorrect repetitions of a song are as significant as correct repetitions. Into their value enters a human element—the personality of the singer. A person of musical gifts and proficiency frequently presents a rendition of a song which contains embellishments. These reveal the succession of tones especially pleasing to the native singer. A person of little musical talent presents an imperfect rendition of a song, yet these imperfections are interesting. They indicate which phase of the song was most difficult for him to acquire and remember, the melody or the rhythm.

The analysis of the Chippewa songs from the land of pine trees, lakes, and hills, in northern Minnesota, shows that in them the descending interval of the minor third occurs with special prominence and frequency; that the majority of the songs begin with a downward progression; and that the intervals of melodic progression are smaller in the older songs. A classification of the songs as melodic and harmonic reveals a possibility that the mental concept of the song has a direct bearing on the form assumed by the melody. The songs said to have been composed during dreams may be considered a spontaneous expression. The majority of these songs are harmonic in structure. The songs whose character and use suggest that their form may have been modified by long repetition are found to be principally melodic in structure.

The value of any specific work lies in the relation of that work to the problems presented by the subject as a whole. Beyond the study of Indian music lies the larger field of research, the development of music, to which the present work is tributary.

RED WING, MINN.

CONTENTS

ILLUSTRATIONS

LIST OF SONGS

1. Arranged in Order of Serial Numbers

Mide' Songs

[a] See footnote, p. 27.

Additional Mídeʹ Songs

SOCIAL SONGS ON WHITE EARTH AND LEECH LAKE RESERVATIONS

Inaʹbúndjĭgañ naʹgúmoʹwĭn (Dream Songs)

Migaʹdiwĭnʹinaʹgûmoʹwĭn (War Songs)

2. ARRANGED IN ORDER OF CATALOGUE NUMBERS

Catalogue no.	Name of singer.	Description of song.	Title of song.	Serial no.	Page no.
1	Gegwe'djiwe'bĭnûñ'	Mĭde'.	"There are spirits"	94	111
2	....do	..do	"They think me unworthy"	95	111
3	....do	..do	"The water birds will alight"	96	111
4	....do	..do	"The sky clears"	97	112
5	....do	..do	"I walk in a circle"	98	112
6	Deda'bicac'.	..do	"Our dwelling is royal"	99	113
7	....do	..do	"Vermilion, I sing of thee"	100	113
8	....do	..do	"There stands a man"	101	113
9	....do	..do	"I stand"	102	113
10	Ge'miwûnac'	..do	"I am named"	103	114
11	....do	..do	"I am unable to harmonize my voice."	104	114
12	....do	..do	"They are feasting with me"	105	114
13	....do	..do	"The sound is fading away"	106	115
15	....do	..do		107	115
16	Na'jobi'tûñ	..do		25	63
17	....do	..do		26	64

Catalogue no.	Name of singer.	Description of song.	Title of song.	Serial no.	Page no.
74	Na'waji'bigo'kwe	Mide'	(b)	72	90
75	....do	....do	(c)	73	90
76	....do	....do	(d)	74	90
78	Mi'jakiya'cĭg	....do	Healing song	77	93
79	....do	....do	Healing song	78	93
86	Cagan'asi	Woman's-dance song	"Where are you?"	185	196
91	....do	Unclassified (a)	Song of thanks for a pony	151	164
92	....do	....do. (b)		152	164
93	....do	....do. (c)		153	165
98	Manido'gicĭgo'kwe	Love song	(No words)	133	148
99	....do	....do	....do	134	149
101	Mrs. English	....do	"My love has departed"	135	150
102	Mrs. Mee	Unclassified (Lullaby)	(No words)	149	163
103	....do	....do	Farewell to the warriors	150	163
104	....do	Love song	"Why should I be jealous?"	136	151
105	Ki'tcĭmak'wa	Unclassified	Call to the dance	146	161
106	....do	Love song	"I do not care for you any more"	137	152
107	....do	....do	"Do not weep"	138	152
108	Ki'ose'wini'ni	Dream song	Duplicate of no. 115 (catalogue no. 209).	198	208
109	....do	Unclassified	"I am as brave as other men"	147	162
110	....do	Love song	"He must be sorrowful"	139	153
112	Maiñ'äns	Moccasin-game song	(No words)	142	157
114	A'gwitû'wigi'cĭg	War song	"The shifting clouds"	131	145
116	Gi'cibäns'	....do	Scalp dance	132	146
122	De'bwawĕn'dûnk	Mide'	First song	16	56
123	....do	....do	Second song	17	57
124	....do	....do	Third song	18	58
125	....do	....do	Fourth song	19	59
126	....do	....do	Fifth song	20	60
127	....do	....do	Sixth song	21	60
128	....do	....do	Seventh song	22	61
129	....do	....do	Eighth song	23	61
130	....do	....do	Ninth song	24	62
131	Gi'wita'binĕs	War song	(No words)	154	176
132	....do	Woman's-dance song	"I have been waiting"	177	192
133	....do	Moccasin-game song	(No words)	168	186
134	....do	....do	"He gave us a double crack"	175	189
135	....do	Woman's-dance song	(No words)	179	193
136	....do	Unclassified	Song of thanks for a pony (no words).	191	202
137	....do	Duplicate	Repetition of no. 115 (catalogue no. 92).	199	209
138	....do	Unclassified	Song referring to a vision	196	205
139	....do	....do	Song referring to an historical incident.	186	198
140	....do	War song	"Inside the cave"	155	177
141	....do	Woman's-dance song	(No words)	180	194
142	....do	Moccasin-game song	....do	169	187
143	....do	....do	"I am standing till daylight"	176	190
144	....do	....do	(No words)	170	187
145	....do	Duplicate (Love song)	Repetition of no. 138 (catalogue no. 107).	200	209
146	....do	Scalp song	(No words)	159	178
147	....do	....do	....do	160	179

Cata- logue no.	Name of singer.	Description of song.	Title of song.	Serial no.	Page no.
148	Gi'wita'binĕs..........	Moccasin-game song....	(No words)................	171	188
149	William Prentiss......	Song of the begging dance.	....do............	187	199
150	.....do................	Moccasin-game song....	....do............	174	189
151	Gage'bĭnĕs...........	Love song.............	"I am going away"........	166	183
152	.....do..............	.....do............	"Come, let us drink"........	167	184
153	.....do..............	Woman's-dance song....	(No words)...........	181	194
154	.....do..............	.....do............	....do............	182	195
155	.....do..............	Love song............	....do............	164	182
157	.....do..............	.....do............	"In her canoe"............	165	183
159	John Mark...........	Woman's-dance song....	(No words)...........	183	195
160	Wabezic'............	Unclassified..........	Friendly song (a) (no words).....	192	202
161	.....do..............	Love song............	(No words)...........	163	182
162	.....do..............	Unclassified..........	Friendly song (b) (no words).....	193	203
163	.....do..............	.....do............	Friendly song (c) (no words).....	194	204
164	.....do..............	.....do............	Friendly song (d) (no words).....	195	204
166	.....do..............	War song.............	"The sky replies"........	162	180
167	.....do..............	.....do............	Scalp song	161	179
168	.....do..............	Unclassified..........	Song of thanks for a gift (no words).	189	201
169	.....do..............	.....do............	(No words)...........	190	201
170	.....do..............	.....do............	Song of the begging dance (no words).	188	200
171	.....do..............	Moccasin-game song....	(No words)...........	172	188
172	Gi'nawigi'cĭg........	War song.............	....do............	156	177
173	.....do..............	.....do............	....do............	157	178
174	.....do..............	Moccasin-game song....	....do............	173	188
175	.....do..............	Woman's-dance song....	"Come, dance"........	178	193
177	.....do..............	.....do............	(No words)...........	184	195
178	.....do..............	War song.............	....do............	158	178
179	Aki'waizi'...........	.....do............	....do............	122	138
181	.....do..............	Moccasin-game song....	....do............	143	158
182	Maiñ'ăns...........	War song.............	....do............	123	138
189	O'dĕni'gûn.........	Mĭde'...............	Song of the four bears............	1	27
190	.....do..............	....do........	Preparatory song............	4	32
191	.....do..............	....do........	Song of the flying feather........	81	97
192	.....do..............	....do........	Song of the man who succeeded...	32	98
193	.....do..............	....do........	Song of a scalp dance...........	83	99
194	.....do..............	....do........	Song of good medicine..........	84	100
195	.....do..............	....do........	Song of the crab medicine-bag....	85	102
197	.....do..............	....do........	Song of the fire-charm.........	86	103
199	.....do..............	....do........	Song of starvation.............	87	104
200	.....do..............	....do........	Song of the owl medicine.........	88	105
203	Nita'miga'bo........	Moccasin-game song....	"If I am beaten"...............	144	158
205	Ga'gandac'..........	War song.............	(No words)...........	124	139
206	.....do..............	Dream song..........	Song of the trees.............	112	126
207	.....do..............	....do........	Song of the thunders...........	113	127
208	.....do..............	....do........	"My voice is heard"..........	114	128
209	.....do..............	....do........	"The approach of the storm".....	115	129
210	.....do..............	....do........	"As the hawk soars"..........	116	130
211	.....do..............	....do........	"In the southern sky".........	117	132
212	.....do..............	....do........	"Manido'listens to me"..........	118	132
213	.....do..............	Dream song (Juggler's song).	The song of Ce'deĕns'...........	111	125
215	.....do..............	War song.............	(No words)...........	125	139
224	.....do..............	Moccasin-game song....	"I have come after your stake"...	145	159

Catalogue no.	Name of singer.	Description of song.	Title of song.	Serial no.	Page no.
229	Ga'gandac'............	War song................	Little Eagle's song	126	140
230	....do................	....do................	(No words)....................	127	141
236	Maiñ'äns..............	Mide'................	Song of the bear path...........	89	106
237	....do................	....do................	Escorting the candidate.........	10	42
238	....do................	....do................	Song of the manido'	2	30
239	....do................	....do................	Dancing song....................	3	31
240	....do................	....do................	"My pan of food"...............	5	34
241	....do................	....do................	"My pipe"......................	6	35
242	....do................	....do................	Song of the za'gimag'	9	41
244	....do................	Dream song	Doctor's song	108	121
245	....do................	....do................	"I go to the big bear's lodge"....	109	121
246	....do................	....do................	"Going around the world".......	110	122
248	....do................	Mide'................	"They are making me old".....	90	107
253	....do................	....do................	"To the spirit land"............	91	108
254	....do................	....do................	Initiation song..................	63	81
255	....do................	....do................	"I will sing"....................	92	109
256	....do................	....do................	"I am walking".................	93	110
259	Henry Selkirk.........	Dream song............	Song of the deserted warrior......	120	134
260	....do................	....do................	Song of the crows...............	119	133
261	....do................	....do................	"I am afraid of the owl".........	121	135
262	....do................	Love song.............	"When I think of him"..........	140	154
271	Ga'tcitcigi'cïg........	War song.............	Song of the loons................	128	142
272	....do................	Unclassified............	Song of We'nabo'jo.............	197	206
274	....do................	....do................	"My music reaches to the sky"..	148	162
275	....do................	Love song.............	(No words).....................	141	154
276	....do................	War song.............	"I will start before noon".......	129	143
277	....do................	....do................	Song of Cïmau'ganïc............	130	143

SPECIAL SIGNS USED IN TRANSCRIPTIONS OF SONGS

(See pp. 5 and 6.)

+ placed above a note indicates that the tone is sung slightly less than a semitone higher than the proper pitch.

− placed above a note indicates that the tone is sung slightly less than a semitone lower than the proper pitch.

(· placed above a note indicates that the note is prolonged slightly beyond its proper time.

·) placed above a note indicates that the note is given less than its proper time.

(.) is used in melody outlines to indicate the pitch of a tone without reference to its duration.

Meaningless syllables are italicized.

Where no words are given beneath the notes it is understood that meaningless syllables were used, except in songs whose words were sung too indistinctly for transcription, such instances being described in the analysis.

CHIPPEWA MUSIC

By Frances Densmore

GENERAL DESCRIPTION OF SONGS

Introduction

The songs comprised in this paper were obtained during 1907, 1908, and 1909, from Chippewa Indians on the White Earth, Leech Lake, and Red Lake reservations in Minnesota, a few songs being also secured from a Chippewa living on the Bois Fort reservation in Minnesota. The Chippewa Indians on the White Earth and Leech Lake reservations may be said to represent the portion of the tribe south of Lake Superior; those on the Red Lake reservation are more nearly connected with the portion of the tribe living north of Lake Superior. Conditions on the White Earth and Leech Lake reservations are different from those at Red Lake, and the personality of the singers presents a marked contrast. For these reasons the social songs are considered in two groups. No Mĭde′ songs were collected at Red Lake.

Chippewa songs are not petrified specimens; they are alive with the warm red blood of human nature. Music is one of the greatest pleasures of the Chippewa. If an Indian visits another reservation one of the first questions asked on his return is: "What new songs did you learn?"

Every phase of Chippewa life is expressed in music. Many of the songs are very old and are found on several reservations; others are said to be the more recent compositions of certain men who composed them "during a dream" or "upon awaking from a dream." It is still customary for the Chippewa to celebrate an important event by a song. On the Leech Lake reservation the writer secured the song which the Indians composed and sang during the disturbance known as the "Pillager outbreak," in 1898. The song relates to the death of Major Wilkinson, an officer of the United States Army, who was shot while leading the troops. The Indians honor his bravery and speak of him with respect. The words of the song evidently refer to the grief of his fellow officers, and are as follows: "One in authority passeth wailing. Thou, O chief, art by nature also a man."

The Chippewa have no songs which are the exclusive property of families or clans. A young man may learn his father's songs, for example, by giving him the customary gift of tobacco, but he does not inherit the right to sing such songs, nor does his father force him to learn them.

The history of the Chippewa songs is well known to the singers, and is further preserved by the Indian custom of prefacing a song with a brief speech concerning it. On formal occasions the Chippewa singer says: "My friends, I will now sing you the song of ——," describing the subject of the song. At the close of the song he says: "My friends, I have sung the song of ——," repeating the title of the song. In this way the facts concerning the song become strongly associated with the melody in the minds of the people.

Chippewa singers often mention the locality from which a song came—Gull lake, Madeline island, or La Pointe. If a song was learned from the Sioux, it is so stated.

An interesting fact concerning Chippewa songs is that the melody is evidently considered more important than the words. In a succession of several renditions of a song it is not unusual to find the words occurring only once. The idea is the important thing, and that is firmly connected with the melody in the minds of the Indians. It is permissible and customary to compose new words for old tunes, but, so far as the writer has observed, these are always similar in general character to the words previously used. These observations do not, of course, apply to the Mïde' songs, which are considered separately. An instance of the changing of words in a song is furnished by one of the love songs (no. 138; catalogue no. 107). As originally recorded the words of this song were: "Do not weep, I am not going to die." On another reservation the same song was found, the words being: "Do not weep, I am not going away;" again: "Do not weep, I am going away but I will return soon." Among a third group of Indians the writer found the song changed again. A certain Indian said that he had recently made some new words for the song. The words referred to a certain incident which he related, their general trend being: "Do not weep, I will take care of you." In all these instances the underlying idea was the same and the general trend of the melody was the same, though different singers gave slightly different passing tones and embellishments. The various changes thus introduced did not affect the identity of the song in the mind of the Indians.

Indian songs are not recorded in a definite system of notation and a standard of absolute exactness is lacking. For that reason it seems desirable that study be concentrated on the melody-trend and the principal rhythm of the song, which show no variation in renditions by different singers. A classified analysis of these unvarying phases may supply data bearing on the natural laws which govern musical expression.

Indian music seems to belong to a period in which habit takes the place of scale consciousness. Habit in the choice of musical intervals is formed by following a line of least resistance or by a definite act of the will; or may be the result of both, the voice at first singing the intervals which it finds easiest and afterward repeating those intervals voluntarily. It is in such ways as these that the tone material comprising Indian songs is probably acquired.

The study of Indian music deals with a free tonal expression, yet this music is recorded at present in the notation of a conventional system. It is acknowledged that ordinary musical notation does not, in all instances, represent accurately the tones sung. According to Ellis,[a] "all these [five-toned] scales are merely the best representations in European notation of the sensations produced by the scales on European listeners. They can not be received as correct representations of the notes actually played." If a new and complete notation were used in recording fractional tones it should be used in connection with delicately adjusted instruments which would determine those fractional tones with mathematical accuracy. The present study is not an analysis of fractional tones, but of melodic trend and general musical character; therefore the ordinary musical notation is used, with the addition of a few signs in special cases.

The songs are recorded on a phonograph provided with a specially constructed recording horn and recorders. Care is taken in selecting the singers and in explaining to them the nature of the material desired, and effort is made to free them from constraint or embarrassment, in order that the recorded song may be free and natural.

Before recording a song the name of the singer, the number of the song, and the tone C' of a pitch pipe are given into the recording horn. These data serve to identify the cylinder record and also to indicate the speed of the phonograph at the time the record is made.

Before transcribing a song the speed of the phonograph is adjusted so that the tone C' as registered on the record shall correspond to

---

[a] In his translation of Hemholtz's The Sensations of Tone as the Physiological Basis of Music, part 3, chapter 14 (footnote, p. 261).

the tone C' as given by the pitch pipe. Thus the pitch and the metric unit of the song are identical in recording and reproducing—a condition essential to accuracy of transcription.

INTONATION

One of the characteristics of Chippewa singing observed during this study is that a vibrato, or wavering tone, is especially pleasing to the singers. This is difficult for them to acquire and is considered a sign of musical proficiency. The vibrato may seem to indicate an uncertain sense of tone, but the singer who uses it is ready to approve the song when sung with correct intonation. He declares, however, that this is not "good singing." A person unaccustomed to Indian singing, even if he have a keen ear, will find difficulty in recognizing a song when it is sung by a typical Indian singer of the old school, yet the Indian is ready to admit that the points of difference are entirely in the rendition.

A kernel of tone on true pitch is evidenced by the following experiment: The phonograph record of an extremely harsh song was selected and duplicated on an electric recording machine, producing a record much softer in that much of the harshness was eliminated, and showing a melody approaching accuracy of pitch. Another discordant song was duplicated on a second phonograph, another record made from this, and so on to the seventh record, which was so clear and melodic as to be easily transcribed. Some of the bytones were lost in each successive duplication, and what remained at last was the principal tone. In each instance this must have been present in the first record, though so obscured as to be almost indistinguishable.

At present the only standard generally available for the measurement of musical intervals is the tempered musical scale. This is artificial, yet its points of difference from the natural scale are intervals less frequently used in primitive music than those which the two scales have in common. Chippewa singers have been found who sang all the intervals correctly except the fourth and seventh.

In his Esthetics of Musical Art, Dr. Ferdinand Hand, of the Universities of Leipzig and Jena, makes the statement that the Swiss and Tyrolese sing the fourth of the scale too high and the seventh too low for our ears. He says also: "Every teacher of singing admits that children have special difficulty in singing these intervals. This is not because they are not in accordance with nature, but are the products of acute reflection and are therefore to be found only where the finer development of the intellect renders them possible."

The descending interval of the minor third occurs with frequency in the Chippewa songs, regardless of the nature of the song. This suggests that it may be an interval either especially pleasing or especially easy for the voice, and not directly connected with the concept of the song.

Accidentals are usually given with more firmness and accuracy than diatonic tones. This may be attributed to one of two causes— either these tones are recognized as deviations from some definite standard, or they are individual tones impressed on the mind of the singers more clearly than other tones, and are therefore given more accurately. Of interest in this connection is the fact that the phonograph record shows the octavo, fifth, and twelfth sung accurately by men who give the other intervals with uncertain pitch. This peculiarity is found in records made by Indians whose environment is primitive and who rarely hear the white man's music. The following system of signs has been adopted: If the singer gives the principal intervals of the scale correctly, but makes deviation in other intervals, these incorrect tones, if raised less than a semitone, are marked + ; if lowered less than a semitone, they are marked −. This tonal peculiarity has been tested in the following manner: Two singers were asked to repeat songs recorded about seven months before; about 20 songs were included in this test, which showed deviation on the same tones in the second as in the first rendition.

RHYTHM

The rhythm of a Chippewa song is as much a matter of composition as the melody and often expresses the idea of the song. The term "rhythm," in this connection, refers to the succession of measures of irregular lengths, as well as to the subdivision of the measure.

The transcription of a song is divided into measures according to the vocal accent. Since a secondary accent seldom occurs, the song is usually divided into measures of two or three counts. In many instances each of these counts is a metric unit and is so indicated by the metronome mark at the opening of the song; in other instances the entire measure constitutes the metric unit. In many songs there is a recurring rhythmic unit composed of one to four or more measures; in other songs there is no recurring rhythmic unit and in many songs of this class the entire melody constitutes a rhythmic unit, complete and satisfactory in itself. Continued repetition of such a song gives to the entire performance the effect of a homogeneous whole.

In many cases a metronome test of the phonograph record shows the drum to have the same pulse or metric unit as the melody. From this fact one would expect to find that the pulse of drum and voice coincide at certain points, but an analysis of phonograph records and observation in the field tend to show that the drum and the voice are independent expressions. This is indicated in the tabulated rhythmic analysis of the songs, and also in the analysis of individual songs. The Chippewa seldom strikes a drum and sounds a tone simultaneously. One phonograph record (no. 124; catalogue no. 205) shows a remarkable peculiarity. The metric units of voice and drum are so nearly alike that the same metronome indication is used for each. At the beginning of the record the drumbeat is slightly behind the voice, but it gains gradually until for one or two measures the drum and voice are together; the drum continues to gain, and during the remainder of the record it is struck slightly before the sounding of the corresponding tone by the voice. The record is not sufficiently long to show whether, in a more extended perform- ance, the drum would have slackened in speed until it again took its place after the voice.

It is worthy of note that appreciable interruptions in regular rhythms are accurately repeated. For instance, in certain songs there occur tones prolonged less than one-half their value; these are marked thus (·. It was found that if the singer sang the song several times he prolonged the tones to exactly the same length in each rendition. Other tones are similarly shortened and are marked thus ·). These also are found to be accurately repeated.

Thus far, observation indicates that the rhythm is the essential part of the Chippewa song. The words of a song may be slightly different in rendition, or the less important melody progressions may vary, but a corresponding variation in rhythm has not been observed. A song, when sung by different singers, shows an exact reproduction of rhythm.

During many of the Chippewa war dances the drum is in even beats, equally accented. The drum rhythm of the woman's dance consists of an accented beat preceded by an unaccented beat; the drum rhythm of the moccasin game is similar, but the unaccented beat in the for- mer corresponds approximately to the third count in a triple measure, while the unaccented beat in the latter corresponds in value to the fourth count in a quadruple measure. Another distinction lies in the manner of beginning these rhythms. In beginning the rhythm of the woman's dance, the drummers give the unaccented beat with a rebound of the stick, so that it seems to be connected with the beat which precedes rather than with that which follows it. As soon as the rhythm is well established, however, the unaccented beat clearly connects itself with the succeeding beat. In the moccasin game the rhythm is unmistakable from the start, the short beat being closely connected with the longer one, which is emphatically accented. These three rhythms, the war dance, the woman's dance, and the moccasin game are the principal rhythms of the drum among the Minnesota Chippewa.

TONE MATERIAL

A wide range of tone material is shown by the songs under observation. Certain songs contain tones whose melodic sequence refers definitely to a keynote or tonic. Other songs contain tones which appear to belong to the system of tones commonly called major or minor keys, but which are used in such melodic sequence that their relation to a keynote or tonic is obscure. The border line between these two classes of songs is not clearly marked. Because the relation of tones to a keynote is not apparent, one scarcely is justified in saying that such relation does not exist, especially as the purpose of the present work is not scale construction, nor scale analysis, but recording, in the simplest and most evident manner, the musical performances of the Chippewa. For this reason no attempt is made to separate these two classes of songs. The distinction will be evident to those who follow closely the transcriptions and analyses. In many instances the sharps and flats at the beginning of the staff indicate that the tones upon those degrees are sharped or flatted, but do not imply that the corresponding key is fully established. For present purposes it is deemed sufficient to analyze the tone material of the songs, with reference to the keynote implied by the beginning and ending of the song and its general melodic trend.

The present system of classification, while carried out consistently, must be recognized as broad in outline and somewhat tentative. The principal change from ordinary terminology is in connection with what are commonly known as the major and minor pentatonic scales. These two consist of the same tones, a major tonality being secured by using as a keynote the lower tone of the group of three tones, and a minor tonality being secured by using as a keynote the upper tone of the group of two tones.

The subject of pentatonic scales is fully considered by Helmholtz,[a] according to whom a scale lacking the second and sixth tones is the second five-toned scale. This is the scale commonly known as the minor pentatonic scale. According to the same author, a scale lacking the fourth and seventh tones is the fourth five-toned scale. This is the scale commonly known as the major pentatonic scale. Following the system set forth by Helmholtz, the terms "second five-toned scale" and "fourth five-toned scale" are used to indicate what are commonly called minor and major pentatonic scales.

A somewhat less important change in terminology is the use of the term "tonality" instead of the more common term "key;" this is fully explained in connection with the first tabulated analysis.

---

[a] In his work The Sensations of Tone as the Physiological Basis of Music (part 3, chapter 14).

Many songs which contain a limited number of tones, too limited to constitute an organized key, still show definite tonality, either major or minor.

STRUCTURE

The sequence of tones in Chippewa songs shows that certain songs are harmonic and others melodic in structure. The following basis of classification has been adopted: Songs are classified as harmonic if their accented tones follow the intervals of diatonic chords, and as melodic if their contiguous accented tones have no apparent chord relationship. In the latter class are included many songs in which the relations of the tones to a keynote is not strongly in evidence.

In many instances the interpretation of the words of these songs has been difficult, the Mĭde' songs requiring special skill in translation.[a]

TABULATED ANALYSIS OF 180 SONGS

The classifications presented are broad in their outlines. Further investigation may make it possible to analyze more closely and to classify more definitely many of these songs.

MELODIC ANALYSIS

TONALITY[b]

	Mĭde' songs.	White Earth and Leech Lake reservations.					Red Lake reservation.					Total.
		Dream songs.	War songs.	Love songs.	Moccasin-game songs.	Unclassified songs.	War songs.	Love songs.	Moccasin-game songs.	Woman's dance songs.	Unclassified songs.	
Major tonality....................	65	12	5	6	2	3	1	3	......	3	4	104
Minor tonality....................	25	2	6	3	2	5	7	2	9	6	6	73
Beginning major, ending minor......							1				1	2
Beginning minor, ending major.....											1	1
Total....................												180

[a] The writer gratefully acknowledges her indebtedness to Mrs. Charles Mee, Mrs. Mary Warren English, Rev. C. H. Beaulieu, and Mr. G. H. Beaulieu for their assistance as interpreters; also to the Rev. J. A. Gilfillan, who for twenty-five years lived on the White Earth reservation, speaking the Chippewa language with a fluency and understanding rarely attained by a member of the white race.

[b] Tonality is defined as "the quality and peculiarity of a tonal system;" key is defined as a "system of tones the members of which bear certain definite relations to each other."

Certain of the songs under analysis show a sequence of tones similar to a major or minor key; in other instances the tone material which comprises a key or scale is present and the songs are clearly major or minor in tonality, yet the arrangement of the tones with reference to a keynote is not apparent. Thus from actual observation we discern the distinction between these two terms.

Since we are considering music of a period in which what we now designate scales and keys were not formulated, the terms "major tonality" and "minor tonality" are used in preference to the common terms "major key" and "minor key."

MELODIC ANALYSIS—Continued

TONE MATERIAL[a]

	White Earth and Leech Lake reservations.						Red Lake reservation.					
	Mide' songs.	Dream songs.	War songs.	Love songs.	Moccasin-game songs.	Unclassified songs.	War songs.	Love songs.	Moccasin-game songs.	Woman's dance songs.	Unclassified songs.	Total.
Fourth five-toned scale	18	8	2	1		1	1	1		3	3	38
Second five-toned scale	11			1		1	2		6	1		22
Major triad and sixth	19	4	1			1	2					27
Major triad, sixth, and fourth	2											2
Minor triad	1				1						1	3
Minor triad and sixth					1							1
Minor triad and fourth	2	1	1	1			2			1		8
Minor triad, second, and fourth					2							2
Minor third and fourth							1					1
Octave complete	3		1	2	1			1				8
Octave complete except seventh	10		1	1						1	1	14
Octave complete except sixth	2					1		1	2		2	8
Octave complete except second			1	1							1	3
Other combinations of tones	19	1	4			3	2	2	1	3	3	38
In two keys	3						1				1	5
Total												180

BEGINNINGS OF SONGS

	Mide' songs.	Dream songs.	War songs.	Love songs.	Moccasin-game songs.	Unclassified songs.	War songs.	Love songs.	Moccasin-game songs.	Woman's dance songs.	Unclassified songs.	Total.
On the twelfth	33	7	4	3	2			3	2			54
On the fifth	29						3	1	3	4	4	44
On the eleventh							1		1			2
On the fourth	1	1	1								1	4
On the tenth		1	2		1							4
On the third					1			1		1	5	8
On the ninth	5		1				1					7
On the second	5				1					1		7
On the octave	11	3	3	5			1	7	1	2	1	34
On the seventh	2								1	1		4
On the sixth	1	2										3
On the tonic							2		2		1	5
In two keys	3						1					4
Total												180

[a] Many songs included in this classification consist of tones which are not clearly referable to a tonic or keynote. The songs are grouped according to the tone material which they contain. Thus, if a melody contains F sharp and C sharp, begins on A and ends on D, it is, in this classification, regarded as being in the key of D.

Certain melodies readily conform to the three principal chords of a key; other melodies containing the same tones have no affiliation for either the principal chords or the closing cadence of the key. This peculiarity is noted in the analysis of the song.

MELODIC ANALYSIS—Continued

ENDINGS OF SONGS

	Mide' songs.	White Earth and Leech Lake reservations.					Red Lake reservation.					Total.
		Dream songs.	War songs.	Love songs.	Moccasin-game songs.	Unclassified songs.	War songs.	Love songs.	Moccasin-game songs.	Woman's dance songs.	Unclassified songs.	
On the tonic	56	10	8	6	3	5	9	3	9	6	8	120
On the fifth	21	3	3	2	1	2	1	1		2	3	39
On the third	10	1	1	1		1		1		1	1	17
In two keys	3						1					4
Total												180

FIRST PROGRESSIONS

	Mide' songs.	Dream songs.	War songs.	Love songs.	Moccasin-game songs.	Unclassified songs.	War songs.	Love songs.	Moccasin-game songs.	Woman's dance songs.	Unclassified songs.	Total.
First progression downward	83	10	9	6	2	4	5	3	2	4	7	135
First progression upward	7	4	2	3	2	4	4	2	7	5	5	45
Total												180

ACCIDENTALS [a]

	Mide' songs.	Dream songs.	War songs.	Love songs.	Moccasin-game songs.	Unclassified songs.	War songs.	Love songs.	Moccasin-game songs.	Woman's dance songs.	Unclassified songs.	Total.
Songs containing no accidentals	73	11	10	4	3	6	9	2	9	8	12	147
Sixth lowered a semitone	4	1	1		1			1		1		9
Fifth lowered a semitone	1											1
Fourth lowered a semitone	1											1
Third lowered a semitone	2	1										3
Second lowered a semitone	3					1						4
Seventh raised a semitone	1											1
Sixth raised a semitone	1	1		3					1			6
Fourth raised a semitone	1			1			1					3
Second raised a semitone									1			1
Fourth and seventh raised a semitone			1									1
In two keys	3											3
Total												180

[a] The principal object of this classification is to show the frequency with which tones diatonically altered occur in these songs. Each accidental is classified according to its interval from the keynote which is implied by the beginning, ending, and general trend of the melody.

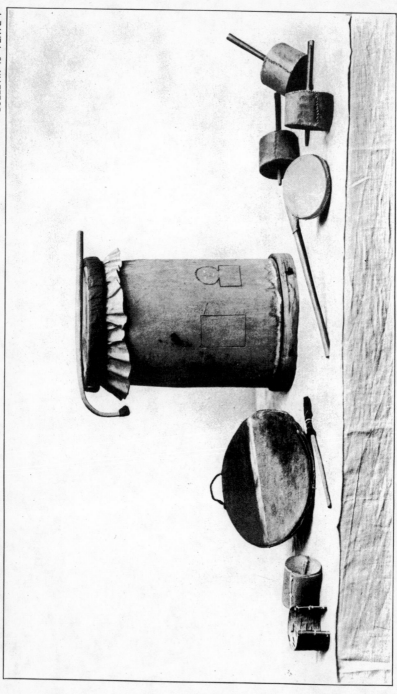

MUSICAL INSTRUMENTS, AND BIRCH-BARK ROLLS CONTAINING MNEMONICS OF SONGS

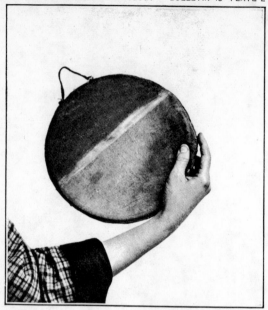

CICI'GWĂN (DOCTOR'S RATTLE), SHOWING MANNER OF HOLD-
ING INSTRUMENT WHEN IN USE

MĬTĬ'GWAKĬK' (MĬDE' DRUM), REVERSE SIDE

MUSICAL INSTRUMENTS

RHYTHMIC ANALYSIS

	Mĭde' songs.	White Earth and Leech Lake reservations.					Red Lake reservation.					Total.
		Dream songs.	War songs.	Love songs.	Moccasin-game songs.	Unclassified songs.	War songs.	Love songs.	Moccasin-game songs.	Woman's dance songs.	Unclassified songs.	
Beginning on accented portion of measure	23	10	9	4	2	5	6	4	9	8	9	89
Beginning on unaccented portion	26	4	2	5	2	3	3	1	......	1	3	50
Transcribed in outline	41											41
Total												180
Metric unit of voice and drum the same	6	1	1	....			3	4	....	2	4	7	28
Metric unit of voice and drum different	23	12	6	....	3	2	2	....	6	4	5	63
Recorded without drum	61	1	4	9	1	3	3	5	1	1	......	89
Total												180

STRUCTURAL ANALYSIS

	Mĭde' songs.	Dream songs.	War songs.	Love songs.	Moccasin-game songs.	Unclassified songs.	War songs.	Love songs.	Moccasin-game songs.	Woman's dance songs.	Unclassified songs.	Total.
Harmonic	20	8	5	....	2	......	1	....	3	......	2	41
Melodic	70	6	6	9	2	8	8	5	6	9	10	139
Total												180

Harmonic.—Songs in which the accented tones follow the intervals of diatonic chord.
Melodic.—Songs in which the accented tones suggest the intervals of a diatonic scale, having no apparent chord relationship to each other.

MUSICAL INSTRUMENTS

The songs of the Chippewa are usually accompanied by either the drum or the rattle, while the Chippewa lover intersperses his songs with the music of the flute.

The drum used in the social dances is about 2 feet in diameter and 10 inches in thickness; it is suspended between stakes, which are driven firmly in the ground. The sides of the drum are decorated with beaded cloth. It is said that in the old days it was customary to make a war drum by driving stakes in the ground and stretching an entire hide over them, binding it in place by means of strong hoops.

The Mĭde'wĭwĭn has its special musical instruments. These consist of the *mĭtĭ'gwakĭk'* (drum) and *cici'gwăn* (rattles). These instruments are shown in plates 1 and 2.

The mĭtĭ'gwakĭk' shown in the illustration is very old. It was purchased on the Red Lake reservation, where it has often been heard at a distance of 10 miles. These drums are not unpleasantly loud, but the sound has great vibration and carries a long distance.

This mĭtĭ'gwakĭk' is made of a basswood log, hollowed by charring and scraping. It is 16½ inches high, 10 inches in diameter at the base, and 8½ inches in diameter at the top. It is decorated with a blue band at the base, four heads representing the four Mĭde' manido', and an oblong said to represent a bag containing yarrow, which signifies life. The heads are outlined in red and the bag in blue. When in use it is partially filled with water (the plug in the side is plainly shown). The top is of untanned deerskin, which is dampened and stretched very tight. At times, instead of being dampened the top of the drum is held toward the fire or in the warmth of the sun, which has the desired effect. Great care is taken in preparing a drum for use, the proper quality of tone being secured by the treatment of the deerskin top.

Four rattles comprise a set as used in the Mĭde'. (See description of Mĭde' ceremony, p. 48.) These are not decorated. Three consist of small wooden drums, each provided with a sewn cover of hide, containing small stones or shot and pierced by a stick which forms the handle. The writer has seen rattles of this type used in the treatment of the sick by means of the Mĭde'. These rattles are used also in the "shooting of spirit power" during a ceremony of the Mĭde'. The fourth rattle is made on a frame of bent wood. Each of these rattles has a different tone, determined by the quantity of stones or shot which it contains.

The round instrument at the right of the drum in the illustration is the rattle used by the *dja'sakid* (doctor or juggler); if the dja'sakid be also a member of the Mĭde'wĭwĭn he may use this as a drum when practising the Mĭde' songs or teaching them to others. As stated elsewhere, the dja'sakid are frequently members of the Mĭde'wĭwĭn, and it was from such a man that this instrument was secured. It is 9½ inches in diameter, one-half inch in thickness, and contains only three or four shot or small stones. Across the face of the drum is a blue band, the smaller segment of the circle being painted green. Larger instruments of the same type are also used by the dja'sakid; many of them are elaborately decorated. The use of this instrument in the treatment of the sick is fully described in the chapter on dream songs. (See p. 119.)

The drum used in the moccasin game is about 15 inches in diameter and 2 inches in thickness. It may have hide stretched over one or both sides and some specimens have small bits of jingling tin set in the hoop. The stick used in beating this drum is similar to the one shown with the dja'sakid instrument.

The courting flute of the Chippewa is usually made of cedar and is similar in construction to the flutes of other Indian tribes.

THE MĬDE′

BELIEFS

The *Mĭde′* (Grand Medicine) is the native religion of the Chippewa. It teaches that long life is coincident with goodness, and that evil inevitably reacts on the offender. Its chief aim is to secure health and long life to its adherents, and music forms an essential part of every means used to that end. Thus far the study of the subject has revealed no reference to war and no allusions to enemies. The element of propitiation is also absent from its teaching and practice.

The organization of this religion is called the *Mĭde′wĭwĭn* (Grand Medicine Society). Both men and women are eligible to membership; a male member is called *Mĭde′wĭnĭ′nĭ*, and a female member *Mĭde′-wĭkwe′*. There are eight degrees in the Mĭde′wĭwĭn, persons being advanced from one degree to another on receiving certain instructions and bestowing valuable gifts. Meetings of the Mĭde′wĭwĭn are held in the spring of each year, members being initiated at that time; it is also permissible to hold initiation ceremonies in the fall. All members are expected to attend one meeting each year for the renewal of their "spirit power." Smaller gatherings may be held at any time for the treatment of the sick, and it is also permissible for a few members of the society to meet at any time for the purpose of singing the songs and strengthening their faith in the beliefs of the Mĭde′. A feast and an offering are inseparable features of all these gatherings.

Ritual exactness is not obligatory in the Mĭde′. Its ceremony of initiation has a general outline which is universally followed, but the details vary in different localities. No ceremonial garments are worn, and there are no ceremonial articles connected with the organization. It is said that each leader has a pipe which he smokes only at meetings of the Mĭde′wĭwĭn, but this seems a matter of custom rather than of requirement. There is nothing which corresponds to an hereditary priesthood, the leaders of a ceremony being men who hold high degrees in the society, and are chosen for the office at each meeting of the society. The selection of songs at the various parts of the initiation ceremony is decided by the leaders of the ceremony, as there are many songs which may be sung.

Since ritual exactness is not obligatory in the Mĭde′, there is no penalty attached to a mistake in the singing of a song. De′bwawĕn′-dûnk, an old member of the Mĭde′wĭwĭn, states that there is a correct way to sing each song and that an effort is made to sing it in this manner because failure to do so is displeasing to the Mĭde′ manido′. Added importance is given to this statement by the fact that De′bwawĕn′dûnk lives on the Bois Fort reservation, where the Indians have had little direct contact with white men and where the old traditions are particularly well preserved.

The emblem of the Mĭde′ is *mi′gĭs*, a small, white shell, which is said to appear upon the surface of the water when the action of a manido′ (spirit) causes the water to seethe. Manido′ in the form of water animals, mermaids, and mermen, also appear to the members of the Mĭde′wĭwĭn for the purpose of imparting instruction when they are in a frame of mind to receive it. Hoping for such a visitation, it is not unusual for a member of the Mĭde′wĭwĭn to sit beside the water for hours at a time, singing Mĭde′ songs and beating the Mĭde′ drum or shaking a rattle.

The healing art of the Mĭde′ is entirely different from that practised by the Chippewa doctors, the method of treatment is different, and the two vocations are distinct, though it is possible for a doctor to be a member of the Mĭde′wĭwĭn. Descriptions of the treatment of the sick by both these methods will be given.[a]

The life enjoined on the members of the Mĭde′wĭwĭn is a life of rectitude. They are taught that membership in the Mĭde′wĭwĭn does not exempt a man from the consequences of his sins. Lying and stealing are strictly forbidden; also the use of liquor.

The Mĭde′ is not without its means of punishing offenders. Those holding high degrees in the Mĭde′wĭwĭn are familiar with the art of subtle poisoning, which may be used if necessary. It is said that they are also able to call down curses on those who displease them. The writer was recently informed of an instance in which a man offended a Mĭde′wĭnĭ′nĭ, who retaliated by saying that a misfortune would soon befall him. In a short time his little daughter died.

SONGS

The songs of the Mĭde′ represent the musical expression of religious ideas. The melody and the idea are the essential parts of a Mĭde′ song, the words being forced into conformation with the melody. To accomplish this it is customary to add meaningless syllables either between the parts of a word or between the words; accents are misplaced and a word is sometimes accented differently in various parts of a song; the vowels are also given different sounds, or changed entirely. Any of these alterations are permissible. In addition to the meaningless syllables used to fill out the measures we find the ejaculations *he hi hi hi*, used in the songs associated with the "shooting of spirit power."

The writer has even been informed that it is permissible for different members of the Mĭde′wĭwĭn holding high degrees to use slightly different words for the songs, but the idea of the song must always remain the same. The words serve as a key to this idea without fully expressing it. Sometimes only one or two words occur in a song. Their literal translation is meaningless, but to an instructed member

---

[a] See pp. 51 and 119.

of the Mĭde′wĭwĭn they bear an occult significance. Many of the
words used in the Mĭde′ songs are unknown in the conversational
Chippewa of the present time. This fact has made it difficult to secure
satisfactory translations of these songs. Nine or ten interpreters
have been employed on many of them, the final translation being
made by three particularly efficient interpreters in consultation with
two members of the Mĭde′wĭwĭn. By this method it has been possible to reach the idea underlying the song.

A Mĭde′ song is not considered complete unless the syllables *ho ho
ho ho* are repeatedly given at the close. When singing these songs
into the phonograph the singers have often requested a signal, so that
they might be sure to record these syllables before the blank was
filled. If necessary they leave a rendition of the song unfinished
in order to record them; some give them also before singing the song.

A member of the Mĭde′wĭwĭn usually begins his performance by
drumming rapidly; then he gives the ejaculations, or speaks to the
Mĭde′ manido′ or makes some remarks concerning the song he is about
to sing; after this he sings the song, the beat of the drum being continuous throughout. The drum appears to be an independent expression,
as in a large majority of instances the metric unit of the drum is
different from that of the voice. (See p. 11.)

The songs of the Mĭde′wĭwĭn are estimated as several hundred in
number. Some have a direct ceremonial use, as in the initiation of
members; others are connected with the use of "medicine," the song
being sung when results are to be accomplished by "spirit power;"
and other songs are known as *ni′miwûg′*, or dancing songs. Certain
ceremonial songs are grouped in series of eight or ten, the members of
the Mĭde′wĭwĭn dancing during the last half of the series.

In the words of these songs the ancient teachings and beliefs of
the Mĭde′ are preserved. The words of the songs frequently furnish
the texts for discourses by the Mĭde′wĭnĭ′nĭ. In some of the series of
songs it is the custom that one song be sung by each man, who follows the song with a discourse based on it.

Many of the songs are taught only to those who pay for the privi-
lege of learning them, and all the songs are recorded in mnemonics on
strips of birch bark. This record serves as a reminder of the essential
idea of the song and is different in its nature from our system of
printing. The Indian picture preserves the idea of the song, while
our printed page preserves the words which are supposed to express
the idea but which often express it very imperfectly.[a]

---

[a] The drawings for songs contained in this paper were made as follows (serial numbers used): Drawings for songs nos. 1, 4, 81–88 by O′dĕni′ gûn; those for songs nos. 16–24 by De′bwawĕn′dûnk; those for
songs nos. 65–69 by Be′cĭgwi′wizäns, and that for song no. 75 by Manido′gicĭgo′kwe—all of whom sang
the songs. The drawings for songs nos. 2, 3, 5–15, 25–64, 70–80 (except no. 75), 89–107 were the work of
Na′waji′bigo′kwe, who sang only a portion of the songs but made the drawings for the remainder on
hearing the phonograph records of the songs.

The drawings of the Mĭde′ songs are universally understood by members of the Mĭde′wĭwĭn. A large number of drawings have been tested in the following manner: A song has been phonographically recorded and the picture drawn on one reservation and later the phonograph record has been played to a member of the Mĭde′wĭwĭn living on a distant reservation. The song has been recognized at once and a picture drawn without hesitation. This picture, on comparison with the first, has been found identical in symbolism, differing only as one person draws better than another. By an inverse test, a song picture has been shown to a member of the Mĭde′wĭwĭn and she has sung the song which was sung on a distant reservation by the person who drew the picture.

There are certain established symbols in the Mĭde′ drawing, the principal ones being the circle, used to represent the earth, the sky, a lake and a hill; and straight or wavy lines, used to represent "spirit power." These symbols are combined with a crude delineation of the objects mentioned in the song.

FIG. 1. Mĭde′ writing.

This system of mnemonics may be used for other purposes than the songs. The writer once asked a woman who is a member of the Mĭde′wĭwĭn to write the Chippewa word *Gi′cĭgo′ikwe* in the Mĭde′ mnemonics. The woman had never heard the word before. It is a proper name combining the words *gi′cĭg* (sky) and *i′kwe* (woman), the vowel *o* being a connective. The woman said that it would require a little time for her to think how to write the word and that no one could be in the wigwam with her when she wrote it. The result is shown herewith (see fig. 1).

The double circle represents the sky, in which the moon is seen; the single circle represents the earth. In each of these circles is the figure of a woman, the two figures being connected by a line which touches the hand of the figure in the earth circle. The explanation given by the woman was as follows:

This name means that there are really two women instead of one. In the sky is one of these women; the other is on the earth. But the woman in the sky is constantly giving spirit power to the one on the earth, which the one on the earth reaches out her hand to receive.

This illustration shows that the Mĭde' writing can be used to express complicated ideas.

The example of song writing here given (fig. 2) shows a delineation of the objects mentioned in the song.

The words of the song are:

Wase' .... Light
Nita'binŏs .... Around you
O'gima .... Chief
I'kwe .... Woman (princess)

This picture was drawn by the same woman as the preceding. She stated that the horizontal line represents the edge of the wigwam, along which are arranged various articles of value indicated by the dots. At each end are torches, the light of which falls

FIG. 2.   Mĭde' song writing.

on the gathered wealth, causing many of the articles to glitter. These articles belong to a woman standing with upraised hands and wearing a pearl necklace with a locket.

In singing this song the woman pointed to one portion of the picture after another, tapping the birch bark lightly as she sang and traversing the row of dots, the horizontal line, the outline of the necklace, and the torches, then beginning again at the row of dots.

The woman who sang this song stated further that "it is a medicine song" and that she could, if desired, furnish some of the medicine for use with the song. "The medicine was in the form of a powder and would be worn in a medicine bag."

No phonograph was available at the time, but the song was noted. It begins on a high tone, descending with frequent intervals of the minor third and glissando progressions, and has a compass of an octave and two tones.

Many of the Mïde' songs are grouped in series, the pictures being drawn on a long strip of birch bark. Midway through such a series a line is drawn. This indicates a pause, after which the people rise, and dance during the remaining songs of the series.

The antiquity of these songs is shown by the fact that many of them are widely known among scattered peoples who came originally from the same locality but have had practically no communication for a long period of time. The preservation of the songs is aided by the mnemonics, and the importance attached to them is shown by the reluctance of the Mïde' Indians to sing them until fully assured of the sincerity and good will of the person making the request.

In analyzing the music as the important part of the expression, the question arises whether the melodic progression or the rhythm is more strongly impressed on the mind of the singer. Which of these elements is to him the more important feature of the song? A careful review of more than a hundred Mïde' songs shows them to consist of simple intervals and complicated rhythms. The tones comprised in the songs are limited in number, many of the songs containing only three or four tones, except as the number is extended by repetition in a lower octave; the variety of rhythms is great, as will be seen in the transcriptions. Accidentals rarely occur in the songs. An accidental in the opening measures of a song is worthy of little consideration, as in many instances the introductory measures are sung only once, and the singer is allowed some freedom in them.

The rhythm of the song is determined by noting the accented tones and dividing the song into measures according to them.

By observation we find that in many of the songs the metric unit is the measure, not the individual count in the measure. In these instances the accented measure beginnings are found to conform to a very slow metronome beat, but the intervening tones are irregular in length and can not be accurately indicated by note values. These songs would resemble chants except for the freedom of their melody progressions.

The next fact which we note in connection with the rhythm is that it is most peculiar in songs which are intended to produce magic and mysterious results. In this class are included songs for the healing of the sick as well as songs used in connection with special "medicine" for success in hunting or other undertakings. In many of these songs there is no repetition of a rhythmic unit, but the entire song constitutes a rhythmic unit, its repeated renditions forming a satisfactory whole.

There are other songs in which two or more measures of varying lengths combine to form a rhythmic unit, which is repeated throughout the song. One measure occasionally constitutes the rhythmic unit, which is continuously repeated.

The rhythm is simplest in the songs used while "shooting" a candidate for initiation into the Mĭde′wĭwĭn. In these songs there is only one object—that the person shall fall unconscious, showing that he is "entirely controlled by the medicine." The rhythm of these songs is an emphatic regular rhythm. When it is desired that a person be energized to some great undertaking the rhythm is irregular but so fascinating in its irregularity that it holds the attention. This is what is always sought—to control the person.

The ni′miwûg′ (dancing songs) are always sung vibrato, with the wavering of voice which would be produced by the motion of the body in dancing. This wavering of the voice is inseparably connected with the song. In all Mĭde′ songs there is a tendency toward uncertainty of intonation. Repetitions of the same tone usually shade downward, and the transition from one tone to another is frequently glissando. By a strange contrast it is found that accidentals, when present, are usually given clearly and correctly. With very few exceptions, the repetition of a song is begun on exactly the same pitch as the first rendition. This frequently involves the ascent of a twelfth and is often made more difficult by the fact that the song ends on a tone below the natural range of the singer's voice. Thus the song as a whole preserves its tonality and repetitions are accurately begun, although the individual tones of the song may be uncertain in intonation. This suggests the possibility that these variations in intonation may be an attempt at ornamentation. The melodic material is extremely limited and this wavering of the voice may seem to add to the effectiveness of the song.

A few points concerning the song as a whole deserve our attention. The repetition of a song is usually continuous with the previous rendition, although a half rest occasionally occurs between the renditions. The repetition of a song frequently opens with a new word and the melody returns to the fifth or sixth measure of the original rendition. Repetitions of a song by different singers are found to be identical in all important respects.

Unimportant phrases near the close of the song frequently vary in number. They are usually reiterations of a word and the exact number seems not essential.

An Indian rarely hums a Mĭde′ song before singing it into the phonograph and the accuracy of his memory is shown by the fact that the song in repetition is never changed in rhythm, the changes, when they occur, being in unimportant note values or melodic progressions.

In summarizing the preceding chapter we find the songs of the Mĭde′ to be essentially a musical expression, the form of the words being subordinate to the form of the melody.

The drum and voice are usually independent in metric units, the drum being a rapid unaccented beat and the voice having a rhythm which bears a relation to the mental concept of the song.

The intonation has been shown to be frequently variable for two reasons: First in imitation of the motion of the body in dancing, and second for the apparent purpose of ornamentation.

No effort has been made by the writer to secure the "bad medicine songs" or songs of cursing. One who has heard a large number of these songs states that they are terrible in their maledictions and represent a phase of life and thought which it were better to leave untouched. They are the weapons of defense in the Mĭde', and all that is believed to have been wrought through them will ever be an unwritten page.

USE OF MEDICINE

The power of the Mĭde' is exerted through a combination of two mediums, music and medicine. The former has been set forth in detail; the latter is less available for analysis, but certain information concerning it has been secured.

The medicine and medicine practice of the Mĭde' should be distinguished from that of the dja'sakid, who are doctors or jugglers. That they may also be members of the Mĭde'wĭwĭn does not change the fact that the two professions are distinct.

The use of medicine in connection with the Mĭde' is as follows: Each member of the Mĭde'wĭwĭn carries in his Mĭde' bag many herbs and other substances supposed to have medicinal value, in addition to the mi'gĭs (small white shells used in the Mĭde'). If a cure of the sick is desired he frequently mixes and sells a medicine after singing the song which will make it effectual.

In the working of a charm it is considered necessary to use both the proper song and the proper medicine. For that reason a small quantity of the medicine is furnished to a person who buys such a song. To accomplish the desired results this medicine should, if possible, come in contact either with the person to be influenced, with some of his personal possessions, or with a small wooden effigy, which the person working the charm makes for the purpose. The medicine may consist of one or more ingredients and may be of greater or less value. Certain herbs enter into the composition of many medicines, while others are rare and difficult to obtain.

In the working of a love charm it is customary to obtain a thread from the clothing of one of the persons to be affected, or, if possible, a loose hair. Two small wooden effigies are made, one representing a man, the other a woman, and the person working the charm binds these together with the thread or hair. The effigies are then placed in a small bag, with some of the proper medicine. This bag is worn around the neck of the person working the charm, who frequently sings the song which is supposed to make the charm effective.

If the intention is to work an evil charm the method of procedure is somewhat similar. An effort is made to secure some personal possession, to which the medicine is applied; if this is impossible, the medicine is applied to a wooden effigy of the person, and the man working the charm sets this figure before him as he sings the songs of cursing. The medicines used in connection with these songs are said to be powerful and subtle vegetable poisons.

It is believed that if a Mĭde′wĭnĭ′nĭ has in his possession any article belonging to a person he can work at any time whatever charm he likes upon that person. It is said that the singer breathes upon his medicine bag before working a charm.

A detailed account of the use of medicine in connection with certain songs is given at the close of this section.

One of the songs used at the dance which follows a Mĭde′ ceremony expresses the idea of a contest between two members of the Mĭde′-wĭwĭn to determine whose medicine is the stronger, the result of the contest to be determined by the effects produced by the two medicines.

The strength of his medicine is the measure of the power of a Mĭde′wĭnĭ′nĭ.

ORIGIN

Narrative by NA′WAJI′BIGO′KWE ("woman dwelling among the rocks")[a]

The Chippewa believe in many manido′, or spirits. The highest of them all is called Kijie′ manido′, literally translated, "Uncreated Spirit." Those connected with the Mĭde′ are (1) Mĭde′ manido′, the Mĭde′ spirit, and (2) four manido′, one at each point of the compass. These are called Wabûnûnk′daci′ manido′, the East spirit; Ca′wanûnk′daci′ manido′, the South spirit; Ningabi′anûnk′daci′ manido′, the West spirit; and Kiwe′dĭnûnk′daci′ manido′, the North spirit. In the Mĭde′ it is also the belief that there are four "layers" beneath the earth and four above the earth. These "layers," or planes, are distinct from each other.

Originally all the inhabitants of the earth (Chippewa Indians) who were to learn the Mĭde′ lived on Madeline island, in Lake Superior, and in that portion of the country. They were selected by the Mĭde′ manido′ to be taught the Mĭde′ religion.

There was first a consultation among the four manido′ (East, South, West, and North). This took place at the center of the earth, not under the earth, but at some place far away. There they sat together and talked and decided to teach the Mĭde′ to these particular Indians.

So the East manido′ was selected to go among these Indians and teach them. Before he left the others he told them that they must get everything ready and decide exactly how the Mĭde′ should be taught to the Indians. Of course the East manido′ could not approach the Indians in his spirit form, so he was born of an old woman who had lived with her husband all her life but had had no children. This old couple lived on Madeline island.

---

[a] The narrator is a prominent member of the Mĭde′wĭwĭn on the White Earth reservation in Minnesota. The narrative was interpreted by Mrs. Mary Warren English, sister of William Warren, the author of "History of the Ojibwa," and is given in the exact words of the interpreter. An Indian who is familiar with the Mĭde′ traditions on the Bois Fort reservation states that this is substantially the belief held there concerning the origin of the Mĭde′.

The people were astonished and said, "He must be a wonderful person to be born in this way," so both mother and child were treated with great respect.

He was indeed a wonderful child. Whatever he said came true. He would say to his father, "Go and get a bear," and his father would find one without any difficulty. It was no effort at all for the family to get enough food. The child grew up rapidly, and when he was a young man he had as his friend and companion one who was his mother's brother's son—his cousin.

When he grew up he began to consider, "I must begin to instruct these Indians in the Mïde'; that is the purpose for which I came."

After thinking this over he said to the old man, his father, "We will go on a journey to the end of the lake;" his mother went with them. The point to which they went was not where Duluth now stands, but was where Superior is located. This was the location of the old town of Fond du Lac.

They reached this place and stayed four days. On the fourth day a terrible storm came from the northeast, sweeping across the lake. During the storm the East manido' said to his father and mother, "My cousin at Madeline island is very ill; we must go back."

His father said, "It is impossible to even put the canoe on the water in such a storm."

Then the East manido' said, "Put the canoe on the water, and the waves will at once subside."

As soon as his father put the canoe on the water the storm subsided.

It was about noon when this happened, and the distance to Madeline island was about 80 miles, but they paddled so fast that they reached there before sundown. When they arrived they found that the cousin had been dead four days, but the body had been kept so that they could see him.

The East manido' told his father and mother and their friends not to weep for the young man. Then the next morning he told the people to make a long lodge extending east and west, such as is now used for the Mïde'. He showed them how to make it with the top open and the sides of birch bark and leaves, and he said that they must all bring tobacco and cooked food. In the center of the lodge he placed a Mïde' pole, and told the Indians to sit in rows around the lodge; he also made a Mïde' drum and rattles, such as are still used.

West of the pole and a few feet away he placed the hewn coffin of the dead man; on the south side of the lodge he seated the relatives and friends.

Then he told his father to take the Mïde' drum and sing.

The old man said, "I do not know how to sing."

His son said, "Just try; make the effort and you will be able to sing."

Then the East manido' spoke to the parents of the dead man and to his own parents, saying, "I am about to leave you. I will be absent four days. You must stay here continuously and do every day as I have told you to do to-day." The old man promised to sing the Mïde' songs and do everything as he had been told to do.

Then the East manido' took vermilion paint and also blue paint and made marks across the faces of the parents of the man and also his own parents—streaks across their foreheads, the lowest red, then blue and red alternately. Then he started away and said he would return on the morning of the fourth day. He went through the air toward the eastern sky. They could see him go.

After he had disappeared the old man took the Mïde' drum and sang more and more Mïde' songs. They came to him one after another. He was assisted by his son. Even while his son was absent he directed him spiritually.

During the four days that the East manido' was absent the sun shone constantly. There was not a cloud and the wind did not blow.

On the morning of the fourth day they looked toward the east and saw the sky streaked with colors like those he had painted on their foreheads. The Indians all looked in that direction with expectation.

All this time the old man had been drumming and singing.

A little before noon they heard a peculiar sound in the sky. It was from the east. Some one was calling *Wa, hi hi, hi,* as they call in the Mĭde′ ceremony. They watched the sky and saw four Indians walking toward them in the sky, giving this call. Each Indian had a living otter in his hand.

The East manido′ came down to the Mĭde′ inclosure, lifted the drapery, and allowed the others to pass in. The four manido′ came in and took their stand at the east end of the lodge. A little beyond the center was the coffin of hewn logs in which lay the body of the young man, who had now been dead eight days.

The four manido′ held the otters with the right hand near the head and the left hand below. These otters were their medicine bags.

The East manido′ stood first in the line. He began to sing, went halfway to the coffin, blew on his medicine bag, and shot from there toward the coffin. Then the top of the coffin burst open, and the East manido′ marched around the lodge and took his place at the end of the line.

Then the next one, the South manido′, did exactly as the East manido′ had done. When he had shot, the young man opened his eyes and breathed. Then the South manido′ took his position at the end of the line.

Next came the West manido′. When he had shot, the young man raised up and looked at the manido′.

Last came the North manido′, and when he had shot the young man rose up entirely well in every respect.

Then these four manido′ began to talk to the Indians, and to tell them that this was the method by which they were to treat the sick and the dead, and that the East manido′ would instruct them in all they were to do.

Then these manido′ told the Indians that they would never see them again. The manido′ would never come to earth again, but the Indians must offer them gifts and sacrifices, which would be spiritually received. They must always remember that the Mĭde′ was given to them by the manido′.

The East manido′ taught them the religion of the Mĭde′ and put souls in their bodies and arranged how these souls should live in the next world. A great many times some of these Mĭde′ people have a trance in which they follow the spirit path and see their dead friends. They also receive messages in dreams. They are especially liable to do this when sorrowing for their friends.

It is told to Mĭde′ members that about halfway to the Spirit Land there is a punishment place where fire burns out all that is evil in them. Sometimes there is so little left of the person that he turns into a frog. There are many little frogs in that place, but the good pass through it unharmed. This is the only phase of punishment taught, except that if a person dies while drunk he will remain drunken forever and his punishment will be an eternal and unquenchable thirst.

Those initiated into the Mĭde′ are instructed how to lead a good life. These instructions are given only to the members. Less heed is paid to the instructions than in the old days, but very sick people are still restored by means of the Mĭde′.

The narrator stated further that she had taken four degrees in the society and received four great instructions, and that she tried to live according to them. She stated that she "could blow on her medicine bag and produce evil results upon those who displeased her, provided they were not of the Mĭde′;" she "would be powerless against a member of the Mĭde′wĭwĭn." She "would not, however, exert this evil power, for it would displease the Mĭde′ manido′. Some do this and it always reacts in evil upon themselves."

Such is the story of the Mĭde′, which the Chippewa believes that he received from the manido′ who came to him from the morning sky.

DESCRIPTION OF DIAGRAM REPRESENTING THE PATH OF LIFE

In the explanation of this diagram[a] (fig. 3) the usual custom of retaining the exact words of the interpreter has been followed.

The description is as follows:

This diagram represents the path of life from youth to old age, the tangent which appears at each angle representing a temptation. There are seven of these temptations.

The first tangent represents the first temptation which comes to a young man. If he yields to it he will not live long.

The second tangent represents the second temptation, and the penalty for this also is that he will not live long.

With the third temptation the element of religious responsibility appears, and the man (supposedly a member of the Mĭde′wĭwĭn) is asked: "How did you act when you were initiated into the Mĭde′wĭwĭn? Were you respectful to the older members, and did you faithfully fulfill all obligations?"

The fourth tangent is placed beyond the angle of the line. It represents a temptation coming to a man in middle life.

FIG. 3. Mĭde′ diagram of the path of life.

With the fifth temptation the man begins to reflect upon his own length of days, and asks himself: "Have you ever been disrespectful to old age?"

The sixth temptation returns to the religious idea, and asks whether all religious obligations have been fulfilled.

The seventh temptation is said to be the hardest of all, and if a man can endure it he will live to the allotted age of man. At this time an evil spirit comes to him, and if he has even so much as smiled during a Mĭde′ ceremony, he must reckon with it then.

The word "temptation," as used in this connection, implies primarily a trial of strength and motive. There seems a significance in the fact that, with the exception of the first and last, these tangents occur after an angle or turn in the line, suggesting that some sharp turn in the life of the man is followed immediately by this testing of his character.

INITIATION CEREMONY OF THE FIRST DEGREE

The following description of an initiation ceremony is compiled from statements made by several members of the Mĭde′wĭwĭn, all of whom belong to the Mille Lac band of Chippewa, but are now living on the White Earth reservation. The entire account has been veri-

---

[a] Drawn by the elder Maiñ′äns, the explanation being interpreted by Mr. John C. Carl, a graduate of Haskell Institute.

MAIÑ'ĂNS

WA'WIEKÛM'ĬG

fied, being translated into Chippewa and pronounced correct by members of the Mĭde'wĭwĭn.[a]

The ceremony described is that of initiation into the first degree. Initiation into the second degree differs slightly from the first, and initiation into the higher degrees is said to be different from the lower degrees in many important respects; yet it is possible for persons to be initiated into different degrees at the same ceremony. It is also possible for a person to take two or even more degrees at the same time, but this requires large gifts and extended instruction and is seldom done.

The first duty of the novitiate is to notify the old man whom he desires as leader of the ceremony. This man consults with the novitiate and selects four others to assist in the ceremony of initiation. These do not usually hold as high degrees as the leader, but they are expected to give part of the instructions and are familiar with the duties of their office. A man is also selected to act as herald and general director of the ceremony. This officer is called oc'kabe'wĭs.

The first duty of the oc'kabe'wĭs is to announce the ceremony to the members of the Mĭde'wĭwĭn and invite them to attend. He carries tobacco, notifies the people that the ceremony is to be held, tells them to smoke the tobacco, and also mentions, in the order of their importance, the persons who will take part in the ceremony.

At the appointed time the people move their lodges and camp near the place where the ceremony is to be held.

The initiators and the friends of the candidate have been preparing for the ceremony and have built the sweat lodge. This is built wherever desired, and there is no prescribed direction for its opening. Four poles are used in its construction, as the candidate is to be initiated to the first degree. Six poles would be used if the second degree were to be taken. These four poles are firmly planted in the ground at points corresponding to the four corners of a square. The poles diagonally opposite are then fastened together, forming the framework of the roof, the binding together of the two poles into one symbolizing the lengthening of life, which is accomplished by means of the Mĭde'. Sheets of birch bark are spread over the poles to form the sides and roof.

The first ceremonial act on the part of the initiators consists in entering the sweat lodge. A fire is built outside the entrance. Stones

---

[a] Accounts of the ceremony were given by two Chippewa bearing the same name, but not related to each other. These were Maiñ'ăns ("little wolf"), an aged man (see pls. 3, 6) who is most desirous that his native beliefs shall be correctly interpreted to his white brethren, and Maiñ'ăns, a younger man, who retains with remarkable accuracy the details of the ceremony as it was given in the old days at Mille Lac.

Wa'wiekûm'ĭg ("the round earth") (see pl. 4) and his wife Na'waji'bigo'kwe ("woman dwelling among the rocks") are members of the Mĭde'wĭwĭn in high degrees and have given valuable assistance in explaining the songs and symbols; also Jiwa'bĭkito' ("resounding metal"), who holds the fourth degree, and De'-bwawĕn'dûnk ("eating noisily"), plate 8, who holds the sixth degree, in the Mĭde'wĭwĭn. Supplementary information has been received from all the singers of Mĭde' songs.

are heated and laid in the center of the lodge and frequently sprinkled with water by means of a wisp of brush, the steam enveloping the bodies of the men. It frequently happens that one or two women are among those who are to assist at the initiation. They do not enter the lodge but stand outside, joining in the songs. Mide' songs are sung in the sweat lodge, and the mĭtĭ'gwakĭk' (Mĭde' drum) is used. The leader of the entire ceremony is usually the leader in the sweat lodge also. There is no prescribed length of time for remaining in the sweat lodge, but several days are allowed for this portion of the ceremony, at least four days being allowed if four men holding high degrees are in attendance.

On the first evening and on each succeeding evening before the initiation the men who are to assist in the ceremony sing in their lodges, and all who desire may enter the lodges and dance. The leader of the entire ceremony sings first in his lodge, drumming on his mĭtĭ'gwakĭk'. The man next in importance answers from his lodge, and when he has finished the other men who are to take part in the initiation sing in their lodges in the order of their importance, "to show how glad they are that this person is to join the Mĭde'wĭwĭn." Then they all sing together, each his own song in his own wigwam.

Each Mĭde'wĭnĭ'nĭ has his own set of songs, some of which he has composed and some of which he has purchased for large sums of money or equal value in goods. It occasionally happens that two men have the same song, but this is a coincidence. It is not permissible for one man to sing a song belonging to another unless he has purchased the right to sing it. The songs owned by individuals are those connected with the use of medicine, and when a man buys a song he receives some of the medicine for use.

During the evenings which precede the initiation ceremony it is customary for members of the Mĭde'wĭwĭn to enter the lodges of the leaders and ask for instruction or information regarding the Mĭde'. For this purpose a person would go, if possible, to the Mĭde'wĭnĭ'nĭ who initiated him, as the men always take an interest in those whom they have initiated and require smaller gifts from them. The person desiring such assistance takes a kettle of food or some other gift, enters the lodge while the man is singing, and waits until he finishes the song, thereupon placing the gift before him and asking the desired instruction or advice, which is willingly given. One who does not wish to ask a favor may enter any lodge and dance without presenting a gift.

The following is an example of the songs which the Mĭde'wĭnĭ'nĭ sing in their lodges during the evenings preceding the initiation ceremony. Other songs for similar use are given at the close of this chapter. It should be remembered that the songs given in connection with this ceremony are representatives of a class and **not** obligatory.

This song was sung by O'děni'gûn ("hip bone"), an old man who is said to be especially skilled in the use of medicine. In connection with the song he gave the following narrative:

There was once an old man who was a member of the Mĭde'wĭwĭn, and knew the use of all kinds of medicines and their songs. This old man had a nephew to whom he taught the songs and the use of the medicines. The young man's name was Awi'-hinedja', and he was anxious to become very powerful. After a time the old man said: "My nephew, I can teach you no more; you know all that I know and now you will be a leader of the Mĭde'wĭwĭn." But the young man was not satisfied. He brought many presents to his uncle in order that his uncle might try to remember still more.

The old man said: "You are certainly very determined," and the young man replied, "I know it."

The old man said: "My nephew, if you are as determined as this you will find out whatever you desire. Come with me."

Then the old man took his nephew far into the woods saying: "We are going where there is a river." So they walked on and on until they came to a rocky gorge. They stood at the edge of the cliff, and looking down they saw a river far below them. There were trees beside the river, but the cliff on which they stood was far above the tops of the trees.

Then the old man said: "Jump down to the river," and the young man jumped down, crashing through the tree tops and falling dead upon the rocks below. His body was so crushed that it was not like a human body any more.

Four bears came and walked around his body, singing this song. When the young man regained consciousness he heard the bears singing; when he opened his eyes he saw the bears walking around him, and when they had walked around him four times he rose up strong and well.

Then the four bears began to walk up the cliff and the young man followed them. The four bears and the young man walked up the sheer face of the cliff as though it were level ground. At the top they found the old man waiting for them.

"Now, my nephew," he said, "you are as great a medicine-man as I."

So Awi'hinedja' became a teacher and leader in the Mĭde'wĭwĭn.

No. 1. SONG OF THE FOUR BEARS　　(Catalogue no. 189)[a]
Sung by O'DĚNI'GÛN

Analysis.—This song follows closely the intervals of the fourth five-toned scale[b] and is sung with the vibrato which characterizes the dancing songs of the Mĭde', making the intonation somewhat indistinct. A comparison between the metric units of voice and drum shows that 3 metric units of the voice are approximately equal to 2 metric units of the drum. This suggests the rhythm commonly known as "two against three," but the voice-pulses are grouped in double measures with

SONG PICTURE NO. 1. This drawing shows the men emerging from the wigwam and also standing at the edge of the cliff. In a similar manner the progress of a narrative is frequently shown in a Mĭde' drawing.

---

[a] The catalogue numbers used throughout this paper correspond respectively with the numbers designating the phonograph records of the songs, which are preserved in the Bureau of American Ethnology.

[b] See p. 7.

few exceptions, and there is no coincidence between voice and drum. The 3–4 measures are unmistakable in rhythm and occur in both renditions of the song. A strong feeling for the submediant is evident in this melody.

The song closes with the exclamatory phrases which characterize the Mĭde′ songs and which can not be accurately transcribed. The notation will, however, give an idea of this peculiarity.

Voice M. M. ♩ = 168
Drum M. M. ♩ = 104
(Drum in unaccented eighth notes)

A - wi-hi - ne - dja *ha* ni - wi - do - se - ma *ha* a - wi-hi-ne - dja

ha ni - wi - do - se - ma *a wi ha* ni - wi - do - se - ma

hi we na hi de - mu - sa *wi hi na* a - wi - hi - ne - dja

ha ni - wi - do - se - ma *a wi ha* ni - wi - do - se - ma

hi we na wa *hi* yû wa *hi* yû

Drum

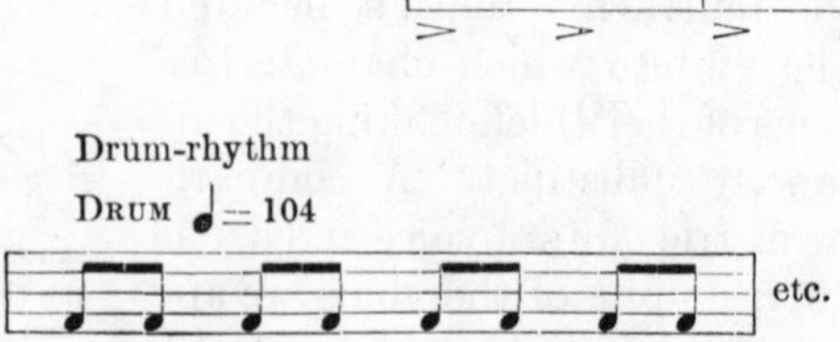

Drum-rhythm
Drum ♩ = 104

etc.

WORDS

Awi′hinedja′.............................. (Man's name)
Ni′widos′ema............................. I am walking with him
Ĭn′ade′musa′............................. Alas! Alas!

After all have been in the sweat lodge a council of the initiators is called by the leader. This is held for the purpose of deciding what part each is to take in the initiation ceremony. The person to be initiated is present at this council.

The council may be held in any of the lodges. The leader sits at the left of the entrance; beside him is his mĭtĭ′gwakĭk′, and before him is spread a blanket, given by the person to be initiated as a part of the prescribed offering. The candidate for initiation sits at the right of the leader; at the opposite side of the lodge sit the other four initiators, while the oc′kabe′wĭs comes and goes as needed.

When all are assembled a discussion is held as to who will be best adapted to certain parts of the ceremony. One man is selected to be the first to "shoot" the candidate for initiation. This man is called ne′mĭta′maûñ′—a special word which can not be literally translated; he was said to be "like the man who sits in the bow of the boat to watch which way the boat is going." The next person to be selected is the man who is to be the last to "shoot" the candidate for initiation. This man is called we′daked′, and is said to be "like the steersman who sits in the stern of the boat and guides it."

After these two have been selected the leader turns to the ne′mĭta′-maûñ′ and says, "You have been appointed by us; do as you think best in the performance of your duties; we do not command you, for we respect you and have confidence in your ability." He then extends his hands over him and places the mĭtĭ′gwakĭk′ before him.

The ne′mĭta′maûñ′ then sings as many songs as he likes, the person to be initiated rising and dancing before him as he sings.

When the ne′mĭta′maûñ′ has finished singing he turns to the man next him and says, " Nikân (my Mĭde′ brother), there must be something in you since you were chosen to take part in this ceremony." He strikes the mĭtĭ′gwakĭk′ three times, saying ho ho ho, and hands it to the man next to him, who sings as he has done and, in turn, passes the drum to the man who sits next to him.

The men of lesser importance are expected to do little except sing a few songs.

This council takes a long time and after it is finished the leader has no further responsibility, though he may be consulted by those to whom he has delegated authority.

Maiñ′ăns stated that when he was one of the initiators he sang the following song, which was taught him by the old man who initiated him into the Mĭde′wĭwĭn. In explanation of the song he said that a manido′ came to teach the Mĭde′ to the Indians, and at that time stopped on a long point of land which projects into Lake Superior at Duluth. The song refers to this incident. (See p. 22). The person to be initiated would not dance during this song.

No. 2. SONG OF THE MANIDO'   (Catalogue no. 238)

Sung by MAIÑ'ĂNS ("LITTLE WOLF")

VOICE ♩ = 152
DRUM ♩ = 152
(Drum-rhythm similar to No. 1)

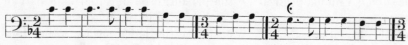

Na-wai - i *he he nĭ mĭ sĭ   nûn na-wai - i he he nĭ mĭ sĭ*

nûn na-wai - i he he nĭ mĭ sĭ   nûn na-wai - i he he nĭ

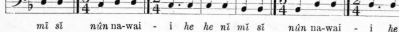

mĭ sĭ   nûn na-wai - i he he nĭ mĭ sĭ   nûn na-wai - i he

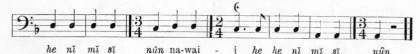

he nĭ mĭ sĭ   nûn na-wai - i he he nĭ mĭ sĭ   nûn

ni - bi - ba - ha - ha - wi - yan e - na - wai

WORDS

Nawaii'............................ On the center of a peninsula
Ni'bawiyăn'......................... I am standing

Analysis.—This song is melodic in structure, begins on the twelfth
and with one exception contains only the tones of the fourth five-toned
scale, the most frequent interval of progression being the
minor third. The notes marked (· were slightly prolonged
in all the renditions. This prolonging of the tone was uniform but not sufficient to be indicated by a note value.
Attention is directed to the fact that with the introduction
of the second word the melody does not begin an entire
repetition but soon returns to a point near the opening of
the song, the remainder of the melody being the same as
in the first.

SONG PIC-
TURE NO. 2.
The Mĭde'
pole and
stone are
shown in
the draw-
ing.

The following song is similar to no. 2, except that the
person to be initiated would dance during this song. It
may also be sung in the *Mĭde'wĭgan* (lodge in which the ceremony
is held) after the initiation.

No. 3. Dancing Song   (Catalogue no. 239)

Sung by Maiñ′ăns

Voice ♩= 108

Drum ♩= 108

(Drum in quarter notes)

Ho wi-gan-e   ho wi-gan-e   ho wi-gan-e   ho wi-gan-e

ho wi-gan-e   ho wi-gan-e   ho wi-gan-e ho wi-gan-e

ho   wi-gan-e   ho wi-gan-e   ho wi-gan-e   ho wi-gan-e

ho o-go-tci-tci-yan-e   wi-gan-e   ho wi-gan-e

ho - wi-gan-e   ho   wi-gan-e   ho   wi-gan-e

ho   wi-gan-e   ho   wi-gan-e   ho   wi-gan-e

ho wi-gan-e   ho wi-gan-e   ho wi-gan-e   ho

WORDS

O′gotcitci′yane′ .... In form like a bird
Siwa′wigane′ .... It appears

Analysis.—This song is based on the second five-toned scale.[a] It
begins on the octave and the principal interval of descent is the
minor third. The long note at the beginning of the measure is often
slightly prolonged. The metric unit of voice and drum is the same,
but the voice deviates somewhat, while the drum is maintained with
mechanical regularity. This song is given with the peculiar vibrato
which characterizes the Mĭde′ dancing songs.

[a] See p. 7.

Before initiation the candidate is taken into the woods by the initiators and given an "instruction," each man talking to him for a long time.   Only one such instruction is given to a candidate for the first degree, the number of instructions corresponding to the degree to be assumed.   In the first degree the instruction is chiefly of a moral nature, the candidate being enjoined to lead a virtuous and upright life.   He is taught also the names and uses of a few simple herbs which he is expected to secure and carry in his Mĭde' bag.   He may find these herbs for himself or procure them from some other member of the order.   In the higher degrees the instructions pertain to the mysteries of the Mĭde', the properties of rare herbs, and the nature of vegetable poisons.

Song picture no. 3.   It is interesting to note that the drawing suggests the skeleton of a bird rather than a living bird.

During the days which precede the ceremony it is customary for the leading members of the Mĭde'wĭwĭn to hold preparatory meetings.   Any man may prepare a feast and invite others to attend, each guest bringing a pan or plate in which he carries away a portion of the food.

At the close of such a meeting the host rises and says, "We will all sing and dance before you go."   The principal guest lifts his pan of food, then all rise and sing the following song, the words of which mean "I am raising it up."   This refers to the pan of food, which is considered to be offered to the manido'.   The same song could be sung if a sick person were to be treated by the Mĭde' and were present in the lodge.   The words would then be understood as referring to the sick person.

After the singing and dancing the principal guest leads and all follow him as he walks around the lodge and out of the door.

No. 4. Preparatory Song   (Catalogue no. 190)
Sung by O'dĕni'gûn

Analysis.—This song moves freely along the tones of the fourth five-toned scale.   The basis of the song consists of two major triads on G flat, one in the upper and one in the lower octave, with E flat as the passing tone, but the presence of A flat as an accented tone classifies the song as melodic rather than harmonic.   We can not safely infer a chord unless more than one tone of it occurs in the melody, and there is no contiguous tone which can be associated with A flat in diatonic chord relation.

Song picture no. 4.   The drawing indicates a small gathering of people at a feast.

The chief musical interest of this song lies in the fact that the metric unit is the measure, not the individual part of the measure.   There is no apparent relation between the metric units of voice and drum.

A variation between the words as sung and the words accompanying the translation will be found in many Chippewa songs. Many words are dismembered and have meaningless vowel sounds inserted between the syllables; in many instances only a portion of a word is used, and the pronunciation is often changed. Throughout this work the words beneath the music are transcribed as given by the singer. The words translated are the correct Chippewa and a comparison between the two will show the changes made by the singer. Thus in the present instance it will be seen that the syllable *hwe* or *wi* is substituted for the two syllables *nin-do*, which are the beginning of the Chippewa word; the syllable *hi* is also inserted in the word. Meaningless syllables are italicized, whether inserted between parts of a word or between the words of the song.

VOICE ♩ = 84
DRUM ♩ = 108
(Drum-rhythm similar to No. 1)

Hwe - na - gi - wi - na   hwe - na - gi - wi - na   .   wi -

na - gi - wi - *hi* - na - *hi* - na   wi - na - gi - wi - na . .   wi -

na - ga - wi - *hi* - na - gi   na   wi - na - gi - na

WORDS

Nindona'giwina'.................... I am raising it (or him) up

On the day before the initiation a feast is given in his own lodge by the candidate for initiation. Invitations are delivered by the oc'kabe'wĭs, and most of the guests are women. A man is appointed leader of this feast, and when it is time for the guests to depart he leads in the singing of two songs, shaking his rattle as he sings. Anyone who knows these songs may join the leader in singing them.

During the first song the guests stand in a line, the leader being next the door, and they dance as they stand in their places, the dance step consisting in the rhythmic transference of the weight from one foot to the other. Each of these songs is sung only once.

Before singing the first song the leader might say, "I have learned this song from an old man, and I will sing it as well as I can." The words of the first song refer to the pan of food which each guest is allowed to take home with him.

No. 5. "MY PAN OF FOOD"   (Catalogue no. 240)

Sung by MAIÑ′ĂNS

VOICE ♩ = 126
DRUM ♩ = 92
(Drum-rhythm similar to No. 1)

Ha ni wa- koñ i - na *ha ha ha ha ha ha ni* wa-koñ . -

VOICE ♩. = 88

na *ha ni* wa- koñ i - na *ha ha ni* wa koñ i -

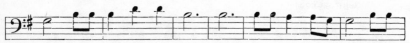

na *ha ni* wa-koñ i - na *ha ha ni* wa- koñ i -na *ha ni*

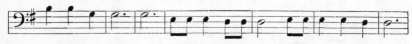

wa-koñ i - na *ha ha ni* wa-koñ i-na *ha ni* wa-koñ i - na

ha ha ni wa-koñ i - na *ha ni* wa - koñ i - na *ha*

nin - do - na - gûn *e he ha ni* wa- koñ i - na *ha ni*

Harmonic analysis:

WORDS

Wa′koñ	On my arm
Ina′	Behold
Nin′dona′gûn	My pan of food

SONG PICTURE
NO. 5. The
man holds
his dish of
food, as
stated in the
song.

Analysis.—This song is plainly harmonic in structure, as the melody tones follow the intervals of the major triad in the upper and lower octaves, the sixth being used as a passing tone. Two renditions of the song were secured, each beginning with several measures in slower time.

The rhythm in these measures is uncertain and can be only approximately indicated, but after the change of time the metric unit is marked by the pulse of the measure beginning, which is very regular.

Before singing the second closing song the leader might say, "I will now depart and announce that the feast is ended."

No. 6. "MY PIPE" (Catalogue no. 241)

Sung by MAIÑ′ĂNS

VOICE ♩ = 108
DRUM ♩ = 96
(Drum-rhythm similar to No. 1)

Nin - do - na - gi - ci - ma *we* nin - do - na - gi - ci - ma *we hi*

o nin-do - na - gi - ci - ma *we* nin - do na - gi - ci - ma

we nin - do - na - gi - ci - ma *we* nin - do - na - gi - ci - ma

we nin - do - na - gi - ci - ma *we* nin-do-pwa-gûn *e* nin - do

WORDS

Nindo′nagicima′................... I am raising
Nin′dopwa′gûn................... My pipe

SONG PICTURE NO. 6. The man raises his dish of food and also his pipe.

Analysis.—The singing of this song was preceded by very rapid drumming, the drum beats being in the value of sixteenth notes, at ♪=144 (two drum beats to each beat of the metronome at 144); with this rapid drumming the ejaculatory *ho ho ho ho* of the Mïde′ was given.

This song begins on the unaccented portion of the measure, which is somewhat unusual. The melody begins on the twelfth and follows the descending intervals of the fourth five-toned scale. The harmonic basis is the same as in the preceding song, but the use of the second as an accented tone places it (according to our present classification) among the songs whose structure is melodic rather than harmonic.

At the close of this song the leader lays down his rattle, raises his hands with palms extended, and motions the people to follow him as he dances out of the lodge.

It is expected that those who have been invited to this feast will build the Mĭde'wĭgan (Mĭde' lodge), where the initiation ceremony is to be held. This is done soon after the close of the feast, and as so many are at work—some cutting the poles and others cutting brush or bringing dry hay—the building of the lodge requires only a short time.

Plate 5 shows a Mĭde' lodge with a ceremony in progress. At this ceremony Wa'wiekûm'ĭg was advanced to a high degree. The structure is made of a framework of poles interlaced overhead to form a roof whose arch suggests the dome of the sky. In unfavorable weather this framework is covered with branches. The size of the lodge varies according to requirement. It is usually from 50 to 100 feet long, 12 to 15 feet wide, and about 8 feet high. In the old days several hundred people attended the Mĭde'wĭwĭn and the lodge at that time is said to have been so long that a person at one end could not hear voices at the other end and could judge the progress of the ceremony only by the sound of the drum.

For an initiation into the first degree the lodge (see fig. 4) extends east and west, with a door at each end. For an initiation into the fourth degree the lodge is built with four doors—east, west, north, and south. If necessary for warmth, two fires are made, one in front of each door. A large stone is placed a short distance west of the fire which burns near the eastern door. This stone symbolizes the power of the Mĭde' as a defense, one man stating that the Mĭde' is like a stone to throw at an enemy. West of the center of the lodge is the pole belonging to the person to be initiated and known as his medicine pole. If he is to take the first degree this pole is decorated with a narrow blue band at the top, below which there is a broad band of red, the remainder of the pole being unpainted. For an initiation into the second degree the pole is decorated with a broader band of blue, the width of the band of red remaining the same. It is also placed nearer the west door. For the third degree an effigy of a bird is placed near the top of the pole, for the fourth degree a crossbar is placed in the same position, and for each succeeding degree there is a prescribed form of decoration.

On the day set for the initiation ceremony, just before sunrise, the oc'kabe'wĭs and the person to be initiated go to the lodge carrying on their backs the gifts which the latter will present to the initiators. They go around the lodge four times, enter the east door, and hang the gifts upon poles provided for the purpose. These gifts consist of blankets and cloth as well as tobacco and food. The oc'kabe'wĭs remains in the lodge to complete the arrangements.

INTERIOR VIEW

EXTERIOR VIEW

MĬDE′ LODGE

These photographs were taken during a Mĭde′ ceremony at Elbow Lake, White Earth reservation,
May, 1909

MAIÑ'ĂNS AS LEADER OF A MĬDE' CEREMONY

Next a dog is killed for the feast. There is nothing ceremonial in either the selection or the killing of the dog; the latter takes place at some distance. The body of the dog is laid at the door of the lodge and the entire procession steps over it, after which it is carried away and cooked.

Early in the morning, before the hour set for the ceremony, the person to be initiated goes to the lodge again, accompanied by the leader, the four initiators, and the oc'kabe'wĭs.

The next event is the sending of the oc'kabe'wĭs with invitations to the members of the Mĭde'wĭwĭn. These invitations are in the form of round sticks about the diameter of a lead pencil and about 6 inches long.

From one lodge to another the oc'kabe'wĭs goes, distributing the sticks to those members of the Mĭde'wĭwĭn who are entitled to attend the ceremony. If a person has committed some offense against the society he is not included in this invitation. The oc'kabe'wĭs counts the sticks as he gives them out and returning reports the number to the initiators, who thus know the number who will be present at the ceremony. Only members of the Mĭde'wĭwĭn are allowed to be present in the lodge during the initiation. This company of people have a leader appointed by the man in charge of the ceremony. They assemble a short distance from the Mĭde'wĭgan, each carrying his medicine bag, and an empty pan in which to carry away a portion of the feast. All are dressed in their finest except two who are called za'gimag', whose duties will be explained. At the proper time the leader moves toward the lodge followed by the company in single file. They march once around the lodge, singing the following song:

No. 7. PROCESSIONAL   (Catalogue no. 54)

Sung by BE'CĬGWI'WIZÄNS ("STRIPED BOY ")

Analysis.—This song begins on the fifth of the key and ends on the fifth, having a range of one octave. The tempo is very rapid, and the song is marked by vigorous accents. The two words are repeated in each line of the song, and pronounced very indistinctly.

At the eastern door the leader of the company pauses and makes a plea to the Mĭde' manido', with right hand extended and left hand shaking his rattle. (See pl. 6.) Three times he advances as though to enter and as many times withdraws as though in fear. The fourth time he puts his head and shoulders through the opening and looks about as though in search of danger. Then he enters the lodge, followed by the company. Main'ăns, the elder, stated that in this

SONG PICTURE NO. 7. The oblong represents the Mĭde'wĭgan. In the center is a long pole on which are hung the gifts to be bestowed by the person initiated. The procession is entering the lodge.

entrance the leader impersonated the bear, who is intimately associated with the Mĭde'.

As the company march around the lodge the leader extends his hands toward the stone, the mĭtĭ'gwakĭk', and the medicine pole. This is an act of reverence.

WORDS

Nĭn'djĭngocka'naki................. The ground trembles
Wapĭn'digeyan'..................... As I am about to enter

While marching around the inside of the lodge the company sings the melody which was sung as they marched around the outside, the following words being substituted:

Cagwani'moyan'.................... My heart fails me
Wapĭn'digeyan' .... As I am about to enter
Manido'wigan'ĭñ.................... The spirit lodge

The company marches around the lodge three times, and while making the fourth circuit they sit down wherever they like.

The diagram (fig. 4) shows the arrangement of the Mĭde'wĭgan and the position of its occupants during the ceremony. The oblong represents the lodge. At each side of the eastern entrance are two figures. The first pair are "fiery dragons which disappear into the ground if the candidate has the proper offering;" the pair nearest the entrance are "servants of the Mĭde' manido', who may refuse to admit the candidate if they are not satisfied with him." The footprints at the entrance indicate that the man who entered impersonated the bear. The candidate sits next to the eastern entrance; beside him are the leader and the oc'kabe'wĭs. The four initiators sit near the western entrance, on the north side of the lodge; their position is, however, not arbitrary. Along the sides of the lodge sit the mem-

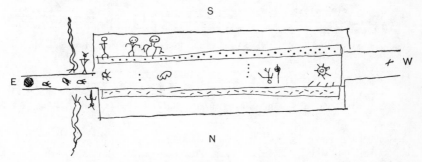

FIG. 4. Diagram showing arrangement of Mĭde'wĭgan during initiation ceremony of first degree. (Drawn by the elder Maiñ'ăns.)

bers of the Mĭde'wĭwĭn. A fire burns near each entrance. The stone near the eastern entrance is shown, also the medicine pole and the pile of gifts beside it. The figure east of the pole shows the second position taken by the candidate for initiation; the dot west of the stone is where the drum is stationed during the initiation; the two dots east of the stone show the position of the drum after the initiation, at which time it is played by the old leader and the oc'kabe'wĭs; the four dots near the center of the lodge represent mi'gĭs and will be explained later. (See p. 48.)

The following song is sung after all are seated.

No. 8. INTRODUCTORY SONG　　　　(Catalogue no. 55)

Sung by BE'CĬGWI'WIZĂNS

Analysis.—The tempo of this song is even more rapid than the preceding, the metric unit being the entire measure. It is based on the major triad in the upper and lower octaves, with the sixth as a connecting tone, the sixth being more prominent than in most songs of similar harmonic structure.

SONG PICTURE NO. 8. The gifts are again shown.

After this song the invitation sticks are collected, counted, tied in a bundle and laid at the foot of the medicine pole.

Next a feast is served, each person receiving his or her portion in the pan brought for that purpose. At this feast the dog is served; portions of rice or other food may be carried away but it is required that all of the dog be eaten in the lodge.

VOICE ♩ = 84
Recorded without drum

A - i -gwû gi - wi - mĭ - de - wi - i - go ni - kân   a - i - gwû

gi - wi-mĭ - de - wi - i - go ni - kân   a - i -gwû gi - wi - mĭ - de -

wi - i - go ni - kân   a - i - gwû gi - wi - mĭ - de - wi - i - go ni - kân.

WORDS

Aigwû′............................ We are now
Giwi′mĭde′wiigo′ .... To receive you into the Mĭde′wĭwĭn
Nikân′........................... Our Mĭde′ brother

Halfway down the lodge sit the za′gimag′, whose faces are not painted.

The leader then dances around the lodge carrying the mĭtĭ′gwakĭk′. He moves along the curves indicated in the diagram (fig. 5). After

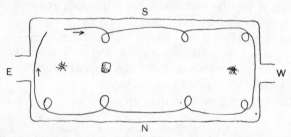

FIG. 5.   Diagram showing course followed by leader during initiation ceremony of first degree.

encircling the lodge he leaves the mĭtĭ′gwakĭk′ in front of the two za′gimag′, who begin to sing the nĭ′mĭwûg′ (dancing songs), during which any persons who wish may rise and dance in their places. There are a large number of these dancing songs and they are greatly enjoyed by members of the Mĭde′wĭwĭn.

Maiñ′ăns, the younger, stated that he sang the following song when he was a za′gimag′. The words contain a reference to water. This reference occurs frequently in the Mĭde′ songs; it will be noted that the water is usually represented as in action—bubbling, flowing, seething, or casting up the white Mĭde′ shells.

No. 9. SONG OF THE ZA'GIMAG'   (Catalogue no. 242)

Sung by MAIÑ'ÄNS

WORDS

Niwa'wacke'abog'.................. A bubbling spring
We'wendji'djiwûñ' .... Comes from the hard ground

Analysis.—This song is an excellent example of the manner in which ejaculations are interpolated into the Mĭde' songs. In portions of the song the rhythm is rigidly maintained. For instance, in the measures containing four quarter notes these notes are of exactly the same length, and the difference between the 3–4 and 4–4 measures is unmistakable, but in the fifth and sixth measures, where there is a repetition of the syllables, the rhythm is irregular.

The pulse of the drum is absolutely regular throughout. The peculiar succession of measure lengths gives an appearance of great rhythmic irregularity, yet the metric unit of the quarter note is, with the exceptions mentioned, quite regularly maintained.

SONG PICTURE NO. 9. The course of the stream is shown.

Other examples of the ni'miwûg are given at the close of this chapter.

The za'gimag' then carry the mĭtĭ'gwakĭk' around the lodge and place it west of the stone, where it remains during the rites of initiation.

The leader then encircles the lodge four times, with right hand extended, left hand shaking the rattle, and head bent forward; this being finished, the oc'kabe'wĭs takes down the gifts from the place where they have been hung; the blankets are folded and laid at the foot of the pole, care being taken to have them placed in the proper order for distribution, the other gifts being conveniently placed on the ground.

The person to be initiated is then escorted to the pole by the leader, moving along the dotted lines indicated in the diagram (fig. 6).

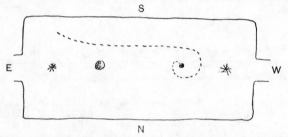

FIG. 6. Diagram showing course followed by candidate, escorted by leader, in dance at Mĭde' initiation ceremony of first degree.

He moves slowly at first, then very rapidly, ejaculating *hi hi hi*, and shaking his rattle.

The candidate is seated on the pile of blankets at the foot of the pole, facing the east.

While escorting the candidate to the pole the following song may be sung:

No. 10. Escorting the Candidate (Catalogue no. 237)

Sung by Maiñ'ăns

Analysis.—This song was sung three times, the transcription being from the third rendition; the others are identical in the pulse of measure beginnings and the outline of intervals, but vary slightly in unimportant note values.

This song is a particularly good example of a feature which characterizes the Mĭde' songs and which has a direct bearing on the problem of musical development. The unvarying portion of the song is the pulse of the measure beginnings, which is uniform in all the renditions, while the pulse of the "counts" in the measures is not mechanically regular and more nearly resembles the rhythm of ceremonial speech. This suggests the possibility that the transition from ceremonial speech to song may be by the adoption of large rhythmic pulses which are first made absolute, the rhythm of the intervening portions being less rigidly controlled and retaining the character of ceremonial speech.

VOICE ♩. = 54
DRUM ♩ = 92
(Drum-rhythm similar to No. 1)

Mĭ-de-wi-ga - a-an gi-wa-ni - no-sĕ   hĕ hĕ   hĕ hĕ   ni-

kâ - â - ân   gi-wa-ni-no-ha-ni-no   ho ho   ho ho   ni-

kâ - â-ân gi - wa-ni-no - sĕ   hĕ hĕ   ni-kâ - â-ân gi-

wa-ni-no - sĕ   hĕ hĕ ni-kâ - â-ân gi - wa-ni-no - sĕ.

WORDS

Nikân'............................Our Mĭde' brother
Giwa'ninosĕ'.........................You are going around
Mĭde'wĭgân.........................The Mĭde' lodge

The rhythm of the drum is mechanically regular and its metric unit has no relation to that of the voice.

After escorting the candidate to the pole the leader summons the men previously selected to perform the rites of initiation. These men move along the northern side of the lodge and take their places at the south side of the eastern door, the man designated as ne'mĭta'maûñ' being first in the line and the man designated as we'daked' being last. Each of these men has a mi'gĭs (a small white shell used in the Mĭde') in his mouth. The ne'mĭta'maûñ' then blows on his medicine bag and dances, standing in his place. He then walks toward the candidate, ejaculating *we ho ho ho ho!* and extending his medicine bag with each ejaculation. As he reaches the candidate he "shoots" him, thrusting the medicine bag toward him and ejaculating with great vehemence. It is difficult to

SONG PICTURE NO. 10. The candidate for initiation is seen approaching the medicine pole. The branches of the sapling are here shown in the drawing, though they are cut when the pole is in use. In this connection they symbolize the life of the tree. (Compare drawings of songs nos. 44 and 55.)

describe this ejaculation, which is not loud but very forceful, with a peculiar throbbing tone. It is exceedingly impressive, and the hearer can not fail to realize that the entire power of the speaker is being projected toward the person under treatment, whether that treatment be intended to remove some inner defect, as in the Mǐde' ceremonies, or to cure some bodily ailment, as in the treatment of the sick.

When the ne'mǐta'maûñ' "shoots" the candidate for initiation the man is said to feel the force of it in some part of his body and indicates his responsiveness by laying his hand on his shoulder, knee, or whatever part may be affected. The ne'mǐta'maûñ' then passes along the northern side of the lodge and takes his place at the end of the line.

The man next to him does precisely what he has done, and is followed by the others, who in turn take their places at the end of the line. After each "shooting" the candidate indicates in what part of his body he feels the effect.

This "shooting" draws heavily on the resources of the person performing it and is very exhausting. A man often calls upon his brethren to assist him. They do not leave their places but are expected to exert their power in his behalf. A woman frequently finds herself unequal to the exertion, although she has been appointed one of the initiators. In that case she may ask a man to take her place by doing the more exhausting portion of the work. She breathes on her medicine bag and hands it to him for his use. They move forward together, he walking close behind her, uttering the ejaculations and moving the medicine bag in the prescribed manner.

Before the we'daked', or the last of the initiators, moves toward the candidate, he may turn to the leader and say, "Now I will stir up the spirit that is in me; I will stand and dance and I ask your assistance." He then dances in his place. In his hands he holds all four of the medicine bags and breathes on them that the power may be intensified to the greatest possible degree. He extends his right arm to its full length and moves toward the candidate, raising the medicine bags and bringing them down with the force of a heavy blow as he ejaculates *wa a hi hi hi wa a hi hi hi!*, throwing all the strength of his being into the motion and the rhythmic sound. Slowly he moves forward. It is the climax of the entire ceremony and the members of the Mǐde'wǐwǐn wait in tense silence until the candidate falls prostrate on the ground, overcome by the "spirit power" of the initiators.

The following is an example of the song sung at this point in the ceremony. Other examples are given at the close of this chapter. A large number of these songs is available; the selection is made by the leader of the ceremony.

No. 11. First Initiation Song   (Catalogue no. 61)

Sung by Be'cĭgwĭ'wizäns

Voice ♩ = 44
Drum ♩ = 96
(Drum-rhythm similar to No. 1)

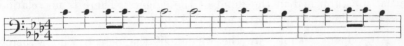

Wa sĭn-don-dĭ-na-wa *ha* ni-kân *i* *na* wa sĭn-don-dĭ-na-

wa *ha* ni - kân *i* *na* wa sĭn - don - dĭ - na - wa *ha*

ni - kân *i* *na* wa sĭn-don-dĭ-na - wa *ha* ni - kân *i* *na*

INTERPOLATION

1st rendition, after 6th measure

wi   *hi*   *na*

2d rendition, last measure

wa   *hi*   *hi*   *hi*   *hi*

3d, 4th and 5th renditions, last three measures

♩. = 44

hi *hi* *hi* *hi* *hi*   *hi*   *hi* *hi* *hi* *hi*   *hi*   *hi* *hi* *hi* *hi*

WORDS

Wasu'...........................	From a long distance
Nindon'dinawa'..................	I am shooting
Nikân'.........................	My Mĭde' brother

SONG PICTURE NO. 11.

Analysis.—This song is sung during the actual "shooting" of the candidate and presents an example of the combination of song and ejaculation which is used at this portion of the ceremony. Six renditions of the song are on the phonograph record and the interpolated syllables differ in the successive renditions. In order to make this clear, the transcription of the song is followed by a transcription of these syllables. The metric pulse of the measure beginning is maintained throughout the ejaculations, although after the second rendition these syllables are given in triple time. This shows the pulse of the measure beginning to be clearly established in the mind of the singer. There is no relation between this and the metric unit of the drum.

After being "shot" by the we'daked' the person who is being initiated falls prostrate on the ground with arms extended. While he lies on the ground the four initiators gather around him, place their medicine bags on his back, and sing the following song:

No. 12. SECOND INITIATION SONG   (Catalogue no. 62)

Sung by BE'CĬGWI'WIZÄNS

VOICE $\ = 72$
DRUM $\ = 92$

(Drum-rhythm similar to No. 1)

Hi wi - na-ke *ni*   *hi*   *hi* wi-na-ke *ni*   *hi* wi-na-ke *ni*

hi   *hi* wi- na-ke *ni*   *hi* wi-na-ke *ni*   *hi*   *hi*-wi- na- ke *ni*

hi wi - na-ke *ni*   *hi*   *hi* wi - na-ke *ni*   *hi* wi-na- ke *ni*

WORDS

Wa'wina'ke...................... I have shot straight

Analysis.—This melody begins on the fifth of the key and ends on the fifth, having a compass of one octave. It contains only the tones of the minor triad and the fourth. There is no relation between the metric unit of voice and drum.

SONG PICTURE NO. 12.

Following this song the four initiators raise the candidate to a sitting posture and a mi'gĭs comes from his mouth. One of the initiators then takes the mi'gĭs and walks once around the lodge. Pausing near the candidate, he breathes on the mi'gĭs and extends it toward the east, breathes on it again and extends it toward the south, repeating the process and extending the mi'gĭs toward the west, north, and the zenith. This being done, the mi'gĭs is said to disappear again into the body of the person being initiated, who falls prostrate as before. While he lies prostrate one of the initiators fastens on his back a medicine bag corresponding to the degree he has taken. In the first degree this bag is made of the white skin of a weasel. The initiators then raise the candidate to his feet and withdraw to the eastern end of the lodge, the following song being sung:

No. 13. THIRD INITIATION SONG (Catalogue no. 63)

Sung by BE′CĬGWĬ′WĬZÄNS

VOICE ♩ = 80
DRUM ♩ = 96
(Drum-rhythm similar to No. 1)

Ha bi - mĭ - ma-dwe - we ni - mĭ - de - wi yan i ha

bi - mĭ - na - dwe - we ni - mĭ - de - wi yan e bi -

mĭ - ma - ha - dwe - we ni - mĭ - de - wa - yan e bi -

mĭ - ma - ha - dwe - we ni - mĭ - de - wa - yan e bi -

mĭ ma - ha - dwe - we we ni - mĭ - de - wa - yan

WORDS

Bi′mĭmadwe′we.................... There comes a sound
Nimĭde′wayan′..................... From my medicine bag

Analysis.—Beginning on the twelfth and moving freely along the descending intervals of the fourth five-toned scale, this song is purely harmonic in character. It begins on the unaccented portion of the measure and contains few interpolated syllables.

After this song the person who is being initiated takes his medicine bag and goes toward the four initiators, "shooting" first the we′daked′, who sits down. After encircling the lodge he "shoots" the next in line, and so on until all are seated, the lodge being encircled after the "shooting" of each man.

SONG PICTURE
NO. 13.

When all are thus seated the person being initiated takes the gifts on his arm and presents the proper articles to the leader, the initiators, and the oc'kabe'wĭs, personally thanking each for his share in the ceremony.

It is considered that after the distribution of these gifts the candidate is fully initiated.

The next event is the showing of their mi'gĭs by the four men who have performed the initiatory rites. The leader requests them to do this. A blanket is spread on the ground east of the medicine pole, and a man is appointed to stand beside the blanket and receive the mi'gĭs. (Fig. 4 shows four mi'gĭs laid in the position indicated.)

The ne'mĭta'maûñ' leads the line of initiators. As they approach the blanket each man in turn makes a rasping noise in his throat and takes a mi'gĭs from his mouth. These shells are received by the man appointed, who lays them in order on the blanket. When all the mi'gĭs have been deposited there the ne'mĭta'maûñ' looks along the line to see that all are ready. The men are watching him, and at his signal they all replace the mi'gĭs in their mouths with a uniform motion.

After showing the mi'gĭs the initiators return to the mĭtĭ'gwakĭk' and sing together. The ne'mĭta'maûñ' holds the stick and plays the drum first, the others shaking their rattles. Then he hands the stick to another of the group, and so on until all have played the drum. Four cici'gwăn (rattles) are used in this portion of the ceremony, no two having exactly the same tone. (See pls. 1, 2.)

The mĭtĭ'gwakĭk' is then removed to a position between the stone and the eastern entrance (see fig. 4); the leader takes his place at one side of it and the oc'kabe'wĭs at the other, the leader pounding the drum and the oc'kabe'wĭs shaking a rattle. When they begin to sing the members of the Mĭde'wĭwĭn sitting on the south side of the lodge spring to their feet, advance toward those on the north side, and "shoot" them with their medicine bags. The latter fall insensible, but in a short time recover consciousness and advance toward those now seated on the south side, "shooting" at them with their medicine bags. These in turn fall insensible, and the "shooting" is continued until all present have been "shot" with the medicine. This ceremony of initiation usually lasts until late in the afternoon.

Meantime food is being cooked outside the lodge and when the "shooting" is finished this feast is served and anyone who likes may freely enter the lodge. This is the social feature of the event. Only members of the Mĭde'wĭwĭn are present at the initiation, but all the members of the tribe may share in the feast and the dance which follow. The nature of this feast is not prescribed. The dog was a feature of the ceremonial feast which took place in the early part of the ceremony. Food for this feast is provided by various members of the tribe and a portion is usually carried home by each person. According to custom, the old men are served first.

The following song is sung when the food and tobacco are brought in and placed before the leading members of the Mĭde'wĭwĭn:

No. 14. First Song of the Feast (Catalogue no. 65)

Sung by Kı'tcimak'wa ("big bear")

Voice ♩ = 69
(Recorded without drum)

Ni-kân-ûg e e nin-da - ca-mi-gog e e ni-kân i hi

na ni - kân-ûg e e nin-da - ca - mi- gog e e ni-kân

a ha ni ni - kân- ûg i hi nin - da - ca-mi-gog

e e ni - kân e he na ni-kân- ûg e he

ni - kân ca - mi - gog e he ni- kân e he na ni - kân-ûg

e e nin-da-ca-mi-gog e he ni - kân-ûg i hi na

WORDS

Nikàn'ûg........................... My Mïde' brethren
Nin'dacà'migog'.................... Have given me this feast

Analysis.—This is a particularly free melody, beginning on the second, ending on the fifth of the key, and
having very little feeling for the fundamental chords of
the key. The intonation usually falls on the second of
two similar tones. The rhythm of the song is peculiar,
the first five measures constituting a rhythmic unit.
The repetition of this unit is regular throughout the
song. A rhythmic unit regularly repeated suggests that
a rhythmic idea or impulse may be the nucleus of the
musical composition. It is of interest therefore to
note the occurrence of the rhythmic unit in this series of songs.

Song picture
no. 14. A
hand is shown
bestowing the
feast, which
the singer
stretches up
his own hand
to receive.

After the feast is served the following song is sung:

12692°—Bull. 45—10——4

No. 15. SECOND SONG OF THE FEAST (Catalogue no. 66)

Sung by KI'TCIMAK'WA

VOICE ♩ = 76
Recorded without drum

Ca - we - ni - mi - wa - ad ni - kân - ûg e he he ca -

we - ni - mi - wa - ad ni - kân - ûg e he he he ca -

we - ni - mi - wa - ad ni - kân - ûg e he he ca - we - ni - mi - wa - ad ni -

kân - ûg e he he ca - we - ni - mi - wa - ad ni - kân - ûg e he he

WORDS

Cawe'nĭmĭwad'..................... I have received great kindness
Nikân'ûg........................... From my Mĭde' brethren

Analysis.—The phonograph record shows an interesting feature of this song which it is impossible to transcribe. On the second and third counts of each measure the tone is sounded slightly before the proper time, giving a peculiar effect of rhythmic irregularity. This may be due to the fact that no drum was used and that the drum is usually struck slightly before the metronome time. The voice may have unconsciously imitated the drum in this respect.

SONG PICTURE NO. 15.
The Mĭde'wĭnĭ'nĭ
holds in his hand the
blankets and other
gifts which he has re-
ceived from the per-
son initiated.

The joyful character of this melody presents a contrast to the serious ceremonial songs which precede it. The tones are those of the fourth five-toned scale and the song is distinctly melodic in character.

After the feast is finished the men who have received gifts carry them to their own lodges with their portion of the feast; later they return to join in the dance, which is of an entirely social nature. At this dance a man may sing his favorite "medicine song" and any others who know the same song may rise and dance. A great variety of Mĭde' songs are used at this final dance.

When it is time for the company to disband, the four initiators stand together at the southeast corner of the Mĭde'wĭgan, the ne'mĭta'maûñ' at the head of the line. The music is very lively and everyone is in the best possible humor. The initiators are the first to leave the lodge, dancing out at the western door, followed by the company and the newly initiated person, the leader being the last to leave the lodge. The person who has been initiated takes with him the medicine pole and the stone, which are his personal property; these he carries to his lodge and makes a feast in their honor. After the feast he takes both the pole and the stone to some secluded place in the woods known only to himself. There he often goes, keeping the place clear of rubbish and undergrowth. The stone remains there always, but the pole may be removed by its owner for use in future ceremonies.

The person who has been initiated also retains as his personal property any songs which he can remember from hearing them sung during the ceremony, it being considered that his gifts to the leaders are sufficient to entitle him to these without further payment.

Each of the men who assisted at the initiation ceremony and received gifts is expected to make a feast after the ceremony and invite the newly initiated. At this feast he gives the newly initiated the mi'gĭs which he exhibited at the ceremony. Thus the initiated receives one mi'gĭs from each of the men who assisted at the ceremony. These he keeps in his Mĭde' bag, adding from time to time such medicines as he has learned to use.

CEREMONY FOR A DYING CHIEF

An opportunity for the writer's personal observation of this ceremony occurred in July, 1907, at Leech Lake, Minnesota, during the last hours of Nigan'ĭbĭnes' ("leading bird of prey"), the hereditary chief of the Pillager band of Chippewa. Nigan'ĭbĭnes' was son of the famous chief Flat Mouth and was always known by his father's name, which is used therefore in this description of the ceremony.

After the agency physicians in consultation had concluded that the old chief could live only a short time, he asked and was granted permission that a Mĭde' ceremony be held in the hope of prolonging his life, or at least of making his last hours more comfortable. Accordingly preparations were begun and a man named Na'joi'se ("two persons walking") was selected as oc'kabe'wĭs, or herald. It was decided also that the leader of the ceremony should be Ge'miwûnac' ("bird that flies through the rain"), the oldest Mĭde'wĭnĭ'nĭ on the reservation, almost totally blind, but supposed to be very powerful (see pl. 9). Invitations were sent to eight members of the Mĭde'wĭwĭn. These invitations were in the form of round sticks, about 5 inches in length. Each member brought his invitation-stick with him, and prior to the ceremony the sticks were tied in a bundle and laid on the ground at the foot of the medicine pole.

For several days before the ceremony the Mĭde'wĭnĭ'nĭ sang with the Mĭde' drum in Flat Mouth's wigwam. The singing was also continued at intervals throughout the entire night. The ceremony took place on the afternoon of July 24, 1907. Early on the morning of that day a Mĭde' lodge was made and Flat Mouth was taken from his wigwam, carried thither, and laid upon a bed of boughs shaded by small birch trees stuck into the ground. The inclosed space was about 60 feet long and 20 feet wide, with rounded corners. At the openings, at the east and west ends, blankets were hung between tall poles. The inclosure was formed of pine branches stuck into the ground and woven together, forming a barrier about 3 feet in height. Flat Mouth was laid in the place of honor at the south side of the eastern entrance. A medicine pole was erected in the center of the lodge about 20 feet from the eastern entrance, and between this pole and the entrance were located a fire, and a kettle in which a dog was cooked.

The ceremony was given according to the fourth degree, which was the degree held by Flat Mouth. The decoration of the pole corresponded to this degree.

In the morning six members of the medicine party entered the lodge, one of whom sang; he was evidently in charge of this part of the ceremony. The songs were unaccompanied, the rattle being used by him while marching and while "treating" Flat Mouth. The rattle was similar to that shown in plates 1 and 2.

After each song the leader led a procession around the lodge, shaking his rattle and ejaculating *Wa hi hi hi hi'*, *Wa hi hi hi hi'*. Behind him came a woman with food in a pan, then a man with a rattle, then a woman, then a man and a woman, each with food in a pan. After circling the lodge several times the party stopped at the eastern entrance and the leader made a speech, to which the others frequently answered *ho'*. Then the leader walked before Flat Mouth, shaking his rattle at arms, limbs, and body with ejaculations of *ho ho ho'*. This continued during the morning.

In the afternoon Flat Mouth was laid upon a bed of boughs in the center of the lodge, west of the medicine pole. At this time the ceremony proper took place, under the direction of Ge'miwûnac', while Na'joi'se continued to act as herald and another member of the party took charge of the cooking of the dog.

The members of the medicine party were in the center of the lodge, the relatives and friends of Flat Mouth being seated along the sides of the inclosure. At the opening of the ceremony Flat Mouth was carried several times around the inclosure on his green blanket and laid gently upon the bed of boughs.

Then a man from Pine Point said he wished to brew a medicine of his own for Flat Mouth. He told of the virtue of this medicine and said that it might not cure Flat Mouth but he believed that it would make him more comfortable. He said that the secret of this medicine was given him in a dream as a boy; that the principal ingredient was part of a large animal which he saw in his dream, and that he always carried this ingredient in his medicine bag.

The consent of Flat Mouth being secured, the man proceeded to brew the medicine. As he did this, he gave the *ya a hi', a hi, a hi, hi hi hi hi*, so frequently heard in the Mĭde'. He was joined by another voice, beginning about a fourth higher and sliding down to a unison.

When the brewing of the medicine was completed Na'joi'se took the steaming cup and carried it five times around the old chief; then he gave the cup to Flat Mouth, who drank the medicine.

This was followed by a "prayer to the medicine pole," interrupted by frequent ejaculations of *he he he*.

Then the feast was served. This consisted of the cooked dog, with the broth. It was required that all of this be eaten in the lodge. There were also bread and wild rice, portions of which were carried away by the guests at the close of the ceremony.

Each member of the medicine party carried a medicine bag, corresponding to his degree in the Mĭde'wĭwĭn. The members now stood in a circle around the chief and each in turn sang a song, after which they marched once around the inclosure. The first few songs were without accompaniment, while the others were accompanied softly by the Mĭde' drum. There was a marked individuality in the songs, suggesting that each person may have been singing his special medicine song. Next the members of the party, each chewing his own medicine, marched around the dying chief, and spit into a box of sawdust at his feet. A man then stirred this mixture, which was rubbed on the soles of Flat Mouth's feet. Each member also laid a pinch of it on his body.

Following this, each of the medicine party sang a song and marched around the chief, "shooting" his medicine bag at him.

Then all marched around the chief, carrying Mĭde' shells in their left hands. Each person laid one shell on the chief's body in passing, and after circling his body took up the shell again. These shells were similar to the mi'gĭs mentioned on page 48.

By this time the old chief was failing so rapidly that it was deemed advisable to carry him into his wigwam. This was done, the men bearing him gently on his green blanket. Then they sang in his lodge. Instead of the Mĭde' drum they used the sharp, thin, doctor's drum and two rattles. The songs were different from those previously used, and of a melancholy cadence, the interval of the sixth being flatted.

Two hours later Flat Mouth died, his death being announced by twenty rifle shots. This is the custom of the tribe, a few shots announcing the death of a child and a larger number that of an adult. As is customary with the tribe, the body was immediately arrayed in the best apparel and ornaments of the deceased; beside it were laid his pipe, fan, and rifle, also a cushion with a woven cover. In the early evening the ceremony was concluded briefly, as few had the heart to dance. Flat Mouth's widow sat next the eastern entrance, where he had lain that morning, and the dancers "shot" their medicine bags at her as they passed. The chief's sister held a Mĭde' shell in her hand and frequently extended it toward Flat Mouth's widow, who breathed on it, whereupon the sister danced again around the drum.

The Mĭde' drum used on this occasion was decorated in black, with a border at the base consisting of a broad band and four deep points. This was said to represent the pointed top of the Mĭde' inclosure. Above this was the recumbent figure of an animal similar to that shown in the drawing of song no. 94 (catalogue no. 1). The top of this drum was of tanned deerskin, held tightly in place by a hoop wound with cloth. The singers stood and held the drum by the corners of the leather which formed the top. Occasionally the widow of Flat Mouth rose and, taking hold of a corner of the leather, stood silently and sadly beside the singers a few moments. There were usually four singers at the drum, one after another acting as leader; each pounded on the drum. One or two rattles were also used.

At the close of the dance the medicine party went to their respective lodges, each carrying a bundle of small gifts. All that night the sound of the Mĭde' drum and the monotonous singing were heard.

The next morning the Mĭde'wĭnĭ'nĭ conducted what corresponded to a funeral ceremony. The lodge was tightly closed, but the voices could be plainly heard. The leaders were rehearsing the beliefs of the Mĭde' and assuring the family of Flat Mouth of their reality. Then they addressed the spirit of the dead chief, as it is believed that the spirit lingers near the body until burial. One after another they sat beside him, telling him to be careful to avoid certain turns in the road to the Spirit Land, or to trust certain spirits who would meet and assist him. They spoke with extreme rapidity, punctuating the words with occasional sharp beats on the drum.

THE BODY OF NIGAN'ĪBĪNES'

At the head is Na'joi'se, the oc'kabe'wis, and at the foot is Ge'miwŭnac', the leader of the Mide' ceremony described on pages 51–55.

DE'BWAWĔN'DÛNK

At the conclusion of this ceremony the writer was permitted to photograph the dead chief. (See pl. 7.) On entering the lodge, the medicine party were found eating the funeral feast, which consisted of fruit, cakes, bread, and rice. The body of Flat Mouth was concealed by a curtain of white cloth. When the feast was concluded several photographs of the dead chief were taken, the upper coverings of the wigwam being removed to admit the light. Immediately afterward the body was lifted on its green blanket and laid in the casket, which was the best that could be purchased at the neighboring town. Beside it, in the casket, were placed the fan, pipe, war bonnet, and cushion. The fan consisted of an eagle wing decorated with dots of red in a design which belonged especially to Flat Mouth, being used by him alone. The cover of the cushion was a bag woven of yarns. This weaving of a bag without a seam is becoming a lost art among the Minnesota Chippewa.

A long procession followed the body of Flat Mouth to the "heathen cemetery," a village of low wooden shelters above the graves. There was no ceremony of any kind when the casket was lowered. The grave was dug very large and almost circular in shape. Visiting the spot a few months later, the writer found that a pointed wooden house had been erected over the grave, according to the custom of the Chippewa. The name Nigan'ĭbĭnes' was painted on a narrow board placed on the peak of the roof, and beside the grave floated an American flag.

Songs for Initiation into the Sixth Degree

Sung by De'bwawĕn'dûnk

The songs of an initiation ceremony differ with the degree which the person assumes, each degree having its special songs. The following songs given by De'bwawĕn'dûnk[a] (pl. 8) are those used when initiating a member into the sixth degree.

Before singing the first song De'bwawĕn'dûnk made a short speech in Chippewa, speaking to the four Mĭde' manido', explaining that he was not going about the city belittling their religion, and begging that they be not offended because circumstances made it impossible for him to smoke the customary pipe before singing. This speech was recorded by the phonograph.

The singer stated that if these songs are to be sung in private or at a small gathering the men lay down their medicine bags, as they are to "sing to the bags." The man who is to sing the first song fills his pipe and smokes it; then he calls on the four Mĭde' manido', who live in the four "layers" beneath the earth. One song is sung by each man.

---

a An old man from the Bois Fort reservation, a most devout adherent of the Mĭde'. These songs were recorded at Washington, D. C., whither De'bwawĕn'dûnk had come with an interpreter on business connected with tribal affairs. The translations were given by his interpreter, Rev. Frank H. Pequette.

No. 16. First Song   (Catalogue no. 122)

Voice ♩ = 144
Drum ♩ = 144
(Drum-rhythm similar to No. 1)

Dji-ca-wa- *he* - nĭ- mĭ - *hi* - gog   *ho ho   ho   ho ho*

ni - *hi* -kâ-hân e   *he he*   dji-ca - we-*he*-nĭ-mĭ-*hi*-gog *ho ho*

ho   ni - *hi* - kâ-hân e   *he he*   ĕ - na-*we*-*he*- bi-wûg *hi   go*

ho   ho ni-kân   e   *he he*   ĕ - na-*we*- *he*-ni - bĭ-wûg   e   *he*

ni-kân e   *he he*   di - bi-sko-*ho*-ka-mĭ - ĭg   e   *he he   e   he he*

ni- *hi* -kâ-hân e   *he he*   ga-ca - we-nĭ-mĭ-wû-ûg e *he he*   *he*

Song picture no. 16. The singer gave the following explanation of this drawing: "The circle is the earth. These three people live in the fourth layer under the earth; from there they sing. This is a sixth degree song and so the people who sing it live in the fourth layer under the earth."

WORDS

Djicawa′nĭmĭgog........	I am blessed
Nikân′ûg	My Mĭde′ brethren
Di′bicoka′mĭg	By the four Mĭde′ spirits
Ĕna′bĭwûg′............	Who live in the four layers
Ga′cawe′nĭmĭwûg′	Of the earth

Analysis.—This song abounds in the interpolated syllables which characterize the Mĭde′ songs. The measure lengths are irregular and their succession appears erratic. However, two records of the song were made, an interval of about a week elapsing between the making of them; on comparison it is found that the records are identical in every respect, except that in the measure marked X the second rendition shows the syllables *ho ho* on the second count. This change is very slight, but as it is the only one which occurs, it is worthy of mention.   In this as in other Mǐde′ songs the pulse is not mechanically regular and the same variations are found in the second as in the first rendition.   This variation usually consists in a very slight prolonging of the accented tones.   This song and the succeeding song contain syncopations, which are extremely rare in the Chippewa songs.

No. 17. Second Song   (Catalogue no. 123)

Voice ♩. = 72
Drum ♩ = 126
(Drum-rhythm similar to No. 1)

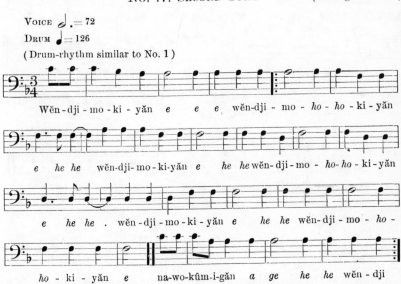

Wĕn - dji - mo - ki - yăn   e   e   e   wĕn-dji - mo - ho - ho - ki - yăn

e   he   he   wĕn-dji- mo - ki-yăn   e   he   he wĕn- dji - mo - ho- ho - ki - yăn

e   he   he .   wĕn - dji - mo - ki - yăn   e   he   he   wĕn- dji - mo - ho -

ho - ki - yăn   e   na-wo-kûm-i-găn   a   ge   he   he   wĕn - dji

WORDS

Nawo′kûmigăn′...................... In the center of the earth
Wĕn′djimo′kiyăn′.................. Whence I come

This and the remaining songs of the set were recorded a few days later than the first song.   At this time tobacco had been provided, which the old chief smoked in silence.   When he was ready, he seated himself before the phonograph and again made a speech, translated as follows:

> I am not doing this for the sake of curiosity, but I have smoked a pipe to the Mǐde′ manido′ from whom these songs came, and I ask them not to be offended with me for singing these songs which belong to them.

SONG PICTURE NO. 17.
The "center of the earth" is plainly indicated in the drawing.

Analysis.—This song is of unusually small compass, and it is interesting to note the drop of a minor third to D with a return to the tonic F. This is rare in the Chippewa songs recorded, but has been noted in other primitive music.   In this song the metric unit is the measure, the pulses of the parts of the measure being less uniform and regular. The song closely resembles a chant.

No. 18. THIRD SONG   (Catalogue no. 124)

VOICE ♩ = 96
DRUM ♩ = 152

(Drum-rhythm similar to No. 1)

Nin - go - *ho* - sa   *ha ha*   nin - go - *ho* - sa   nin - go - *ho* -

sa   *ha ha*   nin - go - *ho* - sa   nin - go - *ho* - sa   nin - go - sa   nin - go -

sa   nin - go - *ho* - sa   nin - go - sa   nin - go - sa   nin - go - sa   nĭ - gĭ

wa - *a*-mĭñ e - bĭd *e*   ma - ni - do   *i ne* nin-go - sa   nin - go - sa

WORDS

Ningo′sa............................. I am afraid of
Nikân′............................. My Mĭde′ brother
Nĭgĭwăm′Ĭñ........................ In my lodge
E′bĭd .... Who dwells

Analysis.—The chief musical interest of this song lies in the fact that the first word is variously accented. We find the musical accent falling on each of the three syllables. In all Mĭde′ songs the words are subordinate to the music, a peculiarity which is well illustrated in this instance. The beginning of the song on the unaccented portion of the measure is somewhat unusual.

The remaining songs of the series are given in outline instead of full transcription. This shows the trend of the melody, but does not indicate either the rhythm or note values. The metronome indication which precedes the songs has no reference to the symbol as written, its only purpose being to show the metric unit of the voice and of the drum, for the purpose of comparison.

SONG PICTURE NO. 18. The Mĭde′ lodge and the person to be initiated are shown.

The beat of the drum is almost uniform throughout the series, being in unaccented strokes, two of which are equivalent to the metronome beat 126 or 132. Thus by metronome test there are approximately four pulses of the drum to one of the voice, but this correspondence is not evident to the ear. The relation between the two is not accurate, for the rhythm of the voice varies, while the drum does not vary, being entirely independent of the voice.

The words of the songs are continually broken and separated by the syllables *hi hi hi*, which occur even more frequently than in the initiation songs of the lower degrees.

Only two of these songs are of minor tonality. One of these, no. 19, is interesting in that the singer began the last half slightly too high, thus changing the key from C minor to C sharp minor. The relations of the tones in the last half are well sustained.

In this series we find three songs containing the tones of the major triad with the sixth added, two instances of the octave complete except the seventh, one instance of the octave complete except the second and seventh, one instance of the octave complete except the fourth and seventh, and two songs of minor tonality.

Musically, the chief value of these songs lies in the relation of voice and drum and in the peculiar ending of the songs. Compare these songs in this respect with the melody outline of songs nos. 25–34. It will be readily seen that the latter have a much stronger feeling for a definite close either on the tonic or with the tones of the tonic chord. An indefinite manner of closing a song may be considered characteristic of a primitive stage of musical culture.

No. 19. FOURTH SONG   (Catalogue no. 125)

VOICE without perceptible metric unit

DRUM ♩ = 126

WORDS

Awe′nen.......................... Who is this
De′wene′......................... Sick unto death
Bema′djiûg′...................... Whom I restore to life

The words of this song refer to the person who is being initiated. Many sick persons are initiated in order that they may be restored to health. The Mïde′ comprehends health of body, mind and spirit in one general idea. It is supposed to benefit the individual as a whole and the lines of demarcation between his various needs are not sharply drawn.

SONG PICTURE NO. 19. On the body of the person to be initiated are seen lines representing the "strength" he is to receive through the Mïde′.

No. 20. FIFTH SONG   (Catalogue no. 126)

VOICE ♩ = 60
DRUM ♩ = 132
(Drum-rhythm similar to No. 1)

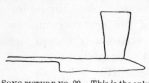

SONG PICTURE NO. 20. This is the only
drawing of a pipe which occurs in
connection with these songs.

WORDS

Niwi′dubima′.......... I am sitting
Nai′ûd................. In the fourth lodge
Opwa′gûn.............. With my pipe

The meaning of the word translated "lodge" is not clearly defined. It refers to a progression in the Mĭde′, a similar idea occurring in songs.

No. 21. SIXTH SONG   (Catalogue no. 127)

VOICE ♩ = 60
DRUM ♩ = 132
(Drum-rhythm similar to No. 1)

WORDS

Ni′jawĕn′imigog′............... They have taken pity on me
Gawa′bikwe′djĭg.............. The white-haired ones

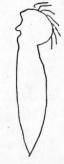

It is said to be the white-haired Mĭde′ spirits who enable the members of the Mĭde′wĭwĭn to attain long life.

The chief purpose of the Mĭde′ is the securing of health and long life to its adherents. Combined with the assurances of its power to confer these benefits are strict injunctions concerning rectitude, obedience to its instructions, and temperance. These qualities doubtless united to produce the promised results.

SONG PICTURE NO. 21. This drawing undoubtedly represents one of the "white-haired Mĭde′ spirits."

No. 22. Seventh Song　　　　(Catalogue no. 128)

Voice ♩ = 60

Drum ♩ = 132

(Drum-rhythm similar to No. 1)

WORDS

Wewĕ′ni............................ Diligently
Bizĭn′dau......................... Listen thou
Kaiya′gigĭdo′djĭg.................. To those who speak

SONG PICTURE NO. 22.
He who speaks and
he who listens are
shown.

No. 23. Eighth Song　　　　(Catalogue no. 129)

Voice ♩ 60

Drum ♩ = 132

(Drum-rhythm similar to No. 1)

WORDS

Ge′ga............................ Almost
Bizĭnda′gonăn′.................... He will listen to us
Manido′.......................... Manido′.

SONG PICTURE NO.
23. This outline
is frequently
used to repre-
sent a manido′.
(Compare draw-
ings of songs nos.
16, 94. and 95.)

Analysis.—This song comprises the compass of an octave, extending from the dominant above to the dominant below the tonic. The melody is based on the tonic triad with the sixth added, and, as frequently occurs in these songs, the entrance of the tonic is delayed. More of the recorded Chippewa songs begin on the twelfth or fifth than on any other tone and the first interval of descent is frequently a minor third. This is repeated several times and is followed by the descent of a major third, which completes the major triad and introduces the tonic.

No. 24. Ninth Song   (Catalogue no. 130)

Voice ♩ = 60

Drum ♩ = 132

(Drum-rhythm similar to No. 1)

WORDS

Ca′cabondeckwa′gwan .. They are going through all the
Manidog′................ Rooms of the Mĭde′ lodge, it appears
Bi′tawaka′mĭg .... The Mĭde′ spirits, who live
A′bidjĭg′................ In the four layers of the earth

Ceremonial Songs

Sung by Na′jobi′tûñ [a]

Song picture no. 24.
The subject recurs to
that of the first song in
the series and the circle
is again shown, with
one of "the people who
live in the fourth layer
under the earth."

The following twenty-six songs consist of four
series, each having its own type of music and its
distinct character of words. The first series may
be sung at the close of a ceremony; the others are
connected with the initiation of members. The
music is the most primitive which the writer recorded, with the possible exception of the songs given by De′bwa-
wĕn′dûnk of the Bois Fort reservation.

series 1—analysis

Musically, the songs in the first series are very similar, yet no
two are exactly alike. The songs were sung firmly and without
hesitation, showing that they were not improvised. Before singing
a song Na′jobi′tûñ sometimes retired to the next room in order quietly
to hum over the song and to be sure that he remembered it correctly.
Many of the songs were sung several times, the renditions being
identical, except occasionally in. unimportant measures near the
close.

The words of the first series relate to the water-spirit—his dwelling, his action, and his manifestation as a male beaver. Mention is
made of the mermen. It is believed that manido′ in the form of
both mermen and mermaids live in the water and at times appear to
the members of the Mĭde′wĭwĭn.

Song no. 33 furnishes an interesting example of the difficulties
encountered in securing translations of these songs. The first interpreter said the last words meant "I will gather it in the place of

---

[a] An old man living at Boy Lake, a portion of the Leech Lake reservation about 30 miles from the
agency, reached only by water. Na′jobi′tûñ ("two men walking") was almost blind and was in every
way the most isolated individual with whom the writer came in contact. He was a firm believer in the
Mĭde′wĭwĭn and its power.

a circle;" later, another interpreter gave as the meaning "a place where the water moved in a circle;" the place was finally identified as a portion of Lake St. Clair where the water is said to form eddies or small circles. This suggests that the song may have come from Walpole island, where many Canadian Chippewa make their home, or from some other group of Chippewa in that vicinity. In this case it is reasonable to assume that the "long rapids" referred to in no. 25 are the rapids at Sault Ste. Marie.

These songs are not fully transcribed, only the outline of the melody being given. This takes no account of rhythm or note values, but shows the melodic trend of the song more clearly than a full transcription. The songs contain frequent interpolations of *hi hi hi hi;* the syllables of the words are repeated; and in many instances the songs resemble chants.

The musical material of many of these songs consists of the major triad with the sixth added, yet the principal interval is the descending minor third. The descent of the minor third characterizes the most primitive music, and the five-toned scale characterizes music which may be termed semideveloped. The major triad with the sixth added is the five-toned scale lacking the second, and in songs nos. 28, 30, and 33 of the present series we find this tone present as a passing tone, thus completing the tone material of the five-toned scale.

In all these songs, except no. 20, the feeling of the tonic chord is very strong. The ending of no. 20, as written, suggests a transition to the relative minor, but as sung it gives us the impression that the song is suddenly left in midair. Yet the ending was conclusive, followed by the customary *ho ho ho ho.* The accidentals in songs nos. 26 and 27 were firmly given, but seem intended as an ornamentation rather than suggesting modulation.

No. 25   (Catalogue no. 16)

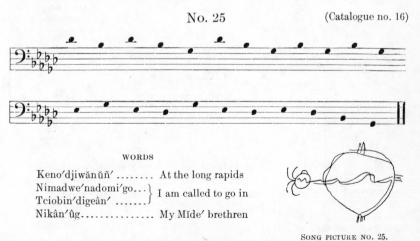

WORDS

Keno'djiwănŭñ' .... At the long rapids
Nimadwe'nadomi'go...⎫
Tciobin'digeân' ....⎭ I am called to go in
Nikân'ûg.............. My Mĭde' brethren

SONG PICTURE NO. 25.

No. 26   (Catalogue no. 17)

SONG PICTURE NO. 26.

WORDS

Kiga′winanân′domigog′.... We may call upon you for assistance
Kikân′ug .... We, your Mĭde′ brethren
Miziwe′mide′wûg.......... Assembled from everywhere

No. 27   (Catalogue no. 18)

WORDS

Daya′wĕngumi′.........⎫ [Free translation]
Daona′gumi′............⎬ When the waters are
Daonun′gumi′..........⎪ calm and the fog rises,
Geundjima′mwekiyân...⎭ I will now and then appear

SONG PICTURE NO. 27. The circle represents the sky, which is overcast with drops of moisture; emerging from this is the face of the manido′. (Compare drawing of song no. 97.)

No. 28   (Catalogue no. 19)

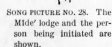

SONG PICTURE NO. 28. The Mĭde′ lodge and the person being initiated are shown.

WORDS

Kigacob′ŭnde′........... You will pass through
Endad′ .... The dwelling of
Manido′.................. The water spirit
Nikân′ .... My Mĭde′ brethren

No. 29   (Catalogue no. 20)

WORDS

Babidiwe′wedjiwăn′..... The sound of flowing waters
Enda′yan............... Comes toward my home

When this is sung the members of the ˙Mĭde′-wĭwĭn rise and dance during the remainder of the series of songs, the change being indicated by a line across the strip of birch bark, between the song pictures.

SONG PICTURE NO. 29. A pointed tipi represents the home of the Mĭde′-wĭnĭ′nĭ. It is interesting to note that the wavy lines indicating the pulsating sound reach the body or heart of the man, not his ears.

No. 30   (Catalogue no. 21)

SONG PICTURE NO. 30. Reference to song no. 34 shows that the speaker is a beaver. This drawing represents his appearance above the water; also one of the "men of the deep."

WORDS

Kayenin′moki′yân .. When I appear
Mamweka′dogowûg′. The men of the deep
Memegwa′siwûg′.... Will be cast up by seething waters

No. 31   (Catalogue no. 22)

WORDS

Memweka′bogowûg′.. They are being cast up by seething
waters
Wabimi′gĭswûg′..... The white Mĭde′ shells

SONG PICTURE NO. 31. On the crest of the waves appear the mi′gĭs, or white Mĭde′ shells.

No. 32   (Catalogue no. 23)

SONG PICTURE NO. 32. The circle represents a lake from which two otters rise.

WORDS

Dabima′mwekiwûg′.. Now and then there will arise out of the waters
Nikân′ûg............ My Mĭde′ brethren
Nigigwûg′........... The otters

No. 33   (Catalogue no. 24)

WORDS

Beba′mamoyân′....... I am gathering
Wananan′dawioyân′ .. That with which
Wawiya′tamŭng′...... I will treat myself
Geŭndĭna′mân........ In the Lake of Eddying Waters, I will obtain it

SONG PICTURE NO. 33. In his hand the man holds some substance gathered from the lake, which is believed to have medicinal properties.

No. 34   (Catalogue no. 25)

WORDS

Kegĕt′.................... Verily
Nimanidon′.............. I am a spirit
Muki′yan .... To be able to become visible
Nabe′mikowiyân′......... I that am a male beaver

SERIES 2—ANALYSIS

SONG PICTURE NO. 34. A beaver is seen rising from the water.

The second series consists of songs used at the initiation of members in the Mĭde′wĭwĭn. In songs nos. 35, 38, and 40 the initiators speak; in nos. 36, 37, and 42 the person to be initiated speaks; and nos. 39 and 41 appear to be the words of a manido′

represented by or existent in the leading man's medicine pouch. The mention of metal in nos. 37 and 42, as well as the mention of the high hill in no. 39, would indicate that the song had been used in a part of the country where minerals and mountains were familiar to the people.

These songs show somewhat better musical material than those in the first series. Two of the songs are on the fourth five-toned scale, five contain the tones of the major triad with the added sixth, thus presenting the partially formed five-toned scale mentioned in the analysis of the first series, while no. 36 contains only the tones of the minor triad.

Song no. 39 of this series is of more than usual interest and is transcribed in full.

No. 35   (Catalogue no. 26)

WORDS

Kigawa′bamäg...... You shall now behold
Mĭde′wĭdjĭg......... They of the Mĭde′

SONG PICTURE NO. 35. This drawing shows the Mĭde′wĭgan, the medicine pole, the stone, and the assembled members of the Mĭde′-wĭwĭn. The candidate for initiation sees and hears the ceremony mentally before entering the lodge. Note the eyes and the ear of the candidate.

No. 36   (Catalogue no. 27)

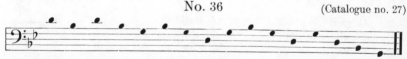

SONG PICTURE NO. 36. The two figures are exactly alike, the heart being shown and the straight lines indicating "strength." Thus the candidate assures himself that he will receive all the benefits enjoyed by other members of the Mĭde′wĭwĭn.

WORDS

Na............................. Listen
Mĭgaye′nin .... I shall also be blessed
Minawĭn′....................... And my life prolonged
Ĕn′dayan′...................... Like
Mĭde′wăg .... Those of the Mĭde′
Endĭwâd′...................... Whom I now behold

The candidate for initiation is assured of the benefits which he will derive from the Mĭde′. This assurance is often needed as the candidate regards the initiation as a difficult ordeal. He has a part which must be properly performed, in which he has been instructed by the initiators.

No. 37   (Catalogue no. 28)

SONG PICTURE
NO. 37. In this
drawing both
straight and
wavy lines
diverge from
the figure.
The wavy
lines are said
to indicate
"the song"
and the
straight lines
to indicate
"strength."

WORDS

Mi'nawina'.................. Is it that
Ain'nweyăn'.................. Which my voice resembles?
Bĭwa'bĭkuñ .... Even metal
Ain'weyăn'................... The sounding of my voice?

No. 38   (Catalogue no. 29)

WORDS

Anindĭ'..................... Where is
Abigwen'.................. The dwelling
Manido'..................... Of the greatest spirit?
Nikân'..................... My Mĭde' brethren
Wabûnâñ'.................. In the east
Abigwen'..................... Is the dwelling
Manido'..................... Of the greatest spirit
Nikân'..................... My Mĭde' brethren
Mĭoma'..................... Here
Abigwen'..................... Is my dwelling
Manido'wĭyân'.............. I who am the greatest spirit

SONG PICTURE NO.
38. It was stated
that the horizon-
tal figure and
head represented
the East man-
ido' and that
the upright fig-
ure and head
represented the
South manido'.

This record was played for Na'waji'bigo'kwe, a member of the Mĭde'wĭwĭn, who drew the pictures for these
series of songs; she said that this is a new form of an old song, and
that the younger men of to-day are arrogant enough to use it, but
that the old and correct form of the song gives the last two words as
follows:

Cawamĭñ'......................... Toward the east
Abigwen'........................... Is his dwelling

No. 39   (Catalogue no. 30)

VOICE ♩. = 69
Recorded without drum

Wa-djĭ-wĭñ ge en-da-nwe-wĭ-da - mâ - ân   wa-djĭ-wĭñ-ge en-da-

nwe-wĭ-da - mâ - ân   wa-djĭ-wĭñ ge en-da-nwe-wĭ-da - mâ - ân

wa-djĭ-wĭñ ge en-da-nwe-wĭ-da - mâ - ân   wa-djĭ-wĭñ ge   en-da-

nwe₁-wĭ-da - mâ - ân   wa-djĭ-wĭñ ge en-da-nwe-wĭ-da - mâ - ân

WORDS

Wadjĭwĭng′.............. From beneath the high
                                  hill
En′danwewĭdamân′ ...... My voice echoes forth

SONG PICTURE NO. 39.
In this drawing the
circle represents a
hill.

Dancing begins with this song and continues during
the remainder of the series.

No. 40   (Catalogue no. 31)

SONG PICTURE NO. 40. In this
drawing the circle represents
the earth; note the interruption of the circle at the lower
edge.

WORDS

Anawĭ′na ....⎫ I will cause it to ap-
Nĭmo′kĭwĭna′ ....⎭   pear
Tĭbĭckoka′mĭg. . . . . . That which is beneath
                                    the earth

Ebĭgwen′.............⎫
Anawĭ′na ....⎬ Although I bring it up
Nĭmo′kĭnĭna′........⎭   to light

No. 41   (Catalogue no. 32)

SONG PICTURE NO. 41. In this drawing the circle represents the sky; note the interruption at the upper edge. Mention of a bird occurs with special frequency in songs of the second, third, and fourth degrees.

WORDS

Nĭpo′nĭyân′........... I am about to alight
Tcĭwa′bamĭyâu′....... That you may see me
Tĭbĭc′koka′mĭg........ Upon the level ground
Tcĭwa′bamĭyâu′....... That you may see me
Nĭpo′nĭyâu′........... I am about to alight
Tcĭwa′bamĭyâu′....... That you may see me

No. 42   (Catalogue no. 33)

WORDS

Wabĭk′................ The strength of metal
Owĭbĭyăn′............ Has entered into my arrow point
Manido′............... A spirit
Ninda′nĭsa′........... I could kill
Wabĭk′................ The strength of iron
Owĭbĭyan′ .... Has entered into my arrow point

SONG PICTURE NO. 42. A bear and an otter are represented in this drawing.

SERIES 3—ANALYSIS

The words of the third series are characterized by very strong affirmation of the power and beauty of the Mĭde′ religion. In this series the affirmative used is *man′dan*, which is the customary word among the Canadian Chippewa, the affirmation used by the Minnesota Chippewa being *kegĕt′*, or *gegĕt′*. This suggests a Canadian origin for the songs.

The translation of no. 50 was the subject of much discussion by the interpreters and members of the Mĭde′wĭwĭn, as the words contain the idea of a year and also the idea of indefinite continuity. It may be best explained as meaning that the power of the inspiration is indefinite, but that it is expected that members will reassemble at the end of a year for the purpose of strengthening and confirming their faith.

Musically, this series presents interesting material. The first two songs are on the second five-toned scale.

The tonality of no. 45 is of unusual interest.

Songs nos. 46 and 47 show the octave complete except the seventh, while nos. 48, 49, and 50 show the incomplete five-toned scale mentioned in the analysis of the first series. The principal interest centers in the first three songs of the series.

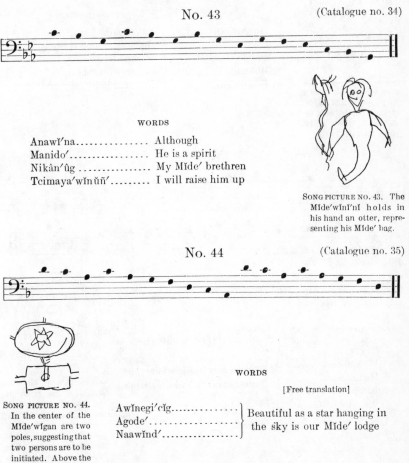

No. 43   (Catalogue no. 34)

WORDS

Anawĭ′na............... Although
Manido′................ He is a spirit
Nikân′ûg .... My Mĭde′ brethren
Tcimaya′wĭnûñ′........ I will raise him up

SONG PICTURE NO. 43. The Mĭde′wĭnĭ′nĭ holds in his hand an otter, representing his Mĭde′ bag.

No. 44   (Catalogue no. 35)

SONG PICTURE NO. 44. In the center of the Mĭde′wĭgan are two poles, suggesting that two persons are to be initiated. Above the lodge is a star in the circle of the sky. (Compare drawings of songs nos. 2 and 10.)

WORDS

[Free translation]

Awĭnegi′cĭg............⎫
Agode′................. ⎬ Beautiful as a star hanging in the sky is our Mĭde′ lodge
Naawĭnd′.............. ⎭

The words of this song are idiomatic and a translation was secured with difficulty. The song was recorded at Leech Lake, where two interpreters worked on it. Later the phonograph record was played for Na′waji′bigo′kwe, at White Earth. She drew the song picture and this translation was finally decided on as giving the essential idea of the song.

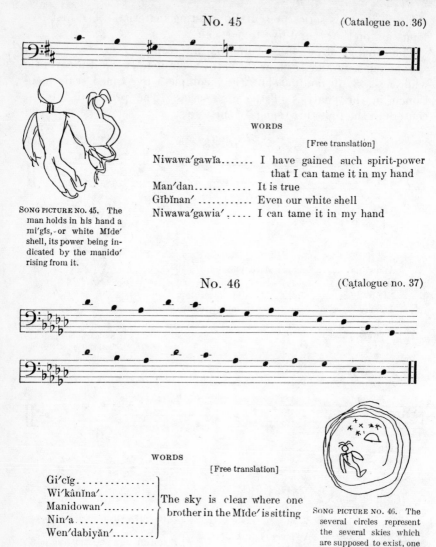

No. 45   (Catalogue no. 36)

SONG PICTURE NO. 45. The
man holds in his hand a
mi'gĭs,- or white Mĭde'
shell, its power being indicated by the manido'
rising from it.

WORDS

[Free translation]

Niwawa'gawĭa....... I have gained such spirit-power
                       that I can tame it in my hand
Man'dan............ It is true
Gĭbĭnan' .... Even our white shell
Niwawa'gawia'..... I can tame it in my hand

No. 46   (Catalogue no. 37)

WORDS

[Free translation]

Gi'cĭg...............⎫
Wi'kànĭna'..........⎪
Manidowan'..........⎬ The sky is clear where one
Nin'a...............⎪ brother in the Mĭde' is sitting
Wen'dabiyăn'........⎭

SONG PICTURE NO. 46. The
several circles represent
the several skies which
are supposed to exist, one
above another. In one of
these the Mĭde' brother is
seen to be sitting, while
beside him are the moon
and the stars.

If the day is fair it is considered that the person to be initiated
will be especially blessed; stormy weather is considered an unfavorable
omen.   The song does not express a desire or hope for fair weather
but affirms it as a fact.   Compare song no. 70.

Dancing begins with this song and continues during the remainder
of the series.

No. 47   (Catalogue no. 38)

WORDS

(Addressed to a sick person whose infirmity makes it impossible for him to walk)

[Free translation]

Anǐ′yǎnkǔn′ .... ⎫ You will recover; you will walk again.
Nin′na .... ⎪ It is I who say it; my power is great
Man′da n............ ⎬ Through our white shell I will enable
Bǐmose′hǐnan′ ...... ⎪ you to walk again
Gibinan′ .... ⎭

SONG PICTURE NO. 47.
The lines on the
man's limbs indi-
cate the "strength"
which he is to re-
ceive through the
Mǐde′, enabling
him to walk. (Com-
pare drawing of
song no. 19, in
which the straight
lines are on the
body, the desired
strength here be-
ing of a more gen-
eral nature.)

No. 48   (Catalogue no. 39)

WORDS

Gego′ .... ⎫ Do not speak ill of the Mǐde′
Ǐnota′waken′ .... ⎭
Nikân′ .... My Mǐde′ brethren
Man′o .... ⎫ Be sure to heed my words
Ǐnota′nǐscǐn .... ⎭
Nikân′ .... My Mǐde′ brethren

SONG PICTURE NO. 48.
In this as in no. 49
wavy lines are used
to represent speech.

Analysis.—The descending minor third is the principal interval in
this song. The tonality is major and the melody follows the tones
of the major triad, the sixth being added in the latter portion of the
song. In common musical terms the song would be said to be in
the key of F, yet the tonic does not appear until the middle of the
song. Comparison will show this to be a marked peculiarity of
Chippewa songs. The progression F–D–F does not occur frequently
in the songs analyzed.

No. 49   (Catalogue no. 40)

SONG PICTURE NO. 49.

WORDS

Gego′.................	} Do not speak ill of the Mĭde′
Ĭnota′waken′.........	
Nikân′................	My Mĭde′ brethren
Nĭngotcĭ′	Wherever you may be
Ikwe′wäñ	Do not speak ill of a woman
Nikân′	My Mĭde′ brethren

No. 50   (Catalogue no. 41)

WORDS

Tcĭ′gĭgĭwa′basogwen′...	We may live by it always
Nikân′..................	My Mĭde′ brethren
Manido′wân............	It is spiritual
Nin′esewĭn′.............	The inspiration we receive

SONG PICTURE NO. 50. In his
hand the Mĭde′ wĭnĭ′nĭ holds
a Mĭde′ shell.

SERIES 4—ANALYSIS

The fourth series is composed of songs which are sung after a man has been initiated and has been given a medicine bag corresponding to the degree he has taken.

Song no. 54 contains a reference to the water spirit.

De′bwawĕn′dûnk stated that song no. 58 refers to a yellow bear, whose shaggy fur resembles feathers. As already stated, the bear is closely connected with the Mĭde′

No. 59 refers to the fact that the white shells used in initiating members into the Mĭde′wĭwĭn are supposed to penetrate the skin, and it is the duty of the initiators, having "shot" these shells, to remove them. The work of these shells is a cleansing work, and if any of them remain in the body it is supposed that the cleansing is incomplete and the person suffers correspondingly. These shells issue from the mouth of the person being initiated.

In the instance of this song one of the shells was difficult to remove and was found to be in the heart of the person under initiation. As an example of this, a woman stated to the writer that her arm had been lame ever since she was initiated into the Mĭde'wĭwĭn. She said that her husband asked her if she was sure that the initiators removed all the shell or "medicine" and stated that if any remained it might produce this lameness, which had continued about thirty years.

The words of no. 60 refer, of course, to a manido'.

These songs are in a different style from the three preceding series, yet it is impossible to indicate this in the melody outline, the progressions being about the same. Most of the songs in this series are chanted in a very dignified and impressive manner, producing a peculiar effect, quite different from that produced by the same tone material in the form of the more rhythmic songs.

No. 51 presents the minor triad with minor seventh added. This combination of tones is fully considered elsewhere in this paper (see p. 130).

No. 52 contains the major triad with the second added, a somewhat unusual feature.

Nos. 53 and 54, one in the major and the other in the minor, show the octave complete except the seventh.

No. 55 is on the fourth five-toned scale, and nos. 56 and 57 are on the second five-toned scale, lacking one tone.

No. 58 is an interesting study of tonality. The ending was given firmly and the melody is particularly effective.

Nos. 59 and 60 consist of the tones of the fourth five-toned scale with the second lowered, the first song being minor and the second major in tonality.

No. 51   (Catalogue no. 42)

WORDS

Umbe'..........................	Come
Nagŭmoda'....................	Let us sing
Umbe'sano'ecigabo'ida.......	Come, we are now standing before you, bending down
Nikân'.........................	My Mĭde' brethren
Kibima'dĭziwĭn'dotamăn'....	We ask long life for you
Misanin'ingegigabo'iyân'.....	That is what I myself am seeking for you

SONG PICTURE NO. 51. In this drawing are shown the Mĭde'wĭgan, the pole, the stone, the oc'kabe'wĭs at the entrance, the leader of the ceremony, and the candidate for initiation. As this series of songs is used for initiation into the second or third degrees, the leader has an assistant who is seated between him and the novitiate.

No. 52   (Catalogue no. 43)

SONG PICTURE NO. 52. The man holds his weasel-skin medicine bag.

WORDS

Ewina′................... Here it is
Hawina′.................. Here it is
A′cigosi′wayân′......... The weasel skin (medi-cine bag)
Geda′bimŭn′............ Through it I shoot the white shells

No. 53   (Catalogue no. 44)

WORDS

Ni′bawiyân′........... Here I stand
Na..................... Behold
Boske′asĭn′............ A stone is filled
Ma′nidowĭd′ .... With spirit power
Nibanin′............... With it I shoot

SONG PICTURE NO. 53. A stone is at the point of the man's arrow.

No. 54   (Catalogue no. 45)

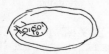

SONG PICTURE NO. 54. The mi′gĭs is shown in the circle of the sea.

WORDS

Nawigitci′gami′we.... In the middle of the sea
Genodog′gitcigâmi′.... The lengthy room of the sea
Andana′biyân′........ There I am sitting

No. 55   (Catalogue no. 46)

WORDS

Waka′oseyân′........... Walking around
Mĭde′watĭgŭñ′.......... The Mĭde′ pole
Manine′amăn′.......... Coming upon it stealthily
Miyûwen′tciayasoseyân′. I make a noise as I fall, leaning
Nigânoseyân′........... When I lead them all

SONG PICTURE NO. 55. Compare song drawings nos. 2 and 10.

In this song the singer represents himself to be a bear, walking around the Mĭde′ pole and trying to strike it. (Compare fig. 6, p. 42.)

No. 56   (Catalogue no. 47)

WORDS

Ninbeba′miseyân′........	I that hasten around
Nabosĕdini′niwejiûd′.....	I shoot at a man and he falls in a trance
Nigagwe′dĭna′.............	Then I feel with my hand
Ninbeba′miseyân′.........	To see if he is still alive

SONG PICTURE No. 56. A wavy line connects the bird and the sky-circle. The double line before this drawing divides the series into two parts, as written on the birch-bark strip. The people dance during the succeeding songs.

No. 57   (Catalogue no. 48)

WORDS

Anima′kizine′........ Going with footwear on his feet

This song is said to be about a bear's paw.

SONG PICTURE NO 57.

No. 58   (Catalogue no. 49)

WORDS

Wa′ciñe′biyân′...........	I who live in a cave
Kimico′misinân′.........	Our grandfather
Onika′sa..................	Arms he has
Omi′gwănŭn′.............	With feathers
Wa′shiñe′biyân′..........	I who live in a cave

SONG PICTURE NO. 58. The "feathered arms" are shown in the drawing.

No. 59   (Catalogue no. 50)

WORDS

Nikân ûn′	My Mĭde′ brother
Na′donamawĭn′	Is searched
Odeĭñ′	In his heart is found
Mi′konamawa′	That which I seek to remove
Migĭsŭn′	A white shell

Song picture no. 59. The mi′gĭs is shown in the heart of the Mĭde′.

No. 60   (Catalogue no. 51)

WORDS

Cĭngus′	Weasel
Nân′domiyan′	Thou art calling me

Song picture no. 60. In his hand the man holds a weasel, representing his Mĭde′ bag.

There is a large number of songs which may be used during the initiation of a member of the Mĭde′wĭnĭn. Each of the old men accustomed to lead the ceremony has his favorite songs and brings with him the birch-bark rolls on which the songs are written. Before each ceremony these rolls are examined and the songs discussed by the initiators but the selection is usually left to the leader.

The three following songs are not parts of series but are detached songs belonging to the portion of the ceremony in which the candidate is "shot" by the initiators.

No. 61. Initiation Song   (Catalogue no. 69)

Sung by A'GWITÛ'WIGI'CĬG ("SKIPPING A DAY")

VOICE ♩ = 96
Recorded without drum

Gi - a - wĭñ nin - da - sa   ya ha   nin   da   gi - a - wĭñ nin - da -

sa ya ha   nin   da   gi - a - wĭñ nin - da - sa ya ha   a   a

ma - ni - do - wĭd nin - da - sa   ya ha   nin   da   gi - a - wĭñ nin - da -

sa ya ha   nin   da   gi - a - wĭñ nin - da - sa ya ha   nin   da

WORDS

Gi'awĭñ'..........................Into thy body
Nindasa'..........................I shoot
Manidowĭd'.......................The spirit

This song is sung while the initiators march around the Mĭde'
lodge, the man to be initiated being seated beside the medicine pole.

Analysis.—A particularly pleasing melody is shown in this song.
The principal tones are those of the major triad, the second and
fourth being used as passing tones. With the exception of the last
measure of each phrase the rhythm is a triple rhythm throughout
the song.

The following narrative concerning the Mĭde' shells was given to
the writer by Mr. Charles Moulton, a member of the Otter Tail band
of Chippewa. Mr. Moulton stated that several years ago in the fall
he shot two ducks. In one of them his wife found two small white
shells of the variety used in the Mĭde', commonly known as Mĭde'
shells. His wife is a granddaughter of De'dadj, the leading Mĭde'-
wĭnĭ'nĭ of the Otter Tail band, and from her childhood has heard the
traditions of the Mĭde'wĭwĭn. She knew that these shells are rarely
found in ducks and that to find two in the same duck was "very great
medicine." Accordingly she showed the shells to De'dadj, who said,
"Put the shells into a box, wrap the box tightly in a cloth, do not
open it for a year, and at the end of that time you will find four

shells in the box instead of two." She followed his instructions. The box was placed at the bottom of a trunk and not disturbed for a year. It was then opened and was found to contain two small shells in addition to the two originally placed there. It was impossible that De'dadj could have put them into the box, as he was almost blind at the time and furthermore did not know where it was hidden.

Mr. Moulton stated that a member of the Mïde'wïwïn would have kept these four shells very carefully, secured small particles of them by rubbing them on a piece of iron and placed these fragments in water as a medicinal drink for the sick.

No. 62. INITIATION SONG   (Catalogue no. 70)

Sung by A'GWITÛ'WIGI'CĬG

VOICE ♩= 76
Recorded without drum

Ni - mĭ - de - wa - yan   e   ni - mĭ - de - wa - yan

e   ni - mĭ - de - wa - yan   e   ni - mĭ - de - wa - yan

e ni-mĭ-de-wa-yan   e ni-mĭ-de-wa-yan e ni-mĭ-de-wa-yan

e   ni - mĭ - de - wa - yan   e   ni - mĭ - de - wa - yan   e

WORDS

Ni'mĭde'wayan'..................... My Mïde' bag

During this song the person to be initiated is "shot" by the initiators.

Analysis.—The tonality of this song is obscure. It is transcribed exactly as sung, the different renditions being identical, yet the key is not definitely established, neither are modulations indicated with sufficient clearness to be safely assumed. The steadily descending progression here found is interesting and the melody itself is unusually attractive.

SONG PICTURE NO. 62. In his hand the man holds the animal which represents his Mïde' bag.

No. 63. Initiation Song   (Catalogue no. 254)

Sung by Main'äns

VOICE ♩ = 168
DRUM ♩ = 176

(Drum-rhythm similar to No. 3)

Ba - do-gwĕn e   gi - bi - nan e   ba - do-gwĕn e   gi - bi - nan

e ba - do-gwĕn e   gi - bi - nan e   ba - do-gwĕn e   gi - bi - nan

e ba - do - gwĕn e   gi - bi - nan e   hĭn de - mu - sa gûn

e gi - wi - ne - wa ba - do-gwĕn e   gi - bi - nan e   ba - do-gwĕn

e gi - bi - nan e   ba - do-gwĕn e   gi - bi - nan e

WORDS

Badogwĕn′	It never fails
Gibiṅan′	The shell
Demusa′	Goes toward them
Gi′winewa′	And they fall

SONG PICTURE NO. 63. This drawing represents a mi′gĭs.

This song is sung during the "shooting" of the candidate for initiation. The song is unusual in that the first descent of the voice is the interval of a fourth. The melody follows closely the minor chord, all other tones being readily identified as passing tones.

No. 64. Initiation Song   (Catalogue no. 67)

Sung by Kĭ′tcimak′wa

Fair weather is symbolic of health and happiness. Thus the words of this song predict health and happiness for the person to be initiated.

Analysis.—An unusual number of vowel syllables are used to fill out the measures of this song. Longer than most Mĭde′ songs, its special musical interest is the manner in which quadruple measures are introduced into a triple rhythm.

Voice ♩= 80

Recorded without drum

We-go-nĕn *i wi ne e e* wa-ya- *he* - *he-he-* da-mo - non *ha ha*

ha ha ha we-go-nĕn *i we ne e he* we-a-wi - *hi* - *hi* - da-mo-

non *ha ha ha ha ha* we-go-nĕn *i we* de *e e e* wa-ya-

we - *he* - e - da-mo - na *ha ha ha ha ha* man-da-gi - cĭg *wi*

e *he he* dji-wa-we - *he* - *he* - na-go - deg *he he he he*

he dji-we-nĕn - i - go-deg *he he* wa-ya-wi - *hi* - en-da-mo-

non *a he he o he* we-go-nĕn *i wi ne e*

e wa-ya-we - *he* - *he* - da-mo - non *ha ha ha ha ha ne*

WORDS

Wegonnĕ′.............. What is this
Wayawĭndamonon′.... I promise you?
Mandagi′cĭg........... The skies shall be bright and clear
for you
Djiwawe′nagodeg′..... This is what I promise you

SONG PICTURE NO. 64.
The wavy line represents the song which, rising to the sky, will make it bright and clear. (Compare drawing of song no. 56.)

Songs to Insure Success

During the dance which follows an initiation ceremony it is customary for the members of the Mĭde′-wĭwĭn to sing the songs of their special medicines. It is said that a man whose hunting medicine is particularly strong may rise and dance and sing his hunting-charm songs and that he may be joined by any other persons whose special medicine pertains to the hunt and who know the same songs.

The following set of five hunting songs were sung by Be'cĭgwi'-wizäns ("striped boy") and are of this character. They were sung by their possessor before starting on a hunting expedition. .

The first, second, and third songs assert the ability of the Mĭde'-wĭnĭ'nĭ to control the wild creatures of the woods; the fourth and fifth songs are concerned with the means which are employed.

No. 65. Hunting Song (a)　　　(Catalogue no. 56)

Sung by Be'cĭgwi'wizäns

Voice ♩ = 152
Recorded without drum

Me - gwû-yak　ka nĭn-don-dji - bi - na　ha　na

me-gwû-yak ka nĭn-don-dji - bi - na　gi-ga-gi - kwa - wi - ni - nâñ

me-gwû-yak ka nĭn-don-dji-bi - na　me-gwû-yak ka nĭn-don-dji - bi -

na　he na　ya me-gwû-yak ka nĭn-don - dji - bi - na　ha　na

me - gwû - yak　ka nĭn - don - dji - bi - na　gi - ga - gi -

kwa - wi - ni - nâñ　me-gwû- yak　ka nĭn-don - dji - bi -

na　me-gwû- yak　ka nĭn - don - dji - bi - na　he na　ya

WORDS

Megwûyak' .... Out of the woods
Nĭndon'djibi'na .... We will bring
Gigagikwa'wininâñ' .... Even as we are telling you

SONG PICTURE NO.
65. The animal is
seen approaching
the hunter.

Analysis.—Attention is called to the varied measure lengths and rapid metric unit in this song. It is also interesting to note that the F flat and succeeding F natural were accurately given.

No. 66. HUNTING SONG (*b*)   (Catalogue no. 57)

Sung by BE'CĬGWI'WIZÄNS

VOICE ♩ = 176
Recorded without drum

SONG PICTURE NO. 66.
Above the singer are
seen his war club and
the resounding sky.

WORDS

Ninba'gaako'kwan . My war club
Gi'cĭguñ .... Resounds through the sky
Dee'dagwe'wesĭñ'.. To summon the animals to my call

Analysis.—The words of this song were too indistinct for transcription. This is an instance in which the entire song constitutes a rhythmic unit. Each tone in the first measure was given with equal accent, the tempo throughout being unusually well marked. The major third is the largest interval occurring in this song.

No. 67. HUNTING SONG (*c*)   (Catalogue no. 58)

Sung by BE'CĬGWI'WIZÄNS

VOICE ♩ = 176
Recorded without drum

Um-be sa ta - di-da ci - ci - gwe ta - di - da *we* gin-

a - ta - gi - ma - ni - do *wa a hi e ha na*

WORDS

Umbe' .... Come
Sa .... Behold
Ata'dida' .... Let us have a contest
Cici'gwe .... O rattlesnake
Gina'tagimanido' .. Most subtle of reptiles
Cici'gwe .... O rattlesnake

SONG PICTURE NO. 67.

This song is addressed to the rattlesnake as being the most dreaded and subtle of reptiles, which always succeeds in whatever it undertakes. The idea of the song is that the Mĭde' has enabled the man to compete successfully with even the wiliest of creatures.

Analysis.—The rhythm of this song is as subtle as the subject. Attention is directed to the melodic and rhythmic effect in the fifth and sixth measures. The minor third is the largest interval occurring in the song.

No. 68. HUNTING SONG (*d*)   (Catalogue no. 59)

Sung by BE'CĬGWI'WIZÄNS

VOICE ♩ = 192

Recorded without drum

A - ya - dja-kûm-ĭg e mo - ki - yăn a - ya - dja-kûm-ĭg

e mo - ki - yăn i hi jañ - we - ci - wa - yăn a i jañ -

we - ci - wa - yăn a i jañ - we - ci - wa - yăn a i e

WORDS

Aya'djawakûm'ĭg...... From all parts of the earth
Mokiyăn'............. I make my appearance
Jañwe'ciwayan'....... Clothed with the skin of the
      marten

The singer stated that the words of this song refer to a Mĭde' bag made of the skin of a marten, which "has power to drive together the animals from all parts of the earth." It will be remembered that the manido' mentioned in the account of the origin of the Mĭde' (p. 23) carried living otters in their hands. Song no. 13 (p. 47) speaks of a sound as coming from the Mĭde' bag, and song

SONG PICTURE NO. 68. "All parts of the earth" are represented by two circles, between which is seen the form of the marten.

no. 60 (p. 78) contains the words, "Weasel, thou art calling me," the song referring to the Mĭde' bag carried by a member of the first degree in the Mĭde'wĭwĭn. In song no. 81 (p. 105) a medicine bag made of the skin of an owl is represented as speaking. A comparison of these songs is of interest.

Analysis.—This is one of the few songs in which the first progression is an upward progression. Rhythm constitutes an important feature of these hunting songs, yet the rhythm of each is distinct and peculiar.

No. 69. HUNTING SONG (e)   (Catalogue no. 60)

Sung by BE'CĬGWI'WIZÄNS

VOICE ♩ = 168

Recorded without drum

A-nun-guñ *we* *he* *na* *a* *ni* *gwe* *he* a-nun-guñ

we *he* *na* *a* *ni* *gwe* *he* a-nun-guñ *we* *he*

na *a* *ni* *gwe* *he* a - we - sin ha-na-ba- mĭg *he* *na*

a *ni* *gwe* *he* a-nun-guñ *we* *he* *na* *a* *ni* *gwe* *he*

SONG PICTURE NO. 69. The correspondence between the man and the star is indicated by a straight line.

WORDS

Anun'guñ .... Like a star
Nĭndina'bamĭg .... I shine
Awesin' .... The animal, gazing, is fascinated by my light

The writer was informed that the use of a light in hunting at night was known by the Indians before the coming of the white man.

Analysis.—This song shows a distinct rhythmic unit of four measures. This unit occurs three times at the opening of the song, is followed by five measures in a different rhythm, after which the rhythmic unit is used in closing the song. Such regularity of musical form is seldom found in these songs.[a] It is also unusual for rests to occur, even the repetitions usually being given with no appreciable pause.

There appears to be no limit to the number of times a song is sung and the continued repetition has a rhythmic swing of its own. At a social dance the drum gives a signal indicating that the song will be sung only once more. This is understood by the dancers, but is scarcely noticed by an outsider. The time for this signal is determined by the man at the drum, who started the song.

---

[a] Songs recently secured show greater regularity.

No. 70. Song for Securing a Good Supply of (Catalogue no. 64)
Maple Sugar

Sung by Kɪ'tcɪmak'wa

Voice ♩ = 72
Recorded without drum

Wĭ-djĭ-ga-wi-ni - na-ha hĭn-dĭ-yan - e wĭ-djĭ-ga-wi-ni-

na-ha hĭn-dĭ-yan - e wĭ-djĭ-ga-wi-ni - na-ha hĭn-dĭ-yan-

e wĭ-djĭ-ga-wi-ni - na-ha hĭn-dĭ-yan - e wĭ-djĭ-ga-wi-ni-

na-ha hĭn-dĭ-yan - e mĭ-tĭ-ga wi-ni - na-ha hĭn-dĭ-yan-

e gi-gi-gog wi-ni - na-ha hĭn-dĭ-yan - e wĭ-djĭ-ga-wi-ni-

na-ha hĭn-dĭ-yan - e wĭ-djĭ-ga-wi-ni - na-ha hĭn-dĭ-yan-e

WORDS

Wĭdjĭga'wiwina'ha .... (Obsolete)
Hĭn'dĭyane' .... (Obsolete)
Mĭtĭgon' .... From the trees
Gion'gigog' .... The sap is freely flowing

Song picture no. 70. From the tree the sap is seen flowing into a bucket. The roots of the tree are shown in the drawing.

The making of maple sugar constituted a pleasant industry among the Chippewa. From their scattered abodes they assembled at the sugar camp in the spring. The events of the winter were fully discussed, and general sociability marked the gathering. Maple sugar is a favorite luxury and is prepared in various attractive forms. An abundant supply is greatly desired, and this song is supposed to secure it.

The words furnish an example of the affirmation which strongly characterizes the Mĭde' songs. There is no request; the song simply asserts that the sap is flowing freely, thus presenting to the mind a vivid picture of the conditions which would produce the desired supply of maple sugar.

Analysis.—This song shows a characteristic tendency to lower slightly the pitch on the second of two similar tones. Throughout the song a double measure is followed by a triple measure. Each rhythm was given distinctly and for that reason it was not deemed advisable to combine two measures in one 5–4 measure. The principal words are mispronounced, as frequently occurs in the Chippewa songs.

LOVE-CHARM SONGS

Sung by NA′WAJI′BIGO′KWE

The love charm is a very popular form of magic among the Chippewa. Of the following set of four love-charm songs no. 72 was first sung for the writer by a woman on the Red Lake reservation, the circumstances being as follows: The writer was engaged in the collection of folk-tales and persuaded this woman to tell a story. She consented with reluctance as it was the summer season and she said that snakes would certainly bite her at night if she told stories in the summer. After writing down a story the writer asked her to tell something about the Mĭde′wĭwĭn and to sing one of its songs. This request was received with still greater reluctance. The woman finally consented to sing one song in some secluded place where she was sure no one could hear her. When asked what the song would be she replied that it was a love-charm song. She was a woman about sixty years of age and was the most dirty and unattractive woman with whom the writer has come in contact. In a thin, nasal tone she sang the song, which was noted down by ear, no phonograph being available. With coy shyness she said the song meant that she was as beautiful as the roses. She also drew a crude picture of the song. Later this picture was shown to Na′waji′bigo′kwe at White Earth. She recognized the picture at once and sang the song into the phonograph. When the transcription of this record was compared with the memorandum made at Red Lake the identity of the song was readily discerned. The singer at Red Lake promised to come back and sing other songs the next day, but some friends who knew that she had sung a Mĭde′ song threatened her with calamity and she did not return. The singer at White Earth said that this is the first of a set of four songs. All were recorded by Na′waji′bigo′kwe, but the first is the most interesting of the set; only the words of the others therefore are given.

Analysis.—One measure constitutes the rhythmic unit in this song, being repeated with absolute regularity. Attention is directed to the range of voice. The singer was a woman, but her voice was in the tenor register. This was found to be the case with the voices of other women who sang the Mĭde' songs, being due, perhaps, to the fact that they were accustomed to singing with the men and adopted a unison tone.

No. 71 (a)

(Catalogue no. 73)

VOICE ♩ = 88
Recorded without drum

A - ni - na - ji - a - ne   a - ni - na - ji - a - ne

a - ni - na - ji - a - ne   a - ni - na - ji - a - ne

a - ni - na - ji - a - ne   a - ni - na - ji - a - ne

a - ni - na - ji - a - ne   o - gĭ - ni - ba - uñ   e

a - ji - na - go - o - yăn   a - ni - na - ji - a - ne

a - ni - na - ji - a - ne   a - ni - na - ji - a - ne

a - ni - na - ji - a - ne   a - ni - na - ji - a - ne

WORDS

A'ninajun'............. What are you saying to me?
Ogĭni'baguñ'........... I am arrayed like the roses
Ajina'gooyan'.......... And beautiful as they

SONG PICTURE NO. 71.
The heart of the fig-
ure is shown. (For
drawing of roses,
compare song no.99.)

No. 72 (b)   (Catalogue no. 74)

WORDS

Niwawin'gawia' .... I can charm the man
Ĕnĭ'nĭwa' .... He is completely fascinated
                          by me

SONG PICTURE NO. 72.
The lines diverging
from the figure of the
man were said to
represent "feeling."
(Compare drawing of
song no. 103.)

No. 73 (c)   (Catálogue no. 75)

WORDS

Ninda'agagia' ....⎤
I'enĭ'ni ....⎮   [Free translation]
Namundj'........ ⎬ I can make that man bashful. I
Ĕn'dogwĕn'....... ⎮   wonder what can be the matter
Wi'agudjiûg' .....⎦   that he is so bashful

SONG PICTURE NO. 73.

No. 74 (d)   (Catalogue no. 76)

WORDS

Mi'sawe'kûmĭg'......... In the center of the earth
A'yagwen'.............. Wherever he may be
Ana'makĭñ'............. Or under the earth

SONG PICTURE NO. 74.

No. 75. Love-charm Song   (Catalogue no. 52)

Sung by Manido'gicĭgo'kwe ("spirit day woman")

Voice ♩ = 72
Recorded without drum

The singer of this and the following song is a woman whose personality is unique and interesting.[a]

Song picture no. 75. The power of the love charm is shown by the manner in which the woman attracts the man, who appears rather reluctant.

Analysis.—It is impossible to indicate by any notation the peculiar nuances of this singer. A slight prolonging of certain tones gives the songs a fascinating effect, heightened by a slight glissando. The songs are also sung with the nasal quality affected by the Chippewa when singing love songs.

Attention is directed to the fact that this, like many other Chippewa love songs, has a slow metric unit.

---

[a] A description of this singer is given in connection with song no. 133. See also pl. 11.

No. 76. Love-charm Song   (Catalogue no. 53)

Sung by Manido'gicĭgo'kwe

Voice ♩= 84
Recorded without drum

Songs Connected with the Cure of the Sick

The treatment of the sick is conducted by the older members of the Mĭde'wĭwĭn, special songs being sung in connection with the use of medicinal herbs. This treatment is frequently given in conjunction with an initiation ceremony, the person being initiated in order to cure him of his bodily illness. Reference is made to song no. 47 (p. 73), the words of which are more characteristic of the Mĭde' than the words of the songs which follow under this heading and which are connected with personal incidents. In song no. 47 the power of the Mĭde' to cure the sick is affirmed and emphasized, it being further stated that the white shell is the means used to that end. This element of affirmation is very strong in the Mĭde' and to it may largely be attributed the power of the Mĭde' over the minds of the Chippewa.

Mi'jakiya'cĭg ("clearing sky"), an aged woman who is a member of the Mĭde'wĭwĭn, sang the two following songs associated with her personal experience.[a]

We'nabo'jo and his grandmother are the principal characters in Chippewa folklore. We'nabo'jo is also connected with the Mĭde', though the connection is not clearly defined.

---

[a] Mi'jakiya'cĭg stated that she was very ill when she was a young woman. Her parents prepared a feast and sent for a Mĭde'wĭnĭ'nĭ. After partaking of the feast the Mĭde'wĭnĭ'nĭ "spoke to the manido'," saying that she wished to have her life prolonged by means of the Mĭde'. He then smoked the tobacco which her father had provided. A few days later a larger feast was held and many members of the Mĭde'wĭwĭn were invited. After all had smoked, the first Mĭde'wĭnĭ'nĭ told them her desire; then he sang these two songs, the people dancing as he sang. Mi'jakiya'cĭg stated further that her health was entirely restored.

No. 77. Healing Song   (Catalogue no. 78)

Sung by Mi′jakiya′cĭg

Voice ♩ = 104
Recorded without drum

We - on - dĭ - kwe - bi - wûg e Wĕ - na - bo - jo i no

na o - kuo - mĭs - ûn ni ne na we - on - dĭ -

kwe - bi - wûg e we - on - dĭ - kwe - bi - wûg e

We′ondikwe′biwûg′..... They are in close consultation
                       with their heads together
We′nabo′jo .... We′nabo′jo
Okwomisûm′............ And his grandmother

Analysis.—Two strongly ascending progressions at
the first of this song mark it as different from the majority of Mĭde′ songs. The dotted quarter at the beginning of each measure forms the foundation of a simple
rhythmic unit which is repeated with little change
throughout the song.

Song picture no.
77. We′nabo′jo
and his grand-
mother are shown
in this drawing.

No. 78. Healing Song   (Catalogue no. 79)

Sung by Mi′jakiya′cĭg

Voice ♩ = 100
Recorded without drum

Ni - ma - ni - do - wi - na - wa ni - kân - ûg i hi e ni - ma - ni -

do - wi - na - wa ni - kân - ûg i hi e ni - ma - ni - do - wi - ta -

wa ni - kân - ûg i hi e ni - ma - ni - do ni - kân - ûg

WORDS

Nimanido′winawa′.................. I see a spirit likeness
Nikân′........................... In my Mĭde′ brother
Nimanido′witawa′ .... He speaks with spirit power
Nikân′........................... My Mĭde′ brother

Analysis.—The rhythmic unit of this song occurs four times and is readily discerned. Attention is directed to the range and tenor register of this song, which was sung by an old woman. The voice was harsh in quality, but fairly accurate in intonation.

No. 79. Healing Song (Catalogue no. 71)

Sung by O′dĕni′gûn

Voice ♩ = 116
Drum ♩ = 116

(Drum-rhythm similar to No. 1)

A - di - zo - ka - nûg a - di - zo - ka - nûg o he o he

nĭn - do - ta - wi - o - ge - djĭ - ga - gi - gi - do - yan

GE'MIWÛNAC'

A'dizoka'nûg................... In a dream
Nĭnan'dotagog'.....................⎫
Djĭgagi'gidoyan'...................⎬ I was instructed to do this
                                  ⎭

Narrative.—The singer gave the following history of this song:

Many years ago there lived at Gull Lake a man named Niogi'cĭg ("four days"). This man had lain for a long time upon a bed of suffering and there seemed no help for him. At last he decided to send tobacco to the Mĭde' men and see if they could help him. They made him a drum and he played on it and sang this song, which he composed himself. The words mean, "It was told me in my dream that I should do this and I would recover."

Analysis.—The rhythm of this song is peculiarly energizing, and when once established would undoubtedly have a beneficial physical effect. The surprising feature of this case, however, is that the song is said to have been composed and the rhythm created by the sick man himself.

A repetition of this song was secured from the same singer after a lapse of several months. The second rendition was identical with the first, beginning on the same tone and showing faulty intonation on the same tones.

No. 80. Healing Song   (Catalogue no. 14)

Sung by Ge'miwûnac'[a]

From the musical and the dramatic standpoint this is one of the finest songs in the entire collection. It is a song which would be sung when a member of the Mĭde'wĭwĭn was dying—when death was expected at any moment. The music in the lodge at the time of Flat Mouth's death was similar to that here given. It represents a type of song which members of the Mĭde'wĭwĭn are especially reluctant to sing.

Analysis.—A peculiar quality of sadness and pleading is found in this song, a quality heightened by the upward progression at the opening of the song and the frequent use of the flatted second. This accidental was always given accurately. Attention is directed to the descent of a perfect fifth, followed by the descent of a perfect fourth, at the close of the song.

---

[a] An aged man, one of the most eminent Mĭde'wĭnĭ'nĭ in northern Minnesota. (Pl. 9.) His name was known on all the reservations and he was held in the same high esteem everywhere. He was in charge of the Mĭde' ceremonies which were held during the last hours of Nigan'Ibĭnes' (see p. 51). The writer had no conversation with him at that time. Returning to Leech Lake several months later she met Ge'miwûnac' again and asked him to sing. It was probably owing to a remembrance of incidents connected with Flat Mouth's death that he was willing to sing this song. He stated that it was similar to those sung during the last hours of Flat Mouth, but that he was then so overcome that he could not recall exactly what songs were used.

VOICE ♩ = 56

Recorded without drum

Ki - ma - ni - do - we   hi na wa ki - ma - ni - do - we

hi na wa ki - ma - ni - do - we   hi na wa ki - ma - ni - do - we

hi   na   wa   ki - ma - ni - do - we   hi   na   wa

hi   ĕn - da - ni - kân e ma - ni - do - wa - ne we hi a we

ma - ni - do - we   hi na wa ki - ma - ni - do - we   hi na wa ki -

ma - ni - do - we   hi na wa ki - ma - ni - do - we   hi na wa hi

WORDS

Kimanido′wihe′..................... You are a spirit
Kimanido′wiĭn..................... I am making you a spirit
Ĕnda′nabiyan′..................... In the place where I sit
Kimanido′wiĭn′..................... I am making you a spirit

SONGS CONNECTED WITH RARE MEDICINES

Sung by O′DĔNI′GÛN

These are examples of the songs which may be sung at the dance following an initiation and also in the lodges during the evenings which precede the ceremony. They are songs which can be sung only by those who purchase the right to sing them. O′dĕni′gûn, who sang all the songs in this group, is said to be "one of the most powerful medicine-men on the White Earth reservation." (See fig. 7, p. 100.)

The word "medicine" as here used refers to any substance by means of which results are supposed to be mysteriously attained. The narratives concerning these songs were given by the singer and are transcribed as nearly as possible in the words of the interpreter.

No. 81. Song of the Flying Feather　(Catalogue no. 191)

Voice ♩ = 100
Drum ♩ = 108
(Drum-rhythm similar to No. 1)

Ya ha ya ha mon o-do-no-dji-i-gon ya ha ya ha

mon a-do-no-dji-i-gon ya ha ya ha mon o-do-no-dji-i-gon

i na ha we a hi a en-di-mu-sa-o-no-dji-găn

ya ha ya ha mon o-do-no-dji-i-gon ya ha ya ha

mon o-do-no-dji-i-gon i na ha we a hi a

HARMONIC ANALYSIS

3 measures　　5 measures　　2 measures　　5 measures

WORDS

Migwûn.................. The feather
O'dono'djiigon'......... Is coming toward
Endimo'nondjiigăn'.... The body of the Mïde'wïnï'nï

Song picture no. 81. In this drawing the persons mentioned in the song are represented twice. The man and his wife are shown in the wigwam; the man is shown also beside the wigwam, while his wife is at a distance. (Compare drawing of song no. 1.)

Narrative.—In a wigwam lived a man and his wife, but after a time the woman ran away. Then the man went to an old Mïde'wïnï'nï and said to him, "My wife has run away; I wish that you would take pity on me and bring her back again."

The old man replied, "Your wife will come back to-night." Then he added, "I am sure of this, because the sound of my drumming is heard all over the world and when she hears it she can not help coming back." So he began to drum and to sing this song, and the man's wife came back to him. Then the old man gave him a charm so that his wife would never run away again.

Explanation of the flying feather and the flying man.—All the old Indians know about the flying man. He was a very powerful Mĭde′ [a] who could cause a feather to come to him out of the air. This feather would come toward him and enter into his body. Then the man could rise up and fly like a bird. The Chippewa depended upon him in the wars with the Sioux, for he could fly through the air and spy out the enemy. Once the Chippewa suspected that the Sioux were near and they sent this flying man to look over the country. As the Sioux were sitting in their camp they saw the flying man coming toward them in the air, and the leader of the Sioux said to his men, "Fill up that pipe as fast as you can;" so they filled the pipe and lighted it. They held the stem of the pipe up toward the flying man. They pointed it at him and he could not see the crowd of Sioux. He did not see them at all. So he returned to his friends and said that he did not see the Sioux anywhere. Then the Chippewa marched across an open field. The Sioux were watching, but they let them pass. Then the Sioux shot and killed them all, even the flying man.

Analysis.—This song is harmonic in character, beginning on the octave, descending a minor third, and then following the tones of the tonic triad. The song contains a short rhythmic unit which occurs five times, giving the song its forceful, energetic character. The rhythm is exceptionally strong and clearly marked throughout the song.

No. 82. Song of the Man Who Succeeded (Catalogue no. 192)

Voice ♩ = 100
Drum ♩ = 108
(Drum-rhythm similar to No. 1)

WORDS

Nin′sa.................... I myself
Ningagwe′djisea′......... Will test my power

Song Picture no. 82.

Narrative.—There was once a man who had never tested the power of his medicine in the hunt. It was a time of starvation in the camp. The man himself was starving. A very old Mĭde′ had been training him for a long time, but the old man lived far away. The man found himself thrown on his own resources. He resolved to do his best, so he composed this song and went forth to hunt. The venture was a desperate one, but he succeeded, and killed a bear. Afterward this was his medicine-song.

---

[a] In conversational Chippewa the term *Mĭde′* is frequently used instead of *Mĭde′wĭnĭ′nĭ*, referring to a male member of the Mĭde′wĭwĭn.

Analysis.—The transcription is from the second of the four renditions on the phonograph record. In the third and fourth renditions the words are slightly changed, thus affecting the note-values, the melodic trend remaining the same. Even in this rendition the words are too broken by interpolated syllables to be transcribed.

The intonation of the first note of the song is always clear. The accidental is also clear, but the intonation is wavering in most of the song. The accidental is the lowered sixth, which occurs frequently in the Chippewa songs under consideration. There is no repetition of a rhythmic unit in this song, although the various parts bear a very close resemblance to one another.

No. 83. Song of a Scalp Dance   (Catalogue no. 193)

Voice ♩ = 104
Drum ♩ = 138
(Drum-rhythm similar to No. 1)

WORDS

Ninga'onde'nimigo' ..... Some will be envious
Gi'witagi'cĭg .... Who are in the sky
Nina'niminan' .... I am dancing around
Inĭ'nĭwi'stigwăn' .... A man's scalp

Narrative.—This song carries us far into the past with its war parties and wild rejoicings of victory. It was sung on the return of the Chippewa from the Sioux country, with scalps. After the usual scalp dances there was held a special dance called a "round dance," because it took place around a grave. If possible, this was the grave of a person killed by the Sioux, often the grave of the person whose death had been avenged by the war. At the close of this "round dance" the poles bearing the

Song picture no. 83. The drawing shows the dancing circle, the men carrying scalps upon poles, the grave of the Chippewa, and the pole at the head of the grave.

scalps were stuck into the ground at the head of the grave, to stay there until the poles should decay and fall. The drawing of the song shows three scalps upheld during the dance, but only one placed at the head of the grave. This may be the scalp of the person who killed the buried Chippewa.

Analysis.—Beginning on the sixth and ending on the third, this melody is somewhat unusual. The voice accent and consequent measure lengths are unmistakable, the only irregularity being in the first two measures after the rest, these measures being a trifle shorter than the metronome time. The drum is exceedingly rapid and the melody in very moderate tempo, a combination often found in songs of mental excitement.

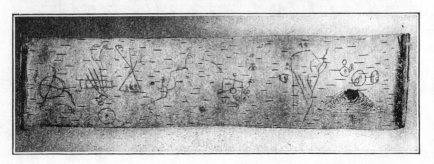

Fɪɢ. 7. Birch-bark rolls containing mnemonics of the songs connected with rare medicines, and used by Oʹdĕniʹgûn when singing these songs.

No. 84. Song of Good Medicine (Catalogue no. 194)

Sᴏɴɢ ᴘɪᴄᴛᴜʀᴇ ɴᴏ. 84. The feathers are seen near the Mĭdeʹwĭnĭʹnĭ.

Narrative.—There were once two men, the elder of whom was very disagreeable toward everyone, and would not believe anything that was told him. The younger man was his constant companion, but was entirely different from him in every respect. One day the younger man secured a thread from the clothing of the elder and took it to an old Mĭdeʹ, asking him to change the disposition of the elder man by means of medicine. The old Mĭdeʹ took a feather, cut the quill, and put the threads inside the quill with a little medicine. Then he fastened the quill together in such a way that the cut was not visible. The old Mĭdeʹ also gave the younger man a feather which looked exactly like the one with medicine in it. On his return the younger man gave his friend the feather containing the medicine and his friend placed the feather in his hair, supposing it to be an ornament. Both men wore the feathers in their hair. After a time the disposition of the elder man began to change. He grew kind and amiable toward everyone until at last he was entirely cured of all his disagreeable qualities. This was the work of the good medicine and the singing of the old Mĭde′.

VOICE ♩= 92
DRUM ♩= 116
(Drum-rhythm similar to No. 1)

[Chippewa words not transcribed]

[Free translation]

I control him by means of the feather so that he will lead a good life

Analysis.—It was extremely difficult to find the metric unit of this song. It was finally found in three consecutive tones which bore an evident metric relation to one another. It was then discovered that the same metric unit underlay the remainder of the song, and working from these three tones it was possible to divide the song into note-values; the notes were then grouped into measures according to the accents. Having transcribed the song according to this process, the rhythm, which seemed hopelessly obscure, was seen to be quite clear. By tapping the rhythm of this song with a pencil one may gain an idea of its peculiarity, and of the unmistakable manner in which the entire song constitutes itself a rhythmic unit. The song was recorded several times, the repetitions being identical in rhythm.

The tone marked ·) was given in every instance less than its proper time.

This song offers a distinct problem in tonality. The tones are those of the fourth five-toned scale on G flat, but the first part of the song affiliates only with the chords of the key of D flat and the last part only with the chords of the key of G flat. Neither key is well established by the melody. In this, as in similar instances, the signature at the beginning of the staff should be understood as affecting the tones on the lines or spaces indicated, but not as implying that the corresponding key is fully established by the melody.

No. 85. Song of the Crab Medicine-bag (Catalogue no. 195)

VOICE ♩ = 104
DRUM ♩ = 116
(Drum-rhythm similar to No. 1)

A - ca wi he he a ne a-ca   we he he a ne hi hi

hi hi hi a-ca we he   he a he a-ca we a ni ni hi   hi hi

hi wa - ca we he he a ni wa-ca we he -he ya we

ni hi hi wa-ca we he he a ni wa-ca we he he a ni

nin-da-we-dja ha ni hi hi ya ha ni hi ni hi hi hi hi hi wa-ca

WORDS

Aca′gecĕn′.......................... Like a crab
Ninda′badjia′...................... I am using it

SONG PICTURE NO. 85.
The drawing represents a Mǐde′ bag with two mǐ′gǐs beside it.

Narrative.—Two women are mentioned in this song. Their grandfather gave them each a medicine-bag made of the skin of a small crab. The two women wore these medicine-bags around their necks and after receiving the bags they never lacked for anything—they had all that they wanted. This was a good kind of medicine-bag, for the crab has claws which hold very tightly, so the medicine-bag enabled the women to hold on to everything that was good.

Analysis.—This song resembles a chant. The accents and the grouping of tones are clearly marked, but the metric unit (♩=104) varies constantly, the variation not being sufficient to be indicated. The first word is so dismembered as to lose its identity, only the first two syllables being retained. The syllable *ne* marks the conclusion of the succession of syllables which represent the word. The second word is mispronounced. The song continues one accidental tone.

No. 86. Song of the Fire-charm   (Catalogue no. 197)

Voice ♩ = 69
Drum ♩ = 126
(Drum-rhythm similar to No. 1)

I - na - ko - ne *ya ha ha* ni - ya - we *he he* i - na - ko - ne

ya ha ha ni - ya - we *he he* i - na - ko - ne *ya ha ha* ni - ya -

we *he he* i - na - ko - ne *ya ha ha* ni - ya -

we *he he* i - na - ko - ne *ya hi hi* ni - ya - we *he he*

ni - ya - we *he he* i - na - ko - ne *ya ha ha* ni - ya

WORDS

Ina′kone′ . . . . The flame goes up
Niyâwiñ′ . . . . To my body

SONG PICTURE NO. 86.
The flames are seen
ascending from a
circle of fire.

Narrative.—The greatest wonder that ever came to the Indians was fire. Like everything else, it came to them through Mĭde′.

Someone asked, "What do you want to do with this?" A man replied, "This fire is for warmth and for cooking." The Indians were afraid of it at first, but soon learned that it was useful.

Once there was a fire burning on the ground and many people were sitting around it. A man rose and walked away and put medicine on his feet. Then he came back and stood in the fire, and he was not burned at all. After he came out of the fire all the people looked to see his feet. He was barefooted, but he was not burned at all. Some tried to find out how he did it. They said that they would walk away and come back and stand in the fire, but the man said that they had better not try it. While he was in the fire he was chewing medicine and spitting the juice on his body, so that, although the flames came up all around his body, he was not burned at all.

Probably some of the very oldest Mĭde′ still have some of this medicine which they can put on their feet and walk in the fire without being burned. They can also put it on their hands and take hold of very hot stones without being burned.

Analysis.—This song differs from other Mĭde′ songs in that the singer sang the song through once, with the portion to be repeated, and then gave the ejaculations *wa hi hi hi hi, wa hi hi hi hi*, after which he began at the beginning and sang the entire song again; this being contrasted with the custom of repeating the last portion of the song an indefinite number of times without a pause. Three complete renditions were recorded by the phonograph. The slow voice-rhythm and rapid drum are found in this as in other songs of mental stress. The pulse of the measure-lengths is uniform throughout the song, though some measures are in 2–4 and some in 3–4 time.

No. 87. SONG OF STARVATION   (Catalogue no. 199)

WORDS

Awĕnĕn′	Who
Gemama′djidod′	Will take
Niau′	My body?
I′kwe	A woman
Ĭnde′musa′ogio′jiton′	Is making the medicine

SONG PICTURE NO. 87.

Narrative.—In the olden times the Indians had no weapons except bows and arrows, and they often suffered greatly for lack of food. In those days they were very jealous of each other because some could get more game than others. Sometimes a man who had plenty of food was later "starved out" by other Indians until he was so hungry that he could eat grass. This was accomplished by means of medicine.

Once a man who was nearly starving went to an old Mĭde′ and asked for his help. The old Mĭde′ said, "Well, my grandchild, I will do what you wish because I fur-

nished to the other parties the medicine which has harmed you." Then the old
Mĭde′ hired a woman to go to the other camp and steal some small object from their
food supply. He wanted her to bring him a small bone from some of their game,
but at the last moment she refused to go. Then he hired another woman. She
worked at the other camp, and she brought the bone which the Mĭde′ wanted. First
the Mĭde′ put medicine on the bone; then he hid it and began to sing this song. In a
short time the people at the other camp could get no game at all. They almost starved,
but the man whom the Mĭde′ was helping could get all the game that he wanted.

Analysis.—The accidental forms the chief musical feature of this
song. The sixth is lowered a semitone each time it occurs except in
the last word. In the first syllable of that word the F sharp is
sung accurately in each rendition of the song, while in the following
measure the tone is about midway between F sharp and F natural.

No. 88. Song of the Owl Medicine (Catalogue no. 200)

Voice ♩ = 104
Drum ♩ = 112
(Drum-rhythm similar to No. 1)

Nin - go - ca nin-ga-gwet - *ni* - se - a　nin - go - ca nin - ga - gwet - *ni* - se -

a　nin - go - ca　nin - ga - gwet - *ni* - se - a　nin - go - ca　nin - ga -

gwet - *ni* - se - a　in - de - mu - sa　*gi we da　ni no gi*　nin -

go - ca　nin - ga - gwet - *ni* - se - a　nin - go - ca　nin - ga -

gwet - *ni* - se - a　nin - go - ca　nin - ga - gwet - *ni* - se - a

WORDS

Nin′goca′	....	I am the one
Ningagwĕt′sea′	....	Who is trying to fly
Inde′musa′	....	He is making it (the medicine)

Narrative.—This song was composed by the same old Mĭde′ as the preceding song
and most of the other songs in this series.

Once a man and his wife came to this old Mĭde′. He could see that they were
starving, and he said, "Stay here at my camp to-night." The snow was 3 feet deep,
and the man and his wife had been obliged to eat most of their dogs. The Mĭde′
gave them food and made them comfortable.

Late that night the old Mĭde′ got ready to sing, and while he was singing he sent an owl over to the camp where the Indians lived who were trying to starve this man and his wife. The owl carried the bad medicine and sat at the head of their camp that night, but they did not know it. This owl was just the dried skin of an owl with the medicine inside of it.

The old rule was that if a man killed an animal he must first divide it among the camps; then he must cook his own share of the meat and invite all the old men to come and eat it with him. If he failed to do this they would be jealous and would "starve him out," as was the case with this man and his wife.

SONG PICTURE NO. 88. The Mĭde′wĭnĭ′nĭ′, the man and his wife, are seen in the wigwam, from which the owl is flying.

After singing this song and sending the owl to the other camp the old Mĭde′ was sure that the man and his wife would have no further trouble. He also gave them medicine to carry, so that they could get near to the animals when they were hunting.

All that the Mĭde′ said was true. The other camp could get no food after the owl went to the camp. The Indians there nearly starved, but the man and his wife had plenty of game.

Analysis.—This song contains no change of rhythm, an unusual feature in a Mĭde′ song. The key of A minor is plainly implied by the melody, although there is very little to establish the key. The song begins on the ninth and ends on the fifth. It contains no repetition, the syllables *ho ho ho ho*, which indicate the conclusion of a song, being given after each rendition.

ADDITIONAL MĬDE′ SONGS

No. 89. SONG OF THE BEAR PATH (Catalogue no. 236)

Sung by MAIÑ′ĂNS

This is said to be the oldest Mĭde′ song known. If this were sung in a Mĭde′ gathering, it would be necessary to make large gifts to the singer, and before singing he would call on the Mĭde′ manido′. No one would sing this song who had not purchased the right to sing it.

Analysis.—The syncopation in this melody, as well as the slight prolonging of many of the tones, makes it difficult of accurate transcription. The melody follows the intervals of the minor triad and fourth, but it is the rhythm which impresses the ear most strongly. This very peculiar rhythm is maintained throughout the various renditions. The tone is wavering, with the vibrato so frequently used in these songs. The seventh of the minor scale does not occur in the song. The seventh of the second five-toned scale is the fifth of the fourth five-toned scale, and is seldom omitted. Its omission seems to indicate a feeling for the minor tonality as such, rather than a use of the tones of the fourth (or major) five-toned scale with a different keynote.

SONG PICTURE NO. 89. In the Mĭde′ there are said to be many "paths;" this song relates to the "bear-path" and a bear is shown in the drawing. Birds are closely associated with the second, third, and fourth degrees, and a bird appears in this drawing, though it is not mentioned in the song.

WORDS

A'nini'kwabikûn'u................ We are following the bear path
Nikân'........................... My Mïde' brother

No. 90. "THEY ARE MAKING ME OLD" (Catalogue no. 248)

Sung by MAIÑ'ĂNS

SONG PICTURE NO. 90.
Through the power
of the Mïde′ a man
lives to be so old
that he leans on a
staff as he walks.

WORDS

Manido′wĭdjĭg′	Those who are spirits
Ningeka′igog′	Are making me old
Endana′bian′	Where I am sitting

Analysis.—This song is purely melodic in character, following the intervals of the second five-toned scale. It clearly illustrates the custom of interpolating syllables in the words of the Mïde′ songs. This is said to be a very old song.

No. 91. "TO THE SPIRIT LAND"   (Catalogue no. 253)

Sung by MAIÑ′ĂNS

VOICE ♩ = 138
DRUM ♩ = 112
(Drum-rhythm similar to No. 1)

WORDS

Aoda′nawĭñe′	To the spirit land
A′nimadja′	I am going
Hĭn′dinosĕ′	I am walking

Before singing this song the singer said, "It is hard now when a man dies, but death was more tragic among the Indians in the old days."

Analysis.—This song has the smallest range of any song analyzed. It was sung five times, each rendition ending on F sharp. The tempo is plainly 5–4, and the pulse of the measure-beginnings is exact, though too slow to be indicated by the metronome. The divisions of the measure are imperfectly indicated by note values, the first tone in several measures being slightly prolonged beyond the value of a dotted quarter. It is these delicate distinctions in time values which give to a song, as sung by the Indian, its peculiar expressiveness and appealing quality. As in other songs of this character, the accidental is the lowered sixth. At first the singer did not sing this accurately, but later gave it with correct intonation.

No. 92. "I WILL SING" (Catalogue no. 255)

Sung by MAIÑ′ĂNS

VOICE ♩ = 84
DRUM ♩ = 92
(Drum-rhythm similar to No. 1)

Ni - da - zon - ga-gi-dăn   e   ni - da - zon - ga-gi-dăn

e   ni-da - zon - ga-gi-dăn   e   ni - da - zon - ga-gi-dăn

e   ni - da - zon - ga-gi-dăn   e   ni - da - zon - ga-gi-dăn

e   ni-da-zon - ga-gi - dăn   e   ni - da - zon - ga-gi-dăn

e   Mĭ - de - wĭ-wĭn   ni-da-zon - ga - gi - dăn   e   ni - da

WORDS

Nidazon′gagidăn′.................... I will sing with the great power
Mĭde′wĭwĭn......................... Of the Mĭde′wĭwĭn

This song was sung during the preparation of the medicines, not during the ceremony of initiation.

Analysis.—This song contains one accidental tone, which occurs only in the introductory measures. Considerable freedom is allowed the singer in beginning a song. The portion of the song following the word "Mĭde′wĭwĭn" is recorded seven times, each repetition returning to the point indicated and completing the circuit with no variation except that the two measures between the double bar and the word "Mĭde′wĭwĭn" are once omitted. The transfer of the accent from the second to the first syllable of the first word is clearly marked. The melodic progressions are of slight importance and the intonation is faulty, the transition from one tone to another being frequently glissando, but the metrical repetition of one word is continuous and emphatic.

SONG PICTURE NO. 92.
Wavy lines represent the song.

No. 93. "I AM WALKING"   (Catalogue no. 256)

Sung by MAIÑ′ĂNS

WORDS

Dabi′nawa′............ Toward calm and shady places
Nin′dinose′.......... I am walking
Mûk′ade′wakûm′ĭg ... On the earth

SONG PICTURE NO. 93.

Analysis.—The rhythm of this song is so irregular as to make it difficult of transcription. The tempo is rapid and the accents are slight. The phonograph record contains four renditions of this song, which are identical in every respect, both the peculiarity of the melody and the variations in rhythm being accurately reproduced. This is the more interesting as the tonality in the first part of the song is so exceedingly irregular.

No. 94. "There are Spirits"   (Catalogue no. 1)

Sung by Gegwe'djiwe'bĭnûñ' ("trial-thrower")

WORDS

Nigĭgwa'niwĭñ......	At Otter Tail
Ea'.................	There
Manido'............	Are spirits
Wenĕnikân'........	Who is this, my Mĭde' brother,
Niwawida'bima'....	That I am sitting with?

In his dream the singer is sitting with the manido' at Otter Tail.

SONG PICTURE NO. 94. The two figures represent Mĭde' manido', or spirits. Plates nos. 1 and 2 show similar figures on a Mĭde' drum. The animal was said to be a "lion," also a "large cat with horns." A similar figure was drawn on the Mĭde' drum used during the ceremony for Nigan'Ibĭnes'. (See p. 54.)

No. 95. "They Think Me Unworthy"   (Catalogue no. 2)

Sung by Gegwe'djiwe'bĭnûñ'

SONG PICTURE NO. 95. The oblong represents the Mĭde'-wĭgan; the two larger figures are manido' and the smaller ones members of the Mĭde'-wĭwĭn.

WORDS

Nin'danawe'nimigog...	They think me unworthy
Nikân'ûg..............	My Mĭde' brethren
Nucke'ekundeg'.......	But look and see
Niwĭ'gĭwam'...........	The length of my wigwam

No. 96. "The Water Birds will Alight"   (Catalogue no. 3)

Sung by Gegwe'djiwe'bĭnûñ'

WORDS

Kegĕt'............................	Surely
Ĭnda'bunisin'dangûg'..............	Upon the whole length of my form
Bĭnes'iwug'.......................⎱	The water birds will alight
Ekwa'yaweyân'...................⎰	

SONG PICTURE NO. 96. The Mĭde'wĭnĭ'nĭ is represented in his own form and also in the form of a fish, upon which the water birds alight. Ability to attract water animals is greatly desired by members of the Mĭde'-wĭwĭn.

No. 97. "The Sky Clears"   (Catalogue no. 4)

Sung by GEGWE'DJIWE'BĬNÛÑ'

WORDS

Kegĕt'............................	Verily
Mijakwat'........................	The sky clears
Nimitĭg'wakĭk'...................	When my Mĭde' drum
Medwe'undjĭn....................	Sounds
Nin'a............................	For me
Kegĕt'............................	Verily
A'nâtĭn'..........................	The waters are smooth
Nimitig'wakĭk'...................	When my Mĭde' drum
Medwe'undjĭn'...................	Sounds
Nin'a............................	For me

SONG PICTURE NO. 97. The arch represents the sky from which rain is falling. The two ovals represent quiet lakes. In his left hand the man holds a Mĭde' drum and in his right hand a stick for beating the drum.

No. 98. "I Walk in a Circle"   (Catalogue no. 5)

Sung by GEGWE'DJIWE'BĬNÛÑ'

WORDS

Nikân'inân'......................	My Mĭde' brethren
Niwa'ninose'.....................	I walk in a circle
Ma'kwa..........................	The bear
A'niija'..........................	Goes on before
Mĭde'wĭgan'igmeduñ.............	To the Mĭde' lodge
Ningĭkĭno'amawa'................	Telling
Gĭtĭna'cina'be...................	The old Indian
Obagi'tciganun'..................	What gifts to give

SONG PICTURE NO. 98. On a pole are hung blankets and other gifts, which are to be distributed according to the directions of the bear. The person to be initiated appears in the drawing, also the bear, which is entering the Mĭde'wĭgan. Curiously, the bear's footprints precede him, indicating the path he is to travel.

No. 99. "OUR DWELLING IS ROYAL"　(Catalogue no. 6)

Sung by DEDA'BICAC' ("BIRD FLYING LOW TOWARD THE EARTH")

WORDS

Ninda'binan' .... Our dwelling
Ogimawân' .... Is royal
Ninda'binan' .... Our dwelling
Ayayado'damiñ' .... Is widely renowned

SONG PICTURE NO. 99.
The Mide'winî'ni is
seen in his own lodge,
roses being introduced
to express the idea of
beauty or luxury.

No. 100. "VERMILION, I SING OF THEE"　(Catalogue no. 7)

Sung by DEDA'BICAC'

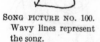

WORDS

Onama'nahomaya' ..... Vermilion, I sing of thee
We'namana'homaya ... O, Vermilion, I sing of thee

Vermilion paint was frequently carried and used by the Mide'.

SONG PICTURE NO. 100.
Wavy lines represent
the song.

No. 101. "THERE STANDS A MAN"　(Catalogue no. 8)

Sung by DEDA'BICAC'

WORDS

Ni'boinî'ni ....⎫
Wanihinî'ni ....⎬ There stands a man
Miwe'djiga'boeyân' ....⎭ It is for him I stand

SONG PICTURE NO. 101.

No. 102. "I STAND"　(Catalogue no. 9)

Sung by DEDA'BICAC'

WORDS

Niba'wiyan' .... I stand
Gidûb'ena' .... Are you present?
Wa'weciga'bowiyan' .... I rise, I stand

12692°—Bull. 45—10——8

No. 103. "I am Named"   (Catalogue no. 10)

Sung by Ge′miwûnac′

WORDS

Nimadwe′winigog′	I am named
Mĭde′winiwûg′	By the leaders of the Mĭde′
Wewûno′dûmowâd′	To receive a share of the offering

SONG PICTURE NO. 103. The many straight lines diverging from the heart and body of the man suggest the importance of being selected to share in the division of the offering.

No. 104. "I am Unable to Harmonize My Voice"   (Catalogue no. 11)

Sung by Ge′miwûnac′

WORDS

[Free translation]

Ningwinanĭ′ĭnwe . . . . ⎫
Gwinawĭ′nowe′ . . . . . ⎪
Ni′tcanicina′be . . . . . ⎬ I am unable to harmonize my
Ĕndanwe′nidûñ′ . . . ⎪ voice with the voices of my
Ni′tcanicina′be . . . . . ⎬ fellow Indians which I
Ĕndanwe′nidûñ′ . . . ⎪ hear at a distance
Ningwa′nanĭ′ina′ . . . ⎭

SONG PICTURE NO. 104. In this song the question is that of beauty, or "harmonizing the voice," and a rose takes the place of the wavy lines which represent a song when sung with the "power of the Mĭde′wiwĭn." The other singers are represented by the figure in the background.

No. 105. "They are Feasting with Me"   (Catalogue no. 12)

Sung by Ge′miwûnac′

WORDS

Niwido′pamĭgog . . .	They are feasting with me
Agwatci′siwayan′ . . .	The outside medicine-bag
Kima′nidom′	You are the spirit
Gigani′nigo′	You will be called

SONG PICTURE NO. 105. This drawing suggests the square bag used by the Chippewa for storing and carrying rice.

No. 106. "The Sound is Fading Away"   (Catalogue no. 13)

Sung by Ge'miwûnac'

WORDS

A'niwe'we...............	The sound is fading away
Na'nowe'we..............	It is of five sounds
Wa'naki'meniwa.........	Freedom
Gï'niwe'we.............	The sound is fading away
Na'nowe'we	It is of five sounds

SONG PICTURE NO. 106.
The five wavy lines
represent the "five
sounds."

No. 107. "You are a Spirit"   (Catalogue no. 15)

Sung by Ge'miwûnac'

SONG PICTURE NO. 107.
The person ad-
dressed is repre-
sented as a manido',
in form like those
that appear in the
water.

WORDS

[Free translation]

Ninma'nidowe'nimïg'.....	
Gima'nido'wiïn'.........	
Nikâne.................	You are a spirit, my Mïde'
Niyûn'.................	brother; you are pre-
Mând ûn'................	pared, my Mïde' brother
Ninikân'................	
Manidowa'nogwen'.......	

Tabulated Analysis of 90 Mïde' Songs

MELODIC ANALYSIS

TONALITY

Major tonality...............................	65
Minor tonality...............................	25
	90

Catalogue numbers of songs

Major tonality.—16, 17, 18, 19, 20, 21, 22, 23, 24, 25, 26, 28, 29, 30, 31, 32, 33, 37, 38, 39, 40, 41, 42, 43, 44, 46, 48, 49, 50, 51, 52, 53, 55, 56, 58, 59, 64, 65, 66, 67, 69, 73, 78, 79, 122, 123, 127, 128, 129, 130, 189, 190, 191, 192, 193, 194, 197, 199, 237, 238, 240, 241, 242, 253, 254. Total, 65.

Minor tonality.—27, 34, 35, 36, 45, 47, 52, 53, 54, 57, 60, 61, 70, 71, 80, 124, 125, 126, 192, 195, 200, 236, 239, 248, 256. Total, 25.

Total number of songs, 90.

TONE MATERIAL

Fourth five-toned scale	18	Octave complete, except sixth	2
Second five-toned scale	11	Octave complete, except seventh	10
Major triad and sixth	19	Other combinations of tones	19
Major triad, sixth and fourth	2	In two keys	3
Minor triad	1		
Minor triad and fourth	2	Total	90
Octave complete	3		

Catalogue numbers of songs

Fourth five-toned scale.—19, 21, 22, 24, 41, 48, 52, 53, 59, 79, 189, 190, 192, 193, 237, 238, 241, 242. Total, 18.

Second five-toned scale.—34, 35, 45, 46, 53, 124, 197, 236, 239, 248, 254. Total, 11.

Major triad and sixth.—16, 17, 18, 20, 23, 25, 26, 28, 29, 31, 32, 33, 39, 42, 122, 129, 130, 191, 240. Total, 19.

Major triad, fourth, and sixth.—127, 128.

Minor triad only.—27.

Minor triad and fourth.—61, 62.

Octave complete.—56, 64, 73.

Octave complete, except sixth.—71, 126.

Octave complete, except seventh.—37, 38, 44, 46, 50, 58, 66, 67, 255, 256. Total, 10.

Other combinations of tones.—30, 36, 40, 43, 49, 51, 54, 55, 57, 60, 65, 69, 73, 78, 80, 123, 195, 199, 200, 253. Total, 19.

In two keys.—70, 125, 194.

Total number of songs, 90.

BEGINNINGS OF SONGS

On the twelfth	33	On the seventh	2
On the fifth (compass less than a twelfth)	29	On the sixth	1
		On the fourth	1
On the ninth	5	In two keys	3
On the second (compass less than a ninth)	5	Total	90
On the octave	11		

Catalogue numbers of songs

On the twelfth.—16, 17, 18, 19, 20, 21, 22, 23, 24, 25, 26, 27, 28, 29, 31, 32, 33, 37, 38, 54, 55, 66, 69, 71, 80, 122, 189, 190, 237, 238, 240, 241, 242. Total, 33.

On the fifth.—30, 39, 41, 42, 43, 44, 46, 47, 48, 50, 51, 52, 60, 61, 62, 63, 67, 73, 78, 79, 80, 123, 126, 127, 129, 130, 197, 255. Total, 29.

On the ninth.—192, 195, 199, 200, 253. Total, 5.

On the second.—36, 40, 59, 65, 194. Total, 5.

On the octave.—34, 35, 49, 58, 64, 124, 191, 236, 239, 248, 254. Total, 11.

On the seventh.—45, 56.

On the sixth.—193.

On the fourth.—57.

In two keys.—70, 125, 256.

Total number of songs, 90.

ENDINGS OF SONGS

On the tonic	56	On the third	10
On the fifth	21	In two keys	3

Total number of songs, 90.

Catalogue numbers of songs

On the tonic.—16, 17, 18, 19, 20, 21, 22, 23, 24, 25, 26, 27, 28, 29, 30, 31, 32, 33, 35, 38, 41, 42, 43, 45, 51, 53, 55, 56, 57, 58, 61, 63, 64, 66, 67, 71, 79, 80, 122, 123, 124, 126, 189, 190, 191, 192, 195, 197, 236, 237, 239, 240, 241, 242, 248, 254. Total, 56.

On the fifth.—34, 37, 39, 40, 44, 49, 54, 59, 60, 62, 65, 73, 127, 128, 129, 130, 199, 200, 253, 255, 256. Total, 21.

On the third.—36, 46, 47, 48, 50, 52, 69, 78, 193, 238. Total, 10.

In two keys.—70, 125, 194.

Total number of songs, 90.

ACCIDENTALS

Songs containing no accidentals....................................... 73
Songs containing accidentals.. 14
In two keys.. 3

90

Table of accidentals, showing catalogue numbers

Accidental.	Number of songs.	Catalogue numbers.
Sixth lowered a semitone....	4	73, 79, 197, 253
Second lowered a semitone....	3	51, 56, 80
Third lowered a semitone....	2	17, 18
Fourth lowered a semitone....	1	50
Fifth lowered a semitone....	1	256
Seventh raised a semitone....	1	71
Sixth raised a semitone....	1	195
Fourth raised a semitone....	1	66
Total....	14	

FIRST PROGRESSION

First progression upward... 7
First progression downward.. 83

90

Catalogue numbers of songs with first progression upward.—54, 59, 78, 80, 194, 197, 248. Total, 7.

RHYTHMIC ANALYSIS

Songs beginning on the accented portion of the measure............ 23
Songs beginning on the unaccented portion of the measure........ 26
Songs transcribed in melody outline............................. 41

90

Metric unit of voice and drum the same............................ 6
Metric unit of voice and drum different.......................... 23
Recorded without drum.. 61

90

Catalogue numbers of songs in which metric unit of voice and drum is the same.—71, 122, 238, 239, 248, 256. Total, 6.

Catalogue numbers of songs in which metric unit of voice and drum is different.—52, 53, 61, 123, 124, 189, 190, 191, 192, 193, 194, 195, 197, 199, 200, 236, 237, 240, 241, 242, 253, 254, 255.   Total, 23.

Catalogue numbers of songs beginning on the accented portion of the measure.—39, 52, 54, 55, 56, 57, 59, 61, 62, 65, 69, 71, 73, 191, 192, 199, 238, 239, 240, 242, 248, 253, 256. Total, 23.

Catalogue numbers of songs beginning on the unaccented portion of the measure.—14, 53, 58, 60, 62, 63, 64, 66, 67, 68, 78, 79, 83, 122, 123, 124, 189, 190, 194, 195, 197, 200, 236, 237, 241, 255.   Total, 26.

Structural Analysis

Melodic	70
Harmonic	20
	90

Catalogue numbers of songs

Melodic.—16, 17, 18, 19, 21, 22, 24, 26, 28, 34, 35, 36, 37, 38, 39, 40, 41, 43, 44, 45, 46, 47, 48, 49, 50, 51, 52, 53, 54, 55, 56, 57, 58, 59, 60, 61, 64, 65, 66, 67, 70, 71, 73, 78, 79, 80, 124, 125, 126, 127, 128, 129, 130, 189, 190, 192, 193, 194, 195, 197, 199, 200, 236, 237, 238, 239, 248, 253, 255, 256.   Total, 70.

Harmonic.—20, 23, 25, 27, 29, 30, 31, 32, 33, 42, 52, 53, 69, 122, 123, 191, 240, 241, 242, 254.   Total, 20.

Total number of songs, 90.

SOCIAL SONGS ON WHITE EARTH AND LEECH LAKE RESERVATIONS

Ina′bûndjĭgañ nagûmo′wĭn (Dream Songs)

The songs in this group are not composed in the usual sense of the term, but are songs which are said to have come to the mind of the Indian when he was in a dream or trance.   Many Indian songs are intended to exert a strong mental influence, and dream songs are supposed to have this power in greater degree than any others.   The supernatural is very real to the Indian.   He puts himself in communication with it by fasting or by physical suffering.   While his body is thus subordinated to the mind a song occurs to him.   In after years he believes that by singing this song he can recall the condition under which it came to him—a condition of direct communication with the supernatural.   It is said that no drum is used at this time, the drum being added when the song is rehearsed and sung afterward.

These dream songs are considered under three divisions: First, songs of the doctor; second, song of the juggler; and, third, songs which were composed during periods of fasting or of mental stress and were used later as war songs or in other connections.   The songs of each division are preceded by an explanation of the circumstances under which they were composed or sung.

1. SONGS OF THE DOCTOR

The Chippewa word *dja'sakid* is applied to two classes of people—doctors and jugglers. It is difficult for us to recognize the relation between these two, for we are accustomed to regard medicine as a science and jugglery as an imposition, but to the Indian mind both are direct demonstrations of supernatural power received and maintained by means of dreams or trances. For that reason it is natural that the same word should be applied to each.[a]

The songs of a Chippewa doctor can not be bought or sold. Each man must bear his own pain or endure his own fasting if he would acquire power over pain in others. Sympathy and affection were very real in the Indian wigwams. Definite knowledge of means for curing the sick was very scanty, and in pathetic helplessness the Indian turned to the supernatural for help. The methods used in the treatment of the sick are repellent. For that reason it is good that we first consider the element of poetry which underlay the best attempts of the old-school Indian doctors to relieve the suffering of their friends.

The fasts which were practised by the Chippewa doctors usually lasted ten days, the time being spent on a mountain or a great rock, or in a tree. A doctor frequently built a kind of nest to which he retired and whither he believed the manido' came to give him the power to do his work.

The Chippewa doctor treats the sick by singing, shaking his rattle, passing his hands over the body of the patient, and apparently swallowing one or more bones, which are afterward removed from his mouth. Each of these phases is considered indispensable to the treatment. The rattle commonly used is shown in plate 1. It is made of deer hide stretched over a wooden hoop and is $9\frac{1}{2}$ inches in diameter and one-half inch in thickness, and contains two or three small shot.

The manner of holding the rattle is shown in plate 2. The discoloration on the front of the rattle and a small hole on the back are indications of its being used in this position. The hole on the back is exactly where the deerskin would be pressed by the second finger. This hole has been roughly patched. The rattle was procured from O'děni'gûn, a man said to be especially skilled in the use of medicine, who sang the Songs connected with Rare Medicines, in the present series (see p. 96).

---

[a] The songs of the Chippewa doctor were recorded by Maiñ'ăns ("little wolf"), the younger, a man of middle age, whose feet were frozen when he was a lad, and who walks on his knees. He related to the writer the story of his experience at the time his feet were frozen. Accompanied by his grandparents he started to walk from one village to another, but a heavy snowstorm and intense cold overtook the little party. His grandparents finally perished of cold and starvation, but he found his way to the village with both feet frozen. Years of suffering followed. When the pain was most severe these songs. Maiñ ăns said, one after another, "rang in his head." He spoke of the condition of intense pain as a dream condition, implying that the intensity of the pain produced a state bordering on unconsciousness. He said that years afterward he became a doctor and these songs were his special "medicine songs" in c. ring the sick.

Two of the bones which are supposed to be swallowed are here shown (fig. 8); these are 2½ inches long and about one-half inch in diameter. The texture of these bones indicates that they are very old. They were procured by the writer from a man on the White Earth reservation who had been a doctor for many years but had given up the practice. His well-worn rattle was also purchased, but this is not shown in the illustration. On another reservation the writer was shown a string of ten or twelve bones which the owner said he repeatedly swallowed in his cures of the sick. Large numbers of bones are often "swallowed," each doctor having a collection of bones for the purpose; a number of these are frequently worn on a string around his neck.

The sick person lies on the ground, the doctor kneeling at his right side. (See pl. 10.) The doctor holds his rattle in his right hand and at

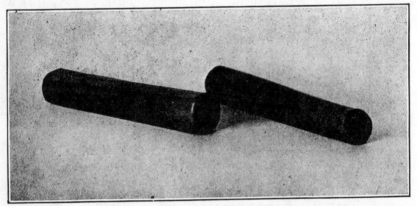

FIG. 8. Bones used by Chippewa doctor in treating the sick.

his left hand is a pan or bowl of water in which lie the bones to be swallowed. The doctor opens his mouth, protrudes his tongue, places the moistened bone on it, and "swallows" it quickly. After shaking the rattle a while he "swallows" another of the bones; usually this procedure is continued until four or five bones have been disposed of in this manner. One doctor stated that the bones lodge in the chest near the shoulder. It is also said that there is a spirit inside the doctor which takes the bones.

After "swallowing" the bones the doctor strikes his breast with the rattle; then he leans over the sick person and strikes his back between the shoulders with the rattle. It is claimed that this enables him to see where the disease is located in the patient.

In giving the following three songs Maiñ'äns stated that he always sang the first song after he had looked at the sick person and decided that he could help him. Afterward he sang the other two songs.

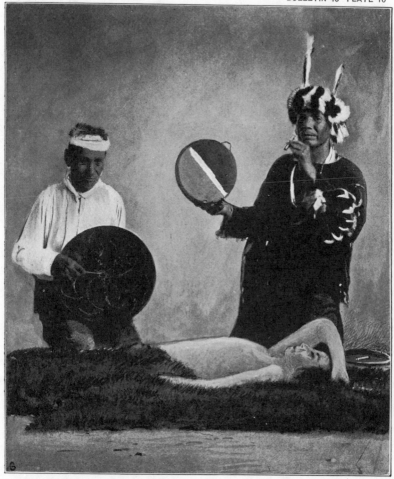

CHIPPEWA DOCTOR TREATING THE SICK

No. 108. DOCTOR'S SONG   (Catalogue no. 244)

VOICE ♩= 76

DRUM ♩= 126

(Drum-rhythm similar to No. 1)

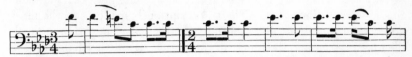

Mĕn - we - we - a - ci - yan a - kĭñ *ge* mĕn - we - we - a - ci -

yan a-kĭñ   *ge*   ke - dan-dji - ka - ba-we-yan a-kĭñ *ge*   men -

we - we - a - ci - yan a-kĭñ *ge* men-we-we - a - ci-yan a-kĭñ *ge*

WORDS

Mĕnwe′wea′ciyan′...............	I am singing and dreaming in my poor way
Akĭñ′..........................	Over the earth
Kedan′djikaba′weyan′............	I who will again disembark
Akĭñ′..........................	Upon the earth

Analysis.—This song was extremely difficult of transcription. When at last the transcription was made it was found that the four renditions of the song were identical except in one or two unimportant measures. The accidental in the first measure was given in all the renditions with good intonation. The metric unit is very slow but is clearly given; the measure accent however is very slight. The rhythmic feeling throughout the song is for the single count rather than for any grouping of counts.

No. 109. "I GO TO THE BIG BEAR'S LODGE" (Catalogue no. 245)

VOICE ♩= 108

DRUM ♩= 132

(Drum-rhythm similar to No. 1)

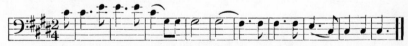

Ki-tci-mak-wa *he* wĭ - gĭ-wăm *e*   bi- *ma* - bĭ - ĭ - ĭn - dĭ - ge

WORDS

Ki′tcimak′wa.......................	The big bear
Wĭ′gĭwăm′..........................	To his lodge
Babĭn′dĭge′........................	I go often

Narrative.—Before beginning this song Maiñ'ăns said, "In my dream I went to the big bear's lodge and he told me what to do. He told me how to swallow the bones and I often go back to his lodge that I may learn from him again. This is what I say in this song which I made up myself. Every dja'sakid has his own animal which he sees in a dream and he learns from this animal what he shall do for the sick person."

Analysis.—This song is so short that the phonograph cylinder contains nine renditions of it. The transcription is made from the most regular rendition, but the intonation is faulty. The singer found much difficulty in starting the song on the octave, owing probably to the presence of the tenth so near the beginning of the song. The tenth is a particularly hard interval to grasp. The rhythm is regularly maintained, especially the rhythmic unit which consists of the dotted quarter or quarter notes preceded by eighths. The subdivision of the third measure shows some indecision; the rhythmic unit has been clearly given out, and the interest lapses slightly until the rhythmic unit again asserts itself.

No. 110. "GOING AROUND THE WORLD"   (Catalogue no. 246)

VOICE ♩ = 72

DRUM ♩ = 138

(Drum-rhythm similar to No. 1)

Ka - wi - ta-kûm-i - gĭc - ka - man a - ki *we*   mĭ - dwe-kûm-i - gĭc-

ka - man a - ki *we*   ka - wi - ta-kûm-i - gĭc-ka - man a-ki *we*

mĭ - dwe - kûm-i - gĭc - ka - man a - ki *we*

mĭ - dwe - kûm - i - gĭc - ka - man a - ki *we*

WORDS

Ka'wita'kûmi'gĭckaman'	....	I am going around
Aki'	....	The world
Midwe'kûmi'gĭckaman'	....	I am going through
Aki'	....	The world

Analysis.—The chief rhythmic phrase of this song is short, clearly
marked, and frequently repeated. It is comprised in the second and
third measures of the song. This recurring phrase is easily traced
and is always given in exact time. The intervening measures are in
less regular time, the words somewhat resembling metric speech and
the note values varying accordingly. They are, however, indicated as
correctly as possible. The use of an accented sixteenth note before
a dotted eighth note is not common in the White Earth songs, but
was frequently found in the songs collected at Red Lake. This song
is melodic in structure, beginning on the sixth and ending on the
third of the fourth five-toned scale.

2. SONG OF THE JUGGLER

The supernatural power of the Chippewa doctor is shown by the
recovery of his patient; the supernatural power of the Chippewa
juggler is shown by a performance which is universal throughout the
tribe. In this performance the juggler frees himself from the tightest
cords, causes his lodge to sway as though blown by a tempest, and
summons the spirits of wild animals whose voices are heard by the
spectators. The accounts of these performances are authentic, but
the ability to perform the feat has never been explained.

The following description of a juggler's performance was given in
connection with the song, the narrator stating that he had seen the
performance by Ce'deĕns' and had heard him sing the song at that
time.

The preparations were as follows: Eight poles were placed upright
in the ground. These poles were 12 to 14 feet high. They were sunk
in the ground 2 or 3 feet and were placed about 2 feet apart. They
were bound together by hoops, eight of which were fastened around
the poles at intervals. After the completion of this framework
Ce'deĕns' sang this song. Then he was bound with ropes made
of the inner bark of the basswood tree, his hands were tied behind
him, his feet were tied, a large stone was placed on his chest, and
he was bound around with stout gill nets, so that he was "like a
ball." Four men carried him eight times around the circle of poles
and then threw him inside the inclosure. One of the four men then
called, "Come, ye people of the sky, come and smoke." In a few
moments the poles began to shake; the whole structure rocked
and swayed as though a tornado were blowing; yet there was no
wind and the sky was cloudless. Soon a voice was heard. The
voice said, "Who is tying up my grandchild? I am going to break
those ropes and throw them over where you are sitting."

The people seated on the ground, watching the performance, heard
the voice, and in a few moments they saw the ropes coming through
the air. These fell near the people, who hastened to examine them

and found that they were indeed the ropes with which the juggler had been bound and that the knots in them were not untied. The ropes had been slipped from the juggler's body and he was free.

The writer was recently informed by a reliable Indian that his uncle was accustomed to perform this feat in the old days, and that after his uncle joined the Christian Church he asked him to explain how he did it. The old man replied that he could not explain it, as he was an entirely different being at that time. His manido' animals were the bear and the snake, and the Indian stated that, as nearly as he could make out, his uncle seemed to imagine himself a snake when giving this exhibition. Two intelligent Indians have given it as their opinion that the juggler imagines himself to be some animal supple and lithe enough to work itself free from the cords, and that this imagination, or mental concept, is so strong that the body responds and does what would be impossible at any other time. It has been frequently suggested that the spectators are hypnotized and imagine they see what they do not see. The foregoing explanation suggests that the hypnotic influence is exerted by the juggler on his own body. Music is considered indispensable to the performance of this feat.

The Indian stated that he had seen the lodge bend like a sapling, so that the top almost touched the ground, when his uncle was giving one of these demonstrations. Afterward three men entered the structure. One stood on the ground, one climbed halfway to the top, and one to the very top. These men tried with all their strength to sway the structure, but could not move it in the slightest degree.

A juggler's performance on the Grand Portage reservation was described to the writer by an eyewitness, who said that "a friend who lived many miles away was suddenly present in the lodge" and that she "heard his voice distinctly." There were also many wild animals in the lodge whose voices she recognized. Spectators are not allowed to enter the lodge, but they hear these voices as they stand outside.

This account shows the association of music and mental influence, which was also mentioned in connection with the medicine songs of the Mĭde'wĭwĭn.

These performances were often given at the time of Mĭde' ceremonies, but were not directly connected with them. As stated elsewhere, the jugglers were not always members of the Mĭde'wĭwĭn.

Attempts were made at times to counterfeit the performances of the jugglers. The following incident was related to the writer:

There was a man who pretended to be a juggler, but the Indians knew that he was a fraud. This man said that he liked to have the lodge built on the shore of the water when he gave an exhibition. That was because it would sway easier if the poles were stuck in soft sand. Once this man was giving an exhibition and he climbed up inside the lodge to shake it. Of course he had to do this because he was not a regular juggler and did not know how to do it right. He was almost at the top and was swaying it back and forth when some boys pulled up the poles and threw the man and his lodge far into the water. No one paid any attention to the man after that.

(Catalogue no. 213)

No. 111. The Song of Ce′deĕns′ (Juggler's Song)

Sung by Ga′gandac′ ("one whose sails are driven by the wind")

Ka-be-bĭn-de-ge no-sĭs *a* ki - wi - gĭ-wăm-iñ

Drum-rhythm

WORDS

Kabebĭn′dige′	I have gone
No′sĭs	My grandchild
Kiwi′gĭwăm′iñ	Into your lodge

Analysis.—This song was sung three times and in each rendition the sixth was lowered a semitone in the first measure and a smaller interval in the remaining portion of the song. The second of the measures containing the words was sung slower to permit the enunciation of the syllables; otherwise the rhythm of the voice was steadily maintained. The drum was silent when the words were sung.

3. DREAM SONGS AFTERWARD USED AS WAR SONGS OR OTHERWISE

Like the other dream songs, these were said to have been composed during a dream or on waking from a dream. Many of them are associated with some animal which becomes the manido' of the dreamer. The words of many of these songs suggest that the dreamer contemplates nature in a certain aspect so long and so steadily that he gradually loses his own personality and identifies himself with it. In other instances he imagines that animals or objects in nature are singing and that he learns their songs. It has not been definitely ascertained whether the singer imagines he repeats the melody or only the words of such songs.

All the dream songs are supposed to be spontaneous melodies, and therein lies their chief importance in connection with the analytical study of Indian music.

No. 112. SONG OF THE TREES   (Catalogue no. 206)

Sung by GA'GANDAC'

VOICE ♩ = 100
DRUM ♩ = 120
(Drum-rhythm similar to No. 111)

No - dĭn   e - ta nin - go - tan

WORDS

Nodĭn'.............................. The wind
E'ta................................ Only
Ningotan'.......................... I am afraid of

Narrative.—The following explanation of this song was given by Maiñ'ăns: The song belonged to a certain man who sang it in the dances which were held before going to war. When this man was a boy he had a dream and in his dream he heard the trees singing as though they were alive; they sang that they were afraid of nothing except being blown down by the wind. When the boy awoke he made up this song, in which he repeats what he heard the trees say. The true meaning of the words is that there is no more chance of his being defeated on the warpath than there is that a tree will be blown down by the wind.

Analysis.—The rhythm of this song is energetic, vivifying, and full of action. The rhythmic unit is short and easily recognized, consisting of a measure in triple time followed by a measure in double time. The song was sung five times, the renditions being identical in every respect. The rhythms of voice and drum are greatly at variance, but each is steadily maintained. The harmonic structure is evident and consists of a major triad in the upper and in the lower octave with the sixth as a connecting tone.

No. 113. SONG OF THE THUNDERS   (Catalogue no. 207)

Sung by GA′GANDAC′

VOICE ♩ = 120

DRUM ♩ = 120

(Drum-rhythm similar to No. 111)

WORDS

Na′nĭngo′dinunk′	Sometimes
Ninbaba′cawen′dan	I go about pitying
Niyau′	Myself
Baba′maciyan′	While I am carried by the wind
Gicĭguñ′	Across the sky

This song forms an example of the strange personation which characterizes many of the dream songs. In this the singer contemplates the storm mystery of the sky until he feels himself a part of it and sings its song.

Analysis.—This song is divided into two parts. The first contains only vowel syllables and consists of nine measures, in which the rhythmic unit occurs twice. This unit is comprised in the first three measures. The second part of the song contains the words. This part of the song constitutes a rhythmic unit in itself. Attention is directed to the harmonic character of the song, although the melody moves with great freedom.

No. 114. "My Voice is Heard"   (Catalogue no. 208)

Sung by Ga'gandac'

Voice ♩ = 112

Drum ♩ = 116

(Drum-rhythm similar to No. 111)

Mi - si - wĕ   a - kĭñ e nin - de - bwe - wi - dûm

WORDS

Misiwč'............................ All over
Akĭñ................................ The world
Nin'debwe'widûm'................. My voice resounds

In this song, as in the preceding, the singer contemplates the storm. He hears the reverberation of the thunder and in his dream or trance he composes a song concerning it.

Analysis.—This song is definitely major in tonality and was sung in exact time throughout. The metric unit of the drum is slightly faster than that of the voice and produces an effect of hurrying the voice. The lowered sixth occurs as an accidental. It is impossible to indicate the exact deviations from pitch and the peculiar portamento of voice used in this song, but the manner of the rendition strongly suggests that they are used to heighten the effect and do not form an actual part of the song.

No. 115. "The Approach of the Storm" (Catalogue no. 209)

Sung by Ga'gandac'

Voice ♩ = 112
Drum ♩ = 116
(Drum-rhythm similar to No. 111)

WORDS

Abitû'................................ From the half
Gicĭguñ'........................... Of the sky
Ebigwěn'........................... That which lives there
Kabide'bwewiduñ'................. Is coming, and makes a noise

The Thunder manido' represents to the Indian the mysterious spirit of the storm, and he imagines that this manido' sometimes makes a noise to warn him of its approach. This is his interpreta-

tion of the distant thunder which precedes a storm. Hearing this,
the Indian hastens to put tobacco on the fire in order that the smoke
may ascend as an offering or signal of peace to the manido'. The
idea which underlies the song is, "That which lives in the sky is
coming and, being friendly, it makes a noise to let me know of its
approach." This means much less to the white race than to the
Indian. We are accustomed to noise; the Indian habitually ap-
proaches in silence, unless he wishes to announce his presence.[a]

Analysis.—This song is harmonic in structure and contains the
tones of the fourth five-toned scale. More than a year before the
making of this record the same song was secured from a younger
singer. On comparing the two records it is found that they differ
much less in rhythm than in melodic progressions. The younger
singer used exactly the same tones, but in some parts of the song he
used the intervals in a slightly different order. The characteristic
rhythm is identical in the two records.

No. 116. "As the Hawk Soars"   (Catalogue no. 210)

Sung by Ga'gandac'

The second word in this song suggests to the Chippewa the course
of a bird which flies forward a short distance, then circles, and then
flies forward again. The Chippewa thought that the hawks were
halfway to the top of the sky because they flew so high, and this
song was probably inspired by the sight of a flock of hawks flying
and circling high overhead.

Analysis.—The harmonic structure of this song divides it into two
parts, the first based on the minor triad with the minor seventh[b]
added, and the second on the tonic triad and sixth. The tones of
the first chord are repeated during fourteen measures, the F sharp
sinking to E on the fifteenth measure. This introduces the tonic
chord in the key of A, and the latter part of the song is composed
of the tones of the tonic triad and sixth in the key of A. The first
part of the song suggests the close attention with which one follows
moving objects; the satisfying resultant chord and the free melody
with its even rhythm suggest the return of the singer's attention to
his song and to his more immediate surroundings.

---

[a] The Indian who composed this song is now a clergyman of the Episcopal Church, Rev. George Smith.
When he was a little boy he often painted his face and fasted five days because he wanted to be a "spirit
man;" when he was 15 or 16 years of age he composed this song in his dream. The preparation for his
life work was according to the native customs, but he is doing that work in the white man's way.

[b] Prof. J. C. Fillmore found this tonality among the Dahomey songs collected at the World's Colum-
bian Exposition at Chicago and Mr. H. E. Krehbiel (in a paper read before the Folk-lore Congress, July,
1894) cited similar instances among the songs of the American negroes. Professor Fillmore recorded a
similar song from the Nass River Indians living in British Columbia. This tonality is found also in the
following songs of the present series: nos. 51, 116, 127, 172.

A correspondence between the idea of a song and its melody or its rhythm can not be taken too literally or pushed too far. Music can not imitate a scene in nature or express a mental concept, yet either may inspire a song. Under such circumstances the song may reflect in some degree the source of its inspiration, yet it would be impossible, in any instance, to infer that source from the character of the song.

Five renditions of this song were secured, the only variations being in the first part; the harmonic material remained the same, but the order of progressions differed slightly. The second part was identical in all the renditions.

Voice ♩ = 112
Drum ♩ = 126
(Drum-rhythm similar to No. 111)

A - bi - ta - - wi - gi - cĭg . . bi -

mi - kwe - kwe - ki - ka - ba - wi - yan

ANALYSIS

14 measures.	1 measure.	2 measures.	3 measures.

WORDS

Abita′wigi′cĭg...................... Halfway up the sky
Bimikwe′kwekika′bawiyan′........ I am flying

No. 117. "IN THE SOUTHERN SKY"   (Catalogue no. 211)

Sung by GA'GANDAC'

VOICE ♩ = 112
DRUM ♩ = 116
(Drum-rhythm similar to No. 111)

A - jig - wa gi -cĭg - uñ . . . ca-wûn - u - bi-

yan

WORDS

Ajig′wa............................ Already
Gi′ciguñ′.......................... In the sky
Cawûn′ubiyan′.................... I am sitting in the south

Analysis.—In harmonic structure this song is similar to the preceding, the first fourteen measures being based on the tones of the minor triad with the minor seventh added, the sixteenth measure containing lower E, the remainder of the song being composed of the tones of the tonic triad. The last part of the song is simpler than that of the preceding song, but the general character is the same. It may be possible that both songs were composed by the same man, this coming first in the order of composition. In this, as in the preceding song, the last part was always sung in exact time.

No. 118. "MANIDO′ LISTENS TO ME"   (Catalogue no. 212)

Sung by GA′GANDAC′

Analysis.—This melody contains only the tones of the major triad and sixth. The song was sung twice, the second rendition beginning on the last count of the fourth measure, suggesting that the first measures are an introduction. The custom of using an introduction to the first rendition of a song has already been mentioned. In this introduction the singer is allowed considerable freedom.

The meaning implied in the Chippewa words is that the manido′ who listens will grant all requests of the singer.

Voice ♩ = 112
Drum ♩ = 120
(Drum-rhythm similar to No. 111)

Nin bi - sĭn - dag   be - cĭg ma - ni - do

WORDS

Nin...................................... To me
Bisĭn′dag............................. He listens
Be′cĭg................................... One
Manido′............................... Spirit

No. 119. Song of the Crows   (Catalogue no. 260)

Sung by Henry Selkirk

Narrative.—The following explanation of the song was given by the singer:

A young man was fasting where his father had taken him. It was in the fall, and the flocks of crows were getting ready to go south. The young man heard the crows in the trees and imagined that he learned this song from them. Afterward the crow was his manido′ because it had given him power to understand the language of the crows. The words of the song mean that the crows are the first birds to come in the spring, and so the old-time Indians thought that the crows brought the spring rains. This was first a dream song and afterward it was used as a war dance.

Analysis.—This melody contains only the tones of the fourth five-toned scale. Both melody and rhythm are of unusual simplicity.

VOICE ♩ = 108

DRUM ♩ = 116

(Drum-rhythm similar to No. 111)

Be - ba - ni - ga - ni   *hi*   nin - di - gog . . bi -

nĕ - si- wûg *e*   nin-wĕn-dji- gi - mi - wûñ an- deg-nin - di - go

WORDS

Be′bani′gani′........................	The first to come
Nin′digog′...........................	I am called
Binĕ′siwûg′.........................	Among the birds
Nin′wĕndjigi′miwûñ′..............	I bring the rain
Andeg′nindigo′.....................	Crow is my name

The two following songs were not composed during dreams, but during great mental stress. They are classed with the dream songs because they are spontaneous melodies, said to have sprung from the lips of the singers without conscious effort on their part. These songs were given by a particularly reliable singer.

No. 120. SONG OF THE DESERTED WARRIOR   (Catalogue no. 259)

Sung by HENRY SELKIRK

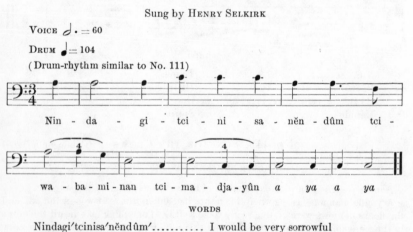

VOICE ♩. = 60

DRUM ♩ = 104

(Drum-rhythm similar to No. 111)

Nin - da - gi - tci - ni - sa - nĕn - dûm   tci -

wa - ba - mi - nan tci - ma - dja - yûn *a* *ya* *a* *ya*

WORDS

Nindagi′tcinisa′nĕndûm′...........	I would be very sorrowful
Tciwa′baminan′....................	To see you
Tcima′djayûn′.....................	Go away

Narrative.—About forty years ago the Chippewa were at war with the Sioux near Turtle mountain in North Dakota. The Chippewa were concealed in a cornfield ready to attack the Sioux when their ambush was discovered, and in the fight one of the Chippewa was shot through the breast. The man's name was No′dinûk′wûm, which means Wind-Thunder. His friends attempted to carry him with them, but it seemed that he would surely die, and their own lives were in danger; so they left him with his face painted and a feather in his hair, to die like a warrior. After they had left him they heard him singing this song. It was an entirely new tune and two of the men remembered it and sang it after they reached home. The song affected the men as no entreaty could have done. They rushed back, dragged the wounded man to the water's edge, lifted him into a canoe, and paddled away safely. The man recovered and now lives at Pine Point. The singer said that he recently saw the man and also the scar of the wound.

Analysis.—The metric unit in this song is the measure, not the individual count in the measure. This unit is regular. The divisions of the measure are not always exact, but are indicated as nearly as possible. The melody tones comprise the minor triad and sixth.

No. 121. "I Am Afraid of the Owl" (Catalogue no. 261)

Sung by HENRY SELKIRK

VOICE ♩ = 152

(Recorded without drum)

WORDS

Eniwek′	Very much
Gaye′	Also
Nin	I
Ko′kokoo′	Of the owl
Ningosa′	Am afraid
Nejike′wûbianin′	Whenever I am sitting alone in the wigwam

Narrative.—The singer stated that he composed this song himself when he was a child. The circumstances were as follows: His mother had gone to a neighbor's, leaving him alone in the wigwam. He became very much afraid of the owl, which is the particular terror of all small Indians, and sang this song. It was just after sugar making and the wigwams were placed near together beside the lake. The people in the other wigwams heard his little song. The melody was entirely new and it attracted them so that they learned it as he sang. The men took it up and used it in their moccasin games. For many years it was used in this way, but he was always given the credit of its composition.

Analysis.—This song contains only three tones and may be said to consist of the minor third with the tone above as a preparatory tone. The chief rhythmic phrase is the quarter note followed by two eighths, a subdivision of a double measure which suggests fear.

Dream Songs— White Earth Reservation

MELODIC ANALYSIS

TONALITY

	Number of songs.	Catalogue numbers.
Major tonality	12	
Minor tonality	2	259, 261
Total	14	

TONE MATERIAL

	Number of songs.	Catalogue numbers.
Fourth five-toned scale	8	206, 207, 209, 210, 211, 244, 246, 260
Major triad and sixth	4	212, 213, 245, 259
Minor triad and fourth	1	261
Other combinations of tones	1	208
Total	14	

BEGINNINGS OF SONGS

	Number of songs.	Catalogue numbers.
Beginning on the twelfth	7	206, 207, 209, 210, 211, 212, 213
Beginning on the tenth	1	244
Beginning on the octave	3	245, 259, 260
Beginning on the sixth	2	208, 246
Beginning on the fourth	1	261
Total	14	

ENDINGS OF SONGS

	Number of songs.	Catalogue numbers.
Ending on the tonic	10	206, 207, 209, 210, 211, 212, 213, 245, 260, 261
Ending on the fifth	1	208
Ending on the third	3	244, 246, 259
Total	14	

FIRST PROGRESSIONS

	Number of songs.	Catalogue numbers.
First progression downward	10	206, 207, 208, 209, 210, 211, 212, 244, 246, 261
First progression upward	4	213, 245, 259, 260
Total	14	

MELODIC ANALYSIS—Continued.

ACCIDENTALS

	Number of songs.	Catalogue numbers.
Songs containing no accidentals	11	206, 207, 209, 210, 211, 212, 245, 246, 259, 260, 261
Sixth lowered a semitone	1	213
Third lowered a semitone	1	208
Sixth raised a semitone	1	244
Total	14	

RHYTHMIC ANALYSIS

Beginning on accented portion of measure	10	
Beginning on unaccented portion of measure	4	211, 212, 259, 260
Total	14	

Metric unit of voice and drum the same	1	207
Recorded without drum	1	261
Metric unit of voice and drum different	12	
Total	14	

STRUCTURAL ANALYSIS

Harmonic	8	206, 207, 209, 210, 211, 212, 213, 244
Melodic	6	208, 245, 246, 259, 260, 261
Total	14	

MIGA'DIWĬN'INA'GŨMO'WĬN (WAR SONGS)

A wide range of material is included in this group. There are songs which have been used to incite war, songs of the warpath, songs concerning the brave deeds of warriors, and songs of the scalp dance. The border line between groups of songs is not absolute and all our classification must be regarded as general in character; thus there are war songs among the dream songs and there is a scalp dance among the "songs connected with special medicines." In these instances the writer has followed the Indian who made the phonograph record. Many songs are used in war dances. The following group may be considered, however, representative of the class.

The drumbeat of the war dance is in even strokes; the drumbeat of the scalp dance is an accented stroke preceded by an unaccented stroke about one-third of its length. These are the ordinary rhythms but they may be varied by drummers of proficiency.

No. 122   (Catalogue no. 179)

Sung by AKI'WAIZI' ("OLD MAN")

VOICE ♩= 69
DRUM ♩= 126
(Drum-rhythm similar to No. 1)

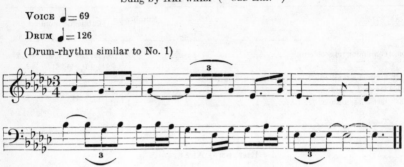

Analysis.—This song is based on the second five-toned scale of E flat, the harmonic divisions being the minor third E flat–G flat followed by the major third G flat–B flat, the song closing with a return of the minor third E flat–G flat.

The rhythm of the voice is plainly ♩ =69, while the beat of the drum is in unaccented eighths, ♩ =126; if the drum were ♩=138 we should have four drumbeats to one melody note, but repeated tests have failed to bring the two parts into this relation. The drum is plainly of a slightly different unit from that of the voice and persistently retains that unit. The tempo of the voice is unusually even in this song.

No. 123   (Catalogue no. 182)

Sung by MAIÑ'ĂNS

VOICE ♩= 76
Recorded without drum

Analysis.—The principal intervals of progression in Chippewa songs are the intervals of the third and fourth. This song is very unusual in that its principal melodic feeling is for the interval of the second. The dominant of the key is unusually prominent. The third of the key does not occur in the song, yet the song is readily accompanied by the tonic, subdominant, and dominant chords of the key. The song contains seven measures and is an excellent example of the entire song constituting a rhythmic unit. Six renditions appear on the phonograph cylinder.

No. 124   (Catalogue no. 205)

Sung by GA′GANDAC′

VOICE ♩ = 200

DRUM ♩ = 112

(Drum-rhythm similar to No. 111)

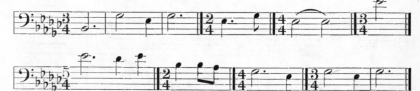

This song is said to have been used about forty-five years ago by Chippewa who were trying to incite the tribe to an attack on the white settlers. The attempt was unsuccessful and it is the pride of the Chippewa that they have never been at war with the white men.

Analysis.—The chief interest of this song lies in the rhythm, the general effect of which is martial and inspiring; yet the measure-lengths are very uneven, producing a rhythm which is fascinating in its irregularity. This is an instance of a special rhythm used for a special purpose. The object of the song was to control the will and influence men to act against their wishes and judgment. In view of this fact the peculiar rhythm of this song is worthy of attention. The tempo is very rapid, adding to the effect of the rhythm. Further consideration of rhythm of this character is given in the chapter on Mĭde′ Songs.

No. 125   (Catalogue no. 215)

Sung by GA′GANDAC′

Analysis.—This song is said to have been learned from the Sioux. Its harmonic structure is interesting. The song is in the key of D flat, the melody showing the octave complete except the seventh. The song is in two parts, each of which opens with the chord of the relative minor. This passes to the tonic major chord by the change from B flat to A flat. The following section of each part contains only the third F–A flat, with B flat as a bytone, yet the major chord of D flat is plainly implied.

HARMONIC ANALYSIS

6 measures   5 measures   5 measures   5 measures

No. 126. LITTLE EAGLE'S SONG   (Catalogue no. 229)

Sung by GA'GANDAC'

This is a song in honor of a warrior named Little Eagle, who died about November 1, 1907, at an advanced age.

O'kitci'ta is a Sioux word. White Earth was the old battle ground of the two tribes and the word suggests that the song was composed by the Sioux, who do not grudge their tribute to a brave man, though he may be their enemy.

Analysis.—The tones of this song are those of the second five-toned scale of F, with G as a passing tone. The unusual interest of the song lies in the E flat of the fourth measure, showing the interval of a whole tone between the seventh and eighth of a minor key. This is a characteristic of early English plain song.

The rhythm of the voice is maintained quite steadily at ♩=72, while that of the drum is ♩=108, each stroke preceded by a short unaccented beat. It will be readily seen that this is in the ratio of two voice pulses to three drum pulses, but the stroke of the drum invariably follows the singing of the tone, and the voice and drum never coincide.   This song shows no descending interval larger than a minor third, and the descent of the minor third occurs seven times in the melody.

VOICE ♩ = 72
DRUM ♩ = 108
(Drum-rhythm similar to No. 111)

O - ki - tci - ta mi - gĭ - sĭns

WORDS

O′kitci′ta.......................... Leader of the warriors
Migĭsĭns′.......................... Is Little Eagle

No. 127   (Catalogue no. 230)

Sung by GA′GANDAC′

VOICE ♩ = 66
DRUM ♩ = 80
(Drum-rhythm similar to No. 111)

HARMONIC ANALYSIS

3 measures   3 measures

This song is said to have been learned from the Sioux. The melody is divided into two parts of three measures each. The first part contains the tones of the minor triad with the minor seventh added, the sixth being used only as a passing tone. This is a very primitive tonality. Among the songs of the Chippewa this tonality is sometimes found in part of a song, but the song usually merges into a diatonic chord before the close. (See songs nos. 116, 117, 172.)

Five renditions of this song were recorded; these are identical except that the first measure occurs only in the first rendition. The harmonic peculiarity of this melody is best seen by playing the chords which form the two parts of the song, as given at the close of the transcription.

No. 128. Song of the Loons   (Catalogue no. 271)

Sung by Ga'tcitcigi'cĭg ("skipping a day")

Voice ♩ = 96
Drum ♩ = 116
(Drum-rhythm similar to No. 111)

Ki - wi -

ta - gi - cĭg *ban* ga - bi - nĕs - i - mo - yan

WORDS

Kiwitagi'cĭg...................... Flying all around the sky
Gabinĕs'imoyan'.................. The loons are singing

This is an old song, which was sung before starting on the warpath. The words refer to the Loon clan or totem which, according to William Warren, was very powerful among the Chippewa, even claiming to be the chief or royal clan.

Analysis.—Harmonic in structure, this song follows the outline of the major triad in the upper and lower octaves with the sixth as a passing tone. This tone material is found in a large number of the songs under analysis and is that of the fourth five-toned scale, lacking the second. It is a form of tone material which appears transitional from the simple major triad to the complete five-toned scale. (See p. 63; also tabulated analysis, p. 9.)

No. 129. "I WILL START BEFORE NOON"   (Catalogue no. 276)

Sung by GA'TCITCIGI'CĬG

VOICE ♩ = 144

DRUM ♩ = 100

(Drum-rhythm similar to No. 111)

WORDS

Tcinau'hwakweg'.................... I will start on my journey before
noon

Tcibwa'wabûmi'igoyan'............ Before I am seen

The singer stated that he learned this song from his father, who was a warrior, and in the old days was often sent in advance of the war party as a scout. Before starting on such an expedition he sang this song. In singing it the words were mispronounced; they contain many interpolated syllables.

Analysis.—This song begins on a very high tone. It is harmonic in structure and is a typical example of a simple song on the fourth five-toned scale.

No. 130. SONG OF CĬMAU'GANĬC   (Catalogue no. 277)

Sung by GA'TCITCIGI'CĬG

In the old days it was customary for a woman to go out and meet a returning war party. If a scalp had been taken she received it at the hand of the leader and danced in front of the war party as it neared the camp, singing and waving the scalp. The song under consideration concerns such an event as this. The singer stated that he had heard it sung by a woman on such an occasion. Sometimes several women went to meet the warriors, but one always preceded the others and received the scalp. The return to the camp was

Voice ♪ = 168

(Recorded without drum)

Ci - mau-gan-ĭc gi - nĭ - ci - wed.

Ci - mau-gan-ĭc gi - nĭ - ci - wed

Ci-mau-gan-ĭc gi - nĭ-ci-wed

Ci-

mau-gan-ĭc gi - nĭ-ci-wed

WORDS

Cĭmau′ganĭc..................... A man's name meaning "soldier"
Ginĭ′shiwed′...................... He killed in war

always followed by a scalp dance. This was sometimes performed
around a pile of presents. Each scalp was fastened to a hoop at the
end of a pole, and anyone to whom this pole was handed was obliged
to hold it aloft as he danced alone around the pile of gifts. This
is an old song in which the name of Cĭmau′ganĭc was introduced in
honor of his special bravery.

Analysis.—In this instance the entire phonograph record is transcribed. It consists of four renditions of the song and clearly shows
the points in which the renditions vary. In this respect it is the
record of a musical performance as well as the record of a song. The
singer imitated the manner in which he had heard a woman sing the
song, the high notes being given in a falsetto voice but with good
intonation. The division of the measures into five counts is not
mechanically accurate throughout the record. In certain measures
the note values correspond exactly to the metronome beat; in others
they vary slightly, but the rhythmic feeling is still that of a five-part
measure. This song is a very free musical expression and is of special
value, both from its structure and from the occasion of its use.

No. 131. "The Shifting Clouds" (Catalogue no. 114)

Sung by A′gwitû′wigi′cĭg

Voice ♩= 126

Recorded without drum

A - ni - go - si - wa - qed   ba - bi - kwa - si - go   *kwe*

WORDS

Ana′qud......................... The shifting
Ba′bikwa′sĭñ.................... Clouds

This is one of the war songs with which a social dance is usually
opened. Most of the singers carry some object in the right hand—a
small gun whittled from wood, a turkey-wing fan, a bow with arrows,

or even a war club with a wisp of hair dangling in imitation of an enemy's scalp. With this they point as if to various objects, as an enemy at a distance or a footprint on the ground. During this song the dancer would point to the clouds.

Analysis.—This song is harmonic in structure. The irregularity of measure lengths is worthy of notice, as is the continuously descending trend of the melody.

No. 132. Scalp Dance   (Catalogue no. 116)

Sung by Gi′cibäns′ ("little duck")

Voice ♩ = 168

Recorded without drum

Yo ho kwe a   yo ho kwe a   yo ho kwe a   yo ho kwe a

ĕ-kwa-wŭg ĕn - do - bi - og   yo ho kwe a   yo ho kwe a

yo   ho   kwe   a   yo   ho   kwe   a   yo   ho   kwe   a

ĕ-kwa-wûg ĕn - do - bi - og   yo ho kwe a   yo ho kwe a

WORDS

Ĕkwawûg′ .... The women
Ĕn′dobiog′ .... Are enjoying it with us

Analysis.—This was sung by an old woman whose voice was about the same register and quality as a man's. A point of interest in this song is that the last tone is approached by an upward progression. The rhythmic unit is short and frequently repeated.

War Songs— White Earth Reservation

Melodic Analysis

TONALITY

	Number of songs.	Catalogue numbers.
Major tonality	5	114, 182, 215, 271, 276
Minor tonality	6	116, 179, 205, 229, 230, 277
Total	11	

Melodic Analysis—Continued.

TONE MATERIAL

	Number of songs.	Catalogue numbers.
Fourth five-toned scale	2	271, 276
Major triad and sixth	1	114
Minor triad and fourth	1	116
Octave complete	1	229
Octave complete except seventh	1	215
Octave complete except second	1	230
Other combinations of tones	4	179, 182, 205, 277
Total	11	

BEGINNINGS OF SONGS

Beginning on the twelfth	4	114, 271, 276, 277
Beginning on the octave	3	116, 182, 229
Beginning on the tenth	2	215, 230
Beginning on the ninth	1	205
Beginning on the fourth	1	179
Total	11	

ENDINGS OF SONGS

Ending on the tonic	8	114, 116, 179, 205, 229, 230, 271, 276
Ending on the fifth	2	182, 277
Ending on the third	1	215
Total	11	

FIRST PROGRESSIONS

First progression downward	9	114, 179, 182, 205, 229, 230, 271, 276, 277
First progression upward	2	116, 215
Total	11	

ACCIDENTALS

Songs containing no accidentals	10	114, 116, 179, 182, 205, 215, 229, 271, 276, 277
Sixth lowered a semitone	1	230
Total	11	

RHYTHMIC ANALYSIS

Songs beginning on the accented portion of the measure	9	
Songs beginning on the unaccented portion of the measure	2	179, 182
Total	11	
Metric unit of voice and drum the same	1	215
Metric unit of voice and drum different	6	179, 205, 229, 230, 271, 276
Recorded without drum	4	114, 116, 182, 277
Total	11	

STRUCTURAL ANALYSIS

	Number of songs.	Catalogue numbers.
Harmonic	5	114, 215, 230, 271, 276
Melodic	6	116, 179, 182, 205, 229, 277
Total	11	

SA'GII'DIWĬN'INA'GŬMO'WĬN (LOVE SONGS)

The love songs mark a distinct phase in the development of music as a means of expression. It is not uncommon to find the words continuous throughout the song with little or no repetition. This characteristic has not been found thus far in any other branch of Chippewa music, and shows that in them the expression by means of words is as free as the expression by means of musical tones. These words are seldom transcribed. From observation the writer believes that the words of a certain melody are often impromptu in exact form, though having a general similarity throughout the renditions by various singers.

The love songs are more free in melody progression than other classes of songs. Many of them have traveled far and are known to be very old. They constitute a favorite form of music among the Chippewa, and are sung with a nasal tone used in no other except the songs of the scalp dance. This resembles the cry of an animal, yet the intervals are given almost as accurately as where a direct singing tone is used.

No. 133   (Catalogue no. 98)

Sung by MANIDO'GICĬGO'KWE ("SPIRIT DAY WOMAN")[a]

Analysis.—This was said to be a very old song. The peculiar quality of tone assumed by the Chippewa in singing their love songs renders it impossible to convey a correct impression by means of notation. This quality is nasal, with a slight drawling and a sliding of the voice from one tone to another.

The range of this song is two octaves, and the intervals are found to be correct, though difficult at first to recognize beneath their disguise of mannerism. The remarkable change of pitch in the tenth measure was given with more accuracy than many less wide intervals, following the general rule that uncommon intervals are more accurately sung than common intervals. A very explosive tone was given on the notes marked with an accent.

---

[a] The singer of this and the following song is a unique personality, living all alone. (See pl. 11.) On each side of her log cabin is a little lake. Back of it stretches the forest, broken only by a wagon road whose single track is marked by stumps beneath and drooping branches overhead. In this desolate place Manido'-gicĭgo'kwe and her dogs guard the timber of her government allotment, the while she gathers roots from which she makes love powders to sell to the children of men. In her hand she usually carries a small hatchet. There is a smoldering fierceness in her small eyes, but her voice in speaking is low and musical and she laughs like a child.

MANIDO'GICĬGO'KWE

TEMPO RUBATO
Recorded without drum

No. 134 (Catalogue no. 99)

Sung by MANIDO′GICĬGO′KWE

TEMPO RUBATO
Recorded without drum

Analysis.—This melody, though apparently simple in outline, is very free in movement. The tones are those of the key of F, yet the melody does not affiliate with the principal chords of that key and shows little feeling for a keynote.

No. 135. "MY LOVE HAS DEPARTED" (Catalogue no. 101)

Sung by MRS. MARY ENGLISH [a]

VOICE ♩ = 132
Recorded without drum

Man-go-dûg-win   nĭn-dĭ-nĕn-dûm man-go-dûg-win nĭn-di-nĕn-dûm,

mi-gwe-na-wĭn   nĭn-ĭ-mu-ce   ĕ-ni-wa-wa-sa-bo-ye-zud.

Ba-wi-tĭñ   gi-nĭ-ma-dja   nĭn-ĭ-mu-ce   a-ni-ma-dja

ka-wĭn-i-na-wa nĭn-da-wa-ba-ma-si   Si   Man-go-dûg-win

nĭn-dĭ-nĕn-dum   man-go-dûg-win nĭn-dĭ-nĕn-dum,

mi-gwe-na-wĭn ka-wĭn-i-mu-ce,   ĕ-ni-wa-wa-sa-bo-ye-zud

WORDS

Part 1

Mangodŭg′win	A loon
Nĭn′dĭnen′dûm	I thought it was
Mi′gwenawĭn′	But it was
Nin′ĭmuce′	My love's
Ĕni′wawasa′boyezud′	Splashing oar

[a] The singer of this song is a sister of William Warren, the historian of the Chippewa. Her family lived on Madeline island when she was a child, and this song came from there. It is a strange experience to talk with one who remembers when there were only one or two boats on Lake Superior, and who stood on the present site of Duluth when it was peopled only by a few Indians. On one occasion Mr. Warren and his sister, with a party of Chippewa, camped where Duluth now stands. As they were taking their departure Mr. Warren stood beside his canoe on the shore, stretched out his hand over the water, and said, "Some day this lake will be a highway of water where hundreds of boats will come and go;" then he pointed to the little group of tipis and said, "My brothers, you and I will never see it, but some day a great city will stand there." The Indians pointed significantly to their foreheads. Their brother had been too long in the hot sun, and even his sister entered the canoe with a heavy heart.

Part 2

Ba'witĭng'............................	To Sault Ste. Marie
Gi'nĭma'dja.........................	He has departed
Nin'ĭmuce'...........................	My love
A'nima'dja.........................	Has gone on before me
Kawĭn'inawa'......................	Never again
Nĭndawa'bama'si..................	Can I see him

Part 3 is similar to part 1.

Analysis.—This is an example of a common form of Chippewa songs, in which the first and last parts are alike, the middle section differing slightly and often being the only part in which words occur. Like most of the love songs, it was sung tempo rubato. The measure-lengths are clearly marked by the accents. This song in a less complete form has been found on other reservations.

No. 136. "Why Should I be Jealous?"   (Catalogue no. 104)

Sung by Mrs. Mee

VOICE ♩ = 88

Recorded without drum

Na - bĭ - sa   nin - do - ma   ge - o - den - da - ma - ban

ma - dja-kwi - wi - jâ - sĭs   a   ya   ya   i   i   ya

WORDS

Nabĭ'sa............................	Why should
Nin'doma'.........................	I, even I
Geoden'damaban'..................	Be jealous
Madjakwi'wijâsĭs'.................	Because of that bad boy?

This song is not without its humorous side. It is said that in the old times an Indian maid would lie face down on the prairie for hours at a time singing this song, the words of which are so very independent and the music so forlorn. The song was as often sung by a young man, the words being appropriately changed.

Analysis.—This is one of the few songs in which the key is fully established, as is shown by the fact that it can be readily accompanied by the three principal chords of the key of A. It is said to be a very old song and to be commonly used in recent times. The latter fact suggests that continuous use under semicivilized conditions may have modified the form of the melody to its present regularity of time and intervals.

No. 137. "I do not Care for You Any More"   (Catalogue no. 106)

Sung by Kɪ'tcĭmak'wa ("big bear")

VOICE ♩ = 52
Recorded without drum

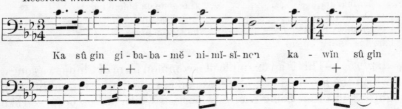

Ka sû gin gi-ba-ba-mĕ-ni-mĭ-sĭ-nc¹   ka - wĭn sû gin

gi- ba- ba - mĕ-ni-mĭ-sĭ-non ba-ka-nĭ - zĭ   be-ba - me - nĭ-mûg nin

WORDS

Kawĭn'..........................	
Sû..........................	
Gin..........................	[Free translation]
Gibaba'mĕnimĭsĭnon'..............	I do not care for you any more
Baka'nĭzĭ'..........................	Some one else is in my thoughts
Beba'menĭmûg'....................	
Nin..........................	

The mournfulness of this song, like the preceding, suggests that the Indian has some difficulty in transferring his affections. Kɪ'tcĭmak'wa, who sang the song, assured me that he was the best singer on the White Earth reservation. His voice is full and resonant. At the dances he sits at the drum for hours at a time, leading both singing and drumming.

Analysis.—E flat is the only tone occurring in this melody which marks it as minor, and this was sung slightly higher than the proper pitch. This song is, however, plainly minor in tonality. Like most of the love songs, it is widely known on the reservation.

No. 138. "Do not Weep"   (Catalogue no. 107)

Sung by Kɪ'tcĭmak'wa

VOICE ♩ = 76
Recorded without drum

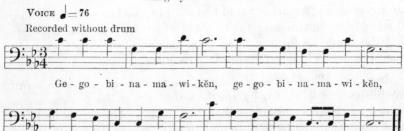

Ge - go - bi - na - ma - wi - kĕn,   ge - go - bi - na - ma - wi - kĕn,

ge - go - bi - na - ma - wi - kĕn,   ka - wĭn go - cu nĭn-da - nĭ - bo - si

WORDS

Gegobina'mawikĕn'................ } Do not weep
Kawĭn'........................... }

Gocu'............................ } I am not going to die
Nĭnda'nĭbosi'.................... }

This song is widely known among the Chippewa. It is one of the sweetest of all their love songs. In it we do not find the fancy of youth but the deeper love and the nearness of the deeper sorrow.

Analysis.—Although this song begins with a downward progression, it is more strongly marked by upward movement than many of the songs. In this and in its plaintiveness lies its chief interest.

Reference is made to song no. 200 (catalogue no. 145), in the section on Red Lake reservation music, which shows a repetition of this song by a singer on that reservation.

No. 139. "HE MUST BE SORROWFUL" (Catalogue no. 110)

Sung by KĬ'OSE'WINI'NI ("GOOD HUNTER")

VOICE ♩ = 76
Recorded without drum

Gi - na - ni - na-wĕn - da - mo - dog   ga - ni - cĭ - wa - na - djĭ - *gi* - gad

me-gwa we-ski - ni - gi-yan *e*

WORDS

Ginani'nawĕn'damodog'............ He [or she] must be very sorrowful
Ganicĭwana'djĭgad'............... Since he [or she] so deceived and
                                     forsook me
Me'gwa.......................... During
We'skinigiyan'.................. My young days

Analysis.—This, like no. 136, may be sung by either a man or a woman. The song is chiefly interesting because of the flatted third as an accidental. The expression of sadness by means of a minor interval is not so characteristic of Indian music as of our own.

No. 140. "WHEN I THINK OF HIM" (Catalogue no. 262)

Sung by HENRY SELKIRK

VOICE ♩ = 62

Recorded without drum

A - no - gi - ya - i - ki-do-pun   e   a - no - gi - ya - i - ki-do-pun

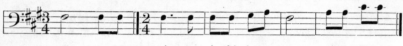

e   a - no - gi - ya - i - ki - do-pun   e   a-wûn-djîc-i-

go - ko nin-gac-ken - dûm   ka - mi-kwe-ni-ma-gĭn   a - no - gi - ya -

i - ki-do - pun   a-djĭc a-no - gi - ya - i - ki-do-pun   e

WORDS

Anogi'yayai'kidopun'.............. Although he said it
A'wûndjĭc'igoko'.................. Still
Ningac'kendûm.................... I am filled with longing
Ka'mikwe'nimagĭn'................ When I think of him

This is one of the old love songs of the tribe and may be sung by either a man or a woman. Several months previous to the making of this record a song resembling it was recorded on the Red Lake reservation. On comparison it is found that the Red Lake song is more elaborate in both rhythm and measure divisions, but the general trend of the melody is the same. See song no. 166 (catalogue no. 151).

Analysis.—The accidental in the second measure of this song is very effective and the compass of the song lacks only one tone of being two octaves. The ability of the singer to "pitch" properly a song of such range is worthy of note.

No. 141   (Catalogue no. 275)

Sung by GA'TCITCIGI'CĬG

Analysis.—A large number of words are used in the Chippewa love songs, but they are in the nature of conversation and do not form a sufficiently important part of the song to be translated. New words are very often composed and names introduced into the song.

This song is said to be very old. In a song of this character the length of the tones varies with the singer and with his mood. This rendition is transcribed as nearly as possible, but one can not be sure that repetitions by other singers would be identical. The song was sung very slowly, with the peculiar nasal tone affected by the Indians when singing love songs.

Love Songs—White Earth Reservation

MELODIC ANALYSIS

TONALITY

	Number of songs.	Catalogue numbers.
Major tonality	3	99, 104, 110
Minor tonality	6	98, 101, 106, 107, 262, 275
Total	9	

TONE MATERIAL

Fourth five-toned scale	1	104
Second five-toned scale	1	262
Octave complete	2	99, 101
Octave complete, except second	1	275
Octave complete, except seventh	1	98
Minor triad and fourth	1	106
Minor triad, second, and fourth	2	107, 110
Total	9	

Melodic Analysis—Continued.

BEGINNINGS OF SONGS

	Number of songs.	Catalogue numbers.
Beginning on the twelfth........................	3	98, 262, 275
Beginning on the octave..........................	5	101, 104, 106, 107, 110
Beginning on the third...........................	1	99
Total........	9	

ENDINGS OF SONGS

Ending on the tonic.............................	6	101, 106, 107, 110, 262, 275
Ending on the fifth.............................	2	98, 99
Ending on the third.............................	1	104
Total............	9	

FIRST PROGRESSIONS

First progression upward.........................	6	98, 99, 101, 104, 262, 275
First progression downward.......................	3	106, 107, 110
Total............	9	

ACCIDENTALS

Songs containing no accidentals..................	4	104, 106, 107, 110
Sixth raised a semitone..........................	3	101, 262, 275
Fourth raised a semitone.........................	1	99
Fourth and seventh raised a semitone.............	1	98
Total............	9	

RHYTHMIC ANALYSIS

Beginning on accented portion of measure.........	4	101, 104, 107, 110
Beginning on unaccented portion of measure.......	5	98, 99, 106, 262, 275
Total............	9	

STRUCTURAL ANALYSIS

Harmonic.............................	None
Melodic..............................	9

ATA'DIWĬN'INA'GÛMO'WĬN (MOCCASIN-GAME SONGS)

The moccasin game is the principal form of gambling practised by the Chippewa at the present time. A characteristic of the moccasin-game songs worthy of special note is the combining of a rapid metric unit of drum with a slow metric unit of voice, strongly indicating the elements of excitement and control which prevail in the game. Words may or may not be used, one instance being shown in which the words occur in different portions of the melody in the varying renditions of the song.

The drumbeat of the moccasin game is a strongly accented stroke preceded by a very short unaccented stroke.

In the moccasin game four bullets or balls are hidden under four moccasins. One bullet or ball is marked and it is the object of the opposing players to locate this with as few "guesses" as possible. The whole village knows by the beat of the drum when a moccasin game is in progress, and the writer can testify to the energy with which the drum is beaten, having sat next to it for a long time, the crowd of interested spectators nearly falling over her head. There was very little air to breathe, but the discomfort was amply repaid by the interest of watching the faces of the players.

No. 142   (Catalogue no. 112)

Sung by Maiñ′ăns

Voice ♩ = 192
Recorded without drum

Analysis.—In this instance an attempt has been made to indicate the embellishing of a melody by means of small melody progressions. Certain tones were sung less than a semitone higher than the pitch indicated and are marked in the usual manner. This song has no words. The melody is of unusual freedom, progressing several times from the highest to the lowest tones. It is peculiar in that the first and last tones are the same.

No. 143   (Catalogue no. 181)

Sung by AKI′WAIZI′

VOICE ♩= 96
DRUM ♩= 116

Drum-rhythm
DRUM ♩= 116

Analysis.—The accidental in this song is the lowered sixth, and it is worthy of note that the accidental was given with more firmness and better intonation than the other tones of the song. Four renditions were secured, the rhythm being regularly maintained. The drum is very sharp and insistent, as in all the moccasin-game songs.

No. 144. "IF I AM BEATEN"   (Catalogue no. 203)

Sung by NITA′MIGA′BO ("LEADER STANDING")

VOICE ♩= 104
DRUM ♩= 120
(Drum-rhythm similar to No. 143)

Nin - gi - wĕ   ni - we - ni - go - yan

WORDS

Nin′gagiwĕ′........................ I will go home
Niwe′nigoyan′.................... If I am beaten
Nin′genadĭn′.................... After more articles
Minawa′geatc′igeyan′............ To wager

Analysis.—Only the first two words appear on the phonograph record, yet five Indians were in the room when the song was recorded and they all agreed that these were the proper words for the song. This is one of the instances in which the melody is evidently more important and constitutes more fully the identity of the song than the words. The melody shows great complexity of rhythm, a feature to be expected from the nature of the words. The tones of the melody are those of the tonic triad.

No. 145. "I HAVE COME AFTER YOUR STAKE" (Catalogue no. 224)

Sung by GA'GANDAC'

VOICE ♩ = 69
DRUM ♩ = 120
(Drum-rhythm similar to No. 143)

Nim - bĭ - na - dĭ - nun   ki - da - di - mi-nûn   *hi   a   ya   a*

ni - ta - wa - ta - gi - yun   *â   ya*

WORDS

Nim'bĭna'dĭnun'	....	I have come after it
Kide'imûn	....	Your stake
Nita'wata'giyun'	....	You good players

Analysis.—The rhythm expresses the idea of this song in a very interesting manner. The voice rhythm is slow, steady, and determined, while the drum rhythm is the quick, energetic beat of the moccasin game.

Moccasin-game Songs—White Earth Reservation

MELODIC ANALYSIS

TONALITY

	Number of songs.	Catalogue numbers.
Major tonality....................................	2	181, 203
Minor tonality....................................	2	112, 224
Total....................................	4	

MELODIC ANALYSIS—Continued.

TONE MATERIAL

	Number of songs.	Catalogue numbers.
Octave complete	1	112
Major triad	1	203
Major triad and sixth	1	181
Minor triad and sixth	1	224
Total	4	

BEGINNINGS OF SONGS

	Number of songs.	Catalogue numbers.
Beginning on the twelfth	2	181, 203
Beginning on the tenth	1	224
Beginning on the second	1	112
Total	4	

ENDINGS OF SONGS

	Number of songs.	Catalogue numbers.
Ending on the tonic	3	112, 181, 203
Ending on the fifth	1	224
Total	4	

FIRST PROGRESSIONS

	Number of songs.	Catalogue numbers.
First progression upward	2	112, 181
First progression downward	2	203, 224
Total	4	

ACCIDENTALS

	Number of songs.	Catalogue numbers.
Songs containing no accidentals	3	112, 203, 224
Sixth lowered a semitone	1	181
Total	4	

RHYTHMIC ANALYSIS

	Number of songs.	Catalogue numbers.
Beginning on accented portion of measure	2	181, 203
Beginning on unaccented portion of measure	2	112, 224
Total	4	
Metric unit of voice and drum different	3	181, 203, 224
Recorded without drum	1	112
Total	4	

STRUCTURAL ANALYSIS

	Number of songs.	Catalogue numbers.
Harmonic..	2	181, 203
Melodic...	2	112, 224
Total..	4	

UNCLASSIFIED SONGS

No. 146. CALL TO THE DANCE   (Catalogue no. 105)

Sung by KI′TCĬMAK′WA

VOICE ♩ = 80

Recorded without drum

This song is sung by riders upon ponies, who go through the village summoning the people to the dance. With his usual conscientious carefulness Ki′tcĭmak′wa sang this into the phonograph with the same shakiness of voice which would be produced by riding on his pony.

Analysis.—The interest of this example lies in the rhythm of the song as a whole. One must have this in mind to appreciate how well it expresses the scene and the action of the rider going his rounds and summoning the people to the dance. Several renditions were given and the melody was accurately repeated.

The song contains no rhythmic unit and the rhythm is remarkably continuous throughout. There is no "stopping place" in the melody, yet the song as a whole can not be said to constitute a rhythmic unit; it simply reflects in its rhythm the motion of the pony and the general gayety of the scene.

No. 147. "I am as Brave as Other Men" (Catalogue no. 109)

Sung by Kı'ose'winı'ni ("good hunter")

Voice ♩ = 92

Drum ♩ = 92

WORDS

Inı̆'nı̆wûg'............................ Men who are brave and heroic
Enĕ'nimowûd'.......................... As you esteem them to be
Migo'................................ Like them
Kayanin'.............................. I also
Enĕ'nimowûd.......................... Consider myself to be

This song is similar to no. 148 and shows the Indian's manner of impressing his greatness on his fellow-men.

A repetition of this song was secured after several months and was found to be particularly correct, even to the time as measured by the metronome.

No. 148. "My Music Reaches to the Sky"   (Catalogue no. 274)

Sung by Ga'tcitcigi'cĭg

Voice ♩ = 104

Drum ♩ = 112

(Drum-rhythm similar to No. 111)

Ge da-mĭn - a - we - we - cka-mûn e a - wadj-i - gi -

nin gi-cĭg

Damĭnwe'weckamûn'.............. Music reaches
Awadj'ginin'...................... My
Gi'cĭg............................ To the sky

This is one of the old songs. It was sung after all had assembled and just before they began to dance. It is said to have been a particular favorite.

Analysis.—Attention is called to the high tones at the beginning of this song. Its structure is similar to that of the preceding song. The measures containing the words are slightly slower than the others, to permit clearness of enunciation.

No. 149. Lullaby   (Catalogue no. 102)

Sung by Mrs. Mee

Voice ♩ = 72
Recorded without drum

This lullaby is very old and is widely used among the Chippewa, the syllables *we we we* corresponding to the "by by" of the white race. The rhythm of this, sung in slow time, is very soothing.

No. 150. Farewell to the Warriors   (Catalogue no. 103)

Sung by Mrs. Mee

Voice ♩ = 76
Recorded without drum

Umbe'........................... Come
A'nimadjag'..................... It is time for you to depart
Wa'sûgi'dija'mĭn................ We are going a long journey

This is a very old song. The writer has talked with those who heard it sung long ago, when a war party left the little Chippewa village.

It was the custom for the women to accompany the warriors a short distance, all singing this song; later the song would be heard again, faintly at first, then coming nearer as the women returned alone, singing still, but taking up the burden of loneliness which is woman's share in war.

Analysis.—Only one other song in the present collection no. 126 (catalogue no. 229) contains the interval of a whole tone between the seventh and eighth. · This interval adds greatly to the effect of the song. The melody is of rare beauty, and is very graceful, despite the wide intervals at the beginning.

No. 151. SONG OF THANKS FOR A PONY (*a*)   (Catalogue no. 91)

Sung by CAGAN′ASI—("ENGLISHMAN")

No. 152. SONG OF THANKS FOR A PONY (*b*)   (Catalogue no. 92)

Sung by CAGAN′ASI

No. 153. SONG OF THANKS FOR A PONY (c)   (Catalogue no. 93)

Sung by CAGAN'ASI

VOICE ♩ = 104

DRUM ♩ = 104

(Drum-rhythm similar to No. 111)

Analysis.—This is a set of three songs which are sung when a pony is given away at a dance. The transaction would not be considered complete unless these or similar songs were sung. This rendition contains no words. A repetition of the same songs on another reservation contains the words "The pony is mine."

Attention is called to the syncopation in the second song. This is unusual, but was accurately given and repeated.

Unclassified Songs— White Earth Reservation

MELODIC ANALYSIS

TONALITY

	Number of songs.	Catalogue numbers.
Major tonality..	3	93, 102, 274
Minor tonality..	5	91, 92, 103, 105, 109
Total..	8	

TONE MATERIAL

	Number of songs.	Catalogue numbers.
Fourth five-toned scale..	1	102
Second five-toned scale..	1	105
Major triad and sixth	2	93, 274
Octave complete except sixth..	1	92
Other combinations of tones..	3	91, 103, 109
Total..	8	

BEGINNINGS OF SONGS

	Number of songs.	Catalogue numbers.
Beginning on the tonic a..	2	102, 103
Beginning on the fifth..	2	91, 274
Beginning on the octave..	1	93
Beginning on the eleventh..	1	109
Beginning on the ninth..	1	92
Total..	7	

a A portion of this melody lies above the keynote and a portion below it.

MELODIC ANALYSIS—Continued.

ENDINGS OF SONGS

	Number of songs.	Catalogue numbers.
Ending on the tonic	5	92, 102, 103, 109, 274
Ending on the fifth	2	91, 105
Ending on the third	1	93
Total	8	

FIRST PROGRESSIONS

First progression upward	4	92, 102, 103, 274
First progression downward	4	91, 93, 102, 105
Total	8	

ACCIDENTALS

Songs containing accidentals	6	92, 93, 102, 103, 105, 274
Fourth raised a semitone	1	109
Second lowered a semitone	1	91
Total	8	

RHYTHMIC ANALYSIS

Beginning on accented portion of measure	5	91, 92, 105, 109, 274
Beginning on unaccented portion of measure	3	93, 102, 103
Total	8	
Metric unit of voice and drum the same	3	92, 93, 109
Metric unit of voice and drum different	2	91, 274
Recorded without drum	3	102, 103, 105
Total	8	

STRUCTURAL ANALYSIS

Harmonic	None	
Melodic	8	

SOCIAL SONGS ON RED LAKE RESERVATION

DESCRIPTION OF THE DANCES, COSTUMES, AND CELEBRATION ON JULY 4, 6, AND 7, 1908

On the evening of July 2, 1908, the writer reached the Red Lake reservation in northern Minnesota for the purpose of studying the music of the Chippewa Indians during the Fourth of July celebration.

A large number of the Indians had already assembled and tipis were hourly added to the groups surrounding the field where the dances were to be held. The conical cloth tipi prevailed, smoke-stained and weatherworn, but a few white tents were pitched at a little distance, showing their occupants to be slightly removed from the older Indian life. Very close together were the tipis of the "old timers." No one need be ignorant of what took place in his neighbor's tipi, although the openings were never exactly opposite each other.

The work of putting up the tipi was usually done by the women, and it was interesting to watch the care with which they erected the three main poles, tied these together near the top, laying the other poles upon their intersection; finally they put one pole in each corner of the smoke-hole flaps of the cloth, spreading the cover neatly over the framework thus constructed, fastening it together over the door, and tying it to the stakes at the ground.

The Indians in the camp numbered about 200, while many more were visiting friends at the agency village.

This celebration was conducted entirely by the Indians, solely for their own pleasure. A subscription had been made by the traders, agency employees, and leading "mixed bloods," which provided food for the camps and prizes for the contest, but the management rested with the Indians. There were no formal exercises and no speeches by white men; indeed, the writer was the only white person there, except the agency employees.

The evening of July 3 found all in readiness. A rope marked off the large dancing circle and outside this were ranged various lemonade stands and a platform for dancing provided with a covering of green boughs.

Although firecrackers were for sale at the stores they seemed to have little attraction for the Indians. Some little boys solemnly fired a few crackers in a secluded lane, and two rockets ascended from the space in front of the Chippewa trading store. Aside from this a dignified silence prevailed.

The writer was awake early on the morning of July 4. It was 3 o'clock; the red dawn lay close to the pine trees in the east, and from the Indian camp arose the deep throb of a drum. Never was national holiday ushered in more impressively. He who sat beside the drum greeted in his own way that which his race honored before they ever saw the Stars and Stripes, and in their tipis his kinsmen waked to say "the day is come."

After breakfast the women were chatting good naturedly over their cooking fires. From one tipi came the jingle of sleigh bells as a brave handled the costume he had prepared for the occasion; near the door of another lay a bundle of bright beaded trappings; everywhere were the dogs and the babies.

It was about 10 o'clock when the parade started. There were no carriages with smiling, bowing speakers prepared to instruct and inspire. About fifty Indians were riding. Their costumes were bright with beadwork and gay streamers adorned the ponies. One man had swathed his pony in a huge American flag, and thus garbed it walked in the rear, following the procession like the spirit of a soldier's horse slain in the border wars.

The little parade took its way down the hill, across the bridge, and up to the agent's office. The leading men drew up their horses in a circle before the door, and each made a patriotic little speech to the agent; then they filed out of the inclosure and across the bridge once more, stopping before one of the stores, where the same programme was repeated. This finished, they went to the other store, a crowd following in their wake. (See pl. 12.)

It was considered that the day was formally and properly opened, and the procession jingled away to the camp.

The noonday sun shone hotly down, dogs and babies sought the shady side of the tipis, yet a general sense of joyous expectancy filled the air. Soon the beat of the drum was heard in the direction of the dancing circle with a low, vibrating *he he* as the singers practised around the drum, a shelter of boughs being provided for their protection.

The war dance began about 2 o'clock. Only a few were present at first, but soon dignified figures were seen coming from the tipis, each wrapped in a bright blanket or bedquilt. An Indian on his way to the dance does not stop to parley or to greet his friends; he sees nothing but the pole which rises high in the center of the circle, and he hears nothing but the throb of the drum. The leading chief, Nae'tawab', did not join the war dance at first. A chair was placed for him at one side of the circle, but he did not hasten his entry.

Throughout this celebration the costumes were more primitive than those seen on other reservations. The difference consisted in a more extensive use of feathers, shell, bone, and horsehair in the decorations. Only two or three men wore felt hats. The wearing of the hat in the dance constitutes a sharply defined line of demarcation between the full-blood and the mixed-blood Indian. On other reservations black felt hats were wound with red yarn, stuck with bright feathers, and adorned with yards of ribbon brilliant and varied in hue, but no such motley garb marred the dignity of the Red Lake dancers. Everyone wore some head covering, but it was of native construction. Stiff moose hair, dyed and fastened on a small wooden frame, constituted a popular headdress. In shape this resembled a huge flat rosette on top of the head with a strip extending down the back of the head to the neck and with one or two heron

INDIAN PARADE

INDIAN DANCE

THE FOURTH OF JULY AT RED LAKE AGENCY

feathers erect on the top. For fastening this on the head it is necessary to braid a small lock of hair on top very tightly, pass it
through a little hole in the wooden frame of the headdress, and
secure it by slipping a wooden peg through the braid. Some wore a
band of fur around the head, and to this part of a horse's mane or
tail was often attached. One man wore a headdress composed entirely of long feathers dyed in bright colors, fastened to a cloth in
such a way that they waved in every breeze and even hung before
his face, almost hiding it from view.

Brown woven underwear was a favorite foundation for a costume,
over which was worn the beadwork consisting of the breechcloth and
leggins and two large flat pockets with broad bands over the opposite shoulder, all of black velvet, on which the white and colored
beads showed effectively. Beaded moccasins completed this portion of the costume. Sleigh bells were a favorite decoration, a band
of them being fastened around each knee and strings of bells to
the waist in the back. One large bell was often worn on each ankle.
Many dancers wore the skins of raccoons or long ribbon streamers
at their elbows; some had the tails of raccoons dragging from their
moccasin heels. A few wore sleeveless velvet jackets beautifully
beaded and with these broad belts of beadwork with knife pouches
on the hip. Small round mirrors were effectively used, being sewed
on bands of cloth to form necklaces. One man wore an "ephod"
of red cloth thickly strewn with little mirrors; this garment, which
was shield-shaped in the back and square in the front, being slipped
over the head, is an article of Chippewa apparel which is rarely seen.
One dancer wore the entire body of an eagle around his neck and
another had that of a huge blackbird on which he had fastened
dots of white. Still another had two strings of claws fastened
across his forehead and temples. Several wore necklaces of bone
with beautifully polished clam shells as ornaments in the front;
others wore the broad silver armlets which were given to the Indians
in the early days. The faces of all were gaily painted. Altogether
it was a brilliant assemblage which sat around the dancing circle.
Some were smoking the red stone pipe with stem of willow; others
were sitting quiet, wrapped in their bright quilts, but when the
familiar *he he* was heard from the singers at the drum they rose
with a rush like a flock of bright birds. Most of the dancers carried
some object in the right hand—a turkey-wing fan, a bow with
arrows, a stone ax, or one of the old clubs to which scalps were once
fastened. One club had a wisp of horsehair dangling unpleasantly
from it. These objects were used in the gestures, which form a
conspicuous feature of the dancing, as the dancers point to some
imaginary enemy in the distance, to a fancied footprint or the
ground, or to the peaceful summer sky. When the dancing had

continued for some time the chief, Nae'tawab', entered the circle, wrapped in a cotton blanket of large pink plaid. Smiling to all, he took the chair placed for him and threw back his blanket, disclosing a magnificent suit of beadwork.

Then began the formal reception of the visiting Indians. This took the form of speeches interspersed with war dances, the speeches being impromptu in the old Indian style.

Nae'tawab' went across the circle to a row of visiting Indians and shook hands with each, giving some pleasant word of greeting. They did not rise when thus addressed. After Nae'tawab' had returned to his seat the drum gave out the rhythm of the war dance, and with an exclamation of *How how* the men sprang to their feet and danced around the drum, each man dancing alone and using his favorite gestures and fancy steps. This gives unlimited scope for the exhibition of individual skill and proficiency. In these dances the men did not all move in the same direction; often those nearest the drum circled toward the east while an outer circle moved toward the west.

As soon as all were seated a speech was made by an Indian from the White Earth reservation. He said: "My friends, there are many white people in the part of the country from which we come and we follow many of their ways when we are at home, but I want to tell you that we have come to this celebration as Indians, not as white men. We wish to be Indians in everything while we are with you and we want you to think of us only as Indians, like those of the old days. I have done."

The seated braves said *How how how*, and then danced again.

After this another man made a speech saying, "My friends, about a month ago my little daughter died. I have been very sad ever since; but as I am with you all here to-day I forget my sorrow and am entirely happy again. I have done."

The braves said *How how how*, and danced again.

There was no apparent order in these speeches. The speakers walked back and forth before their little audience, using simple gestures and sometimes waiting to hear *How how* after a particularly telling sentence. Patriotic speeches were made exhorting the Indians to appreciation of the day and emphasizing the fact that their gathering formed a part of a great celebration which extended all over the United States.

Nae'tawab' reserved his speech until the last, delivering with great oratorical effect a speech such as a chief should make. He stated especially that there would be no festivities on the following day, as it was Sunday, and he wished his people to show due respect to the Ruler of All by strictly observing the day.

Then they danced for the rest of the day, singing the various war-dance songs familiar to Chippewa on the several reservations.

At about 8 o'clock in the evening the sound of the drum was heard. A crowd from the camp was moving toward an old store, Nae'tawab' leading and the drum in the midst. Before this building they stopped and began to dance around the drum, all singing the high droning melody of the "begging dance." Soon a shifting of the crowd showed that they were going toward the Chippewa trading store. Nae'tawab' was the leader, dancing and waving a little flag. Standing before the store he faced the Indians, dancing with all his might and urging them to sing louder and louder. Soon the trader brought out a box of oranges which he distributed; then the melody changed slightly to the "thanks-for-a-gift" song, and the crowd passed on to another store.

The scene presented a picture never to be forgotten. A bright light from the store windows flooded the grotesque crowd, while beyond were the gathering shadows of the night. Nae'tawab', growing more and more excited, was on the platform before the store waving his flag and dancing. His suit of beaded velvet glistened in the light and his dancing was wonderfully graceful.

Later they took their way up the hill toward the camp. Singing their strange, high melody, they vanished in the night and only the song remained.

On Sunday the camp was quiet. Monday morning saw the festivities resumed. Dancing began about 10 o'clock and lasted until late at night. The feast was one of the chief events of this day and consisted of boiled beef and soup. The beef is cut in pieces the size of a man's hand and boiled until there is very little taste in it. When served, it is dry and can be taken in the fingers. The broth is served separately as a drink, some of it being taken home by the people, who bring little pails for the purpose.

At this dance a huge kettle containing the meat was brought into the dancing circle. One of the men in charge of the feast then selected five or six of the older men and led them one at a time to the kettle, where they seated themselves and began to eat. The first men thus selected were not in dancing costume, and the writer was told that they were thus honored because of their bravery in the old days. When one of them had finished eating he selected someone from the circle to take his place at the kettle, leading him forward with some little pleasantry. The Chippewa are a people whose smiles come very readily when they are at ease and with their friends. Portions of the meat were also passed to those who sat in the dancing circle, and the kettle was removed when the feast was finished and the dance resumed.

On Monday a pony was given away. It was done very simply. A "woman's dance"[a] was in progress, and a woman walked across the

---

circle and handed a little stick to a man, who took it and danced with
her. The writer was told that he afterward gave her an equivalent
in beadwork. It is the invariable custom that a valuable gift must
receive an equal return and such an exchange at a dance is usually
arranged between the parties beforehand.

The principal "woman's dance" was held on Tuesday. Almost
every woman brought a bag of gifts. This she laid on the ground
beside her. In beginning this dance the drum gave the proper
rhythm and the singers began one of the "woman's-dance" songs.
Three young men rose together and rushed across the circle with the
swoop peculiar to Chippewa dancers when making a concerted movement. Stopping in front of three women, they danced before them,
laid down their gifts, and then rushed back again, seating themselves
and instantly looking as though nothing had occurred. During the
dance it is not customary for a man to ask a woman to dance unless
she has previously asked him to do so. This was evidently a kind
of preliminary demonstration. It was half an hour before the dance
was fairly started. At first the circle was small, only large enough
to reach around the drum, but later it occupied the larger part of
the inclosure. In this dance the people faced the drum, moving
slowly, the women with a sidewise shuffling step, the men often using
the step of the war dance.

The "woman's dance" is a merry one, and this was for pleasure
rather than for the gifts, so it was continued longer than usual. If an
exchange of gifts is the important part, it is arranged that each dance
shall last only two or three minutes, the dancers then seating themselves and gifts being once more presented. The gifts at this dance
consisted principally of calico, though some large pieces of beadwork
and one pony were given away. Nae'tawab' presented his pink plaid
blanket to one of the women. It is the custom for a dancer to hold
aloft the gift he or she has received that all may see it. To the
spectator this is more interesting when the gifts are more varied and
frequent, consisting of pipes, bead pouches, bead chains, strings of
sleigh bells, and beaded jackets. The writer has even seen a man on
a similar occasion "dance away" his beaded velvet costume, one
piece at a time, finally leaving the circle wrapped in a blanket.

The dancing, which began in the morning, was continued with little
intermission until after midnight. The scene was lighted by a full
moon, round and red above the pine trees. Hour after hour was
heard the tireless throb of the drum and the shrill voices of the
singers; at last they ceased and the camp fell asleep—all but the dogs,
which barked until nearly daybreak. At last they too were quiet, and
one was reminded of the words of an old Chippewa war song, "When
the dogs are still I will be ready to do mischief." A gray light strug-

gled across the sky. It was the hour most dreaded in Indian warfare, the hour when so many terrible attacks were made. Yet in forgetfulness of the past and without fear of the future the little village slept.

THE SINGERS OF RED LAKE

The personality of an Indian singer must be taken into consideration when analyzing his songs. This is the more important if the singers are of a primitive type. Under such conditions one encounters strongly marked individualities, each of which may offer its particular sort of song or sing familiar songs in its own particular way.

The songs secured at Red Lake are placed in their several classes, but a description of the singers is herewith presented, in order that those who wish to judge a song by the personality of the singer may have an opportunity of doing so.

Six singers were employed, and 48 songs recorded, this material being representative of the culture on this reservation.

1. GI'WITA'BINĔS ("SPOTTED BIRD")

This singer was a man about 50 years old, who combined the old and the new modes of Indian life and thought. He spoke English fluently and sent his children to the government schools, yet his special pride was his singing, which he said was in the "regular old Indian way."

These facts regarding his personality must be taken into consideration in an estimate of his songs.

He recorded 18 songs, 6 of which were major and 12 minor in tonality. They were divided as follows: 6 moccasin-game songs, 3 woman's dances, 2 war songs, 2 old scalp dances, 1 song concerning a vision, 1 song concerning an historical event, and 3 repetitions of songs secured elsewhere.

All the songs except the first one were accompanied by the drum. In most instances the repetitions of the song filled the entire phonograph cylinder.

The value of this series of 18 records lies in its relation to the style of Indian singing as well as to accurate preservation of melodies. Gi'wita'binĕs varied the songs which he sang five or six consecutive times, frequently repeating certain phrases or the last half of the song, and embellishing the melody. In transcribing these songs that portion of the record has been selected on which the song was evidently sung through once in a direct way, no attempt being made to transcribe variations therefrom which were clearly made for effect.

It is worthy of note that in these songs the pulse of the measure beginning is always repeated accurately, no matter how much the subdivision of the count, the less important melody progressions, or the order of phrases may vary. The significance of this can be appreciated only after an examination of the songs, and those who wish to follow closely this study of rhythm may tap the rhythm of the songs with a pencil, following the note values as definitely as possible. It is not necessary that one should be able to hear mentally the melody; the general progression can be seen by the position of the notes on the staff.

In these, as in songs previously considered, the tempo of the drum is steadily maintained, the tempo of the voice varying somewhat from the metronome indication.

The special points of interest in this group are:

(1) Two songs on the second five-toned scale, nos. 80 and 169.

(2) Two songs based on the tonic and submediant chords, nos. 186 and 159.

(3) A slow melody with a very quick drum, no. 171.

(4) A song interrupted by sharp ejaculations repeated on the same tone, no. 176.

(5) Range of the singer's voice from C sharp on the bass clef to B on the treble clef. Many songs have the compass of a twelfth.

(6) A rhythm of three pulses of the drum equivalent to two of the melody, a rhythm in which the pulse of the drum has no apparent relation to that of the melody, a practice of letting the drum follow the voice and of using an accented sixteenth note followed by a dotted eighth are of frequent occurrence, but are found in the work of other singers also.

2. WABEZIC′ ("MARTEN")

Wabezic′ was a most interesting character. He was part Cree and belonged to the Pembina band living farther north, but he married a Chippewa woman and now lives at the village of Sandy River, on the Red Lake reservation. He could neither speak nor understand English. Wabezic′ was short in stature and different in feature from the Chippewa. He was a wiry, active little man, with quick, keen eyes, a good dancer, and had the general appearance of a man accustomed to depend on his own resources. He said that he was named Wabezic′ because he was so small.

This singer gave twelve songs, five of which were major and six minor in tonality. One was so wandering as to suggest a possibility that it was incorrectly remembered. It is transcribed, however, as it was sung. The main characteristics of these songs are the persistence with which the drum beat follows the voice, the frequent descent of the minor third, and the tenacity with which the rhythm is maintained even when the melody is imperfectly repeated.

This singer was an excellent subject, but it was difficult for him to sing so many songs without preparation; thus some of the songs are sung more firmly and repeated more accurately than the others.

3. GI'NAWIGI'CĬG ("EAGLE DAY")

This singer was an old man who could neither speak nor understand English and was almost totally blind. He sang seven songs, six of which were minor and the other merged into minor at the close. He was a typical old Indian and most of his songs are of value.

Musically these songs differ little from those of Wabezic'.

4. GAGE'BĬNES ("THE EVERLASTING BIRD")

This singer was a young man, a mixed-blood, who had a pleasing voice and a particularly agreeable manner, both in singing and speaking. His features suggested the possibility of some negro ancestry and his songs have a suggestion of the plaintive quality and peculiar swing of negro melodies.

He sang the plaintive songs so well that he was encouraged to keep to that style; he gave eight songs in all, five of which were love songs and the other three woman's dances.

It is noteworthy that two of the most plaintive songs were major in tonality. Three of the songs were major, three were minor, and two were duplicates.

These songs have a wide range, some of them having a compass of a twelfth. The love songs usually begin on a high note and the minor third is much used in the descending progression.

5. WILLIAM PRENTISS

This singer was a young man, one of the best dancers and also considered one of the best singers. He spoke English freely and was very intelligent. He only sang two songs. One (no. 187) was the "begging song" used on the evening of July 4; the other (no. 174) is of interest, as the rhythm so closely resembles that of negro music. Both the songs given by this singer were minor in tonality.

6. JOHN MARK

This young man recorded only one song. This shows an interesting rhythm and a graceful melody, but as the voice was not adapted to the phonograph no further records were made. The importance of rhythm is shown by the fact that singers who recorded only a few songs usually gave songs of very peculiar rhythm. This suggests that the rhythm is more readily remembered than the melody. It has already been noted that in renditions of the same song by different singers the rhythm shows less variation than the melody.

In all the songs recorded at Red Lake the intonation is most accurate on the octave and fifth (or twelfth) and most noticeably uncertain on the fourth and seventh. Accidentals are usually given with special firmness and accuracy. Secondary accents are seldom found; thus the songs are divided into measures of 2–4 rather than 4–4 time.

The rhythmic peculiarities of certain songs, which resemble the rhythmic peculiarities of negro music, may be traceable to a vestige of negro ancestry among the Chippewa of northern Minnesota. Similarly, the melodic as well as the rhythmic features of certan songs, which suggest what is commonly known as "Scotch music," may be traceable to songs heard years or even generations ago from Scotch traders, many of whom were connected with the Hudson's Bay Company. This is offered as a tentative explanation. If it be true, it is an interesting point that both these elements should have left a rhythmic stamp on the music of a locality. The melodic resemblance is less important, as the tonality commonly known as the "Scotch scale" is found in the music of many primitive peoples.

WAR SONGS

No. 154
(Catalogue no. 131)

Sung by GI'WITA'BINĖS

Recorded without drum

Analysis.—This song was said to come from Standing Rock, South Dakota, and is one of the Sioux songs adopted by the Chippewa, though always credited to the Sioux. No words were used. The song was sung four times, without the drum. The length of the notes of the first ten measures varied slightly in the renditions, but from the tenth measure to the close the rhythm was regular and the tempo as indicated, ♩=80. It is a peculiar rhythm, which makes the exactness of its repetition more interesting. In each rendition the difference between the flat and the natural in the fourth measure from the last is worthy of note.

No. 155. "Inside the Cave"   (Catalogue no. 140)

Sung by Gi′wita′binĕs

A - pic-kwe- ka - mi-gaug *e*   a - bi-dog ni - mi - co - mis

WORDS

Apickwe′kamigaug′	....	Inside the cave
Abidog′	....	That is where, it seems,
Ni′mico′mis	....	My grandfather is

This is a very old song. The phonograph record was played for a man on the White Earth reservation, who recognized it at once and said "That is an old Chippewa war-dance song of the days before they were friendly with the Sioux."

Analysis.—This song was sung five times and in four of these renditions the last part is repeated as marked.

The beat of the drum is in quarter notes, preceded by an unaccented stroke.

No. 156   (Catalogue no. 172)

Sung by Gi′nawigi′cĭg

Voice ♩ =̲ 92

Drum ♩ = 96

(Drum-rhythm similar to No. 1)

This song shows a very rapid drum beat with a slow melody rhythm. In the beat of the drum we find an impetus to quickened pulse and rapid action, while the slower melody rhythm suggests con-

trol and restraint. It is worthy of note that the tones marked (·
were prolonged equally in each repetition, but not sufficiently to be
indicated by a note value.

No. 157   (Catalogue no. 173)

Sung by GI′NAWIGI′CĬG

VOICE ♩ = 168
Recorded without drum

This song contains three instances of a sixteenth note accented and
followed by a dotted eighth. This subdivision of the count thus far
has been found only at Red Lake and is not a characteristic of Chippewa music.

No. 158   (Catalogue no. 178)

Sung by GI′NAWIGI′CĬG

VOICE ♩ = 104
Recorded without drum

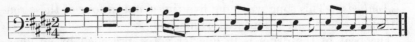

This, a short song, was sung seven times with no material variation.

No. 159. SCALP SONG   (Catalogue no. 146)

Sung by GI′WITA′BINĔS

VOICE ♩ = 104
DRUM ♩ = 116
(Drum-rhythm similar to No. 111)

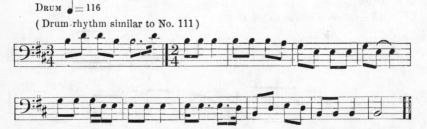

Analysis.—This song contains only the tones of the fourth five-
toned scale on G and ends on the third tone of that key, and the only
two chords agreeable to the melody are the tonic and submediant
chords. This melody is characterized also by the descent of the minor
third. There is no interval in the song larger than the minor third.

No. 160. Scalp Song   (Catalogue no. 147)

Sung by Gī′wita′binĕs

VOICE ♩ = 120
DRUM ♩ = 120

(Drum-rhythm similar to No. 111)

Analysis.—This song was sung four times, and no two renditions are identical, the differences consisting mainly in the interpolation of long repetitions of the same tone and in a variety of ornamental phrases. The rendition selected for transcription is the one containing the least of such material.

No. 161. Scalp Song   (Catalogue no. 167)

Sung by Wabezic′

VOICE ♩ = 112
DRUM ♩ = 112

Analysis.—This song contains only the tones of the minor chord, and the fourth of the scale, which is used as a passing tone. It was

sung four times. The intonation was wavering but the rhythm was repeated exactly. The record shows the drum to be perceptibly behind the voice, yet having the same metric unit.

No. 162. "THE SKY REPLIES"   (Catalogue no. 166)

Sung by WABEZIC'

VOICE ♩ = 108
DRUM ♩ = 108
(Drum-rhythm similar to No. 111)

WORDS

Weja'wŭckwago'deg	The blue, overhanging
Gi'cĭg	Sky
Nina'pomigwûn'	Answers me back

The singer said that he once killed a Sioux and sang this song with the scalp.

This song was sung very firmly, without hesitation, and with good intonation. The three records are identical in every respect. The drum beat always followed the voice. The words were not sung clearly enough to be transcribed.

War Songs—Red Lake Reservation

MELODIC ANALYSIS

TONALITY

	Number of songs.	Catalogue numbers.
Major tonality	1	140
Minor tonality	7	146, 147, 166, 167, 172, 173, 178
Beginning major and ending minor	1	131
Total	9	

MELODIC ANALYSIS—Continued.

TONE MATERIAL

	Number of songs.	Catalogue numbers.
Fourth five-toned scale	1	140
Second five-toned scale	2	172, 178
Minor third and fourth	1	173
Minor triad and fourth	2	147, 167
Other combinations of tones	3	131, 146, 166
Total	9	

BEGINNINGS OF SONGS

	Number of songs.	Catalogue numbers.
Beginning on the octave	7	146, 147, 166, 167, 172, 173, 178
Beginning on the fifth	1	140
Beginning major and ending minor	1	131
Total	9	

ENDINGS OF SONGS

	Number of songs.	Catalogue numbers.
Ending on tonic	9	

ACCIDENTALS

	Number of songs.	Catalogue numbers.
Songs containing no accidentals	9	

FIRST PROGRESSIONS

	Number of songs.	Catalogue numbers.
First progression upward	4	131, 146, 172, 173
First progression downward	5	140, 147, 166, 167, 178
Total	9	

RHYTHMIC ANALYSIS

	Number of songs.	Catalogue numbers.
Beginning on accented portion of measure	6	131, 146, 147, 166, 167, 178
Beginning on unaccented portion of measure	3	140, 172, 173
Total	9	
Metric unit of voice and drum the same	4	140, 147, 166, 167
Metric unit of voice and drum different	2	146, 172
Recorded without drum	3	140, 173, 178
Total	9	

STRUCTURAL ANALYSIS

	Number of songs.	Catalogue numbers.
Harmonic	1	140
Melodic	8	131, 146, 147, 166, 167, 172, 173, 178
Total	9	

LOVE SONGS

No. 163   (Catalogue no. 161)

Sung by WABEZIC'

The singer said that " in this song a young man asked a young girl to go and walk with him and said that if she did not come this evening he would come and ask her again to-morrow evening."

In this transcription the sharps and flats indicate the pitch of the tones, but do not imply an established key.

No. 164   (Catalogue no. 155)

Sung by GAGE'BINĔS

This song is an interesting example of a plaintive melody in a major key.

No. 165. "In her Canoe" (Catalogue no. 157)

Sung by Gage′binĕs′

VOICE ♩ = 60
Recorded without drum

WORDS

Miau′	I see her
Nin′imu′ce	My sweetheart
Kaniwa′wasa′boye′su	Paddling her canoe

This is a song of a young man who stands on the shore watching the maiden of his heart as she paddles her canoe on the lake.

The song is slow and is a good example of a plaintive melody in a major key.

No. 166. "I am Going Away" (Catalogue no. 151)

Sung by Gage′binĕs′

VOICE ♩ = 72
Recorded without drum

WORDS

First verse

Umbe	Come
Ma′noni′gamadja′	I am going away
Ma′no	I pray you
Bïn′a	} Let me go
Nin′gama′dja	
Neyab′ninga′wicin′	I will soon return
Ge′go	Do not
Mawi′micikĕn′	Weep for me

Second verse

Na	Behold
Tci′miwĕnda′min	We will be very glad
Tciwa′bundiyung′	To meet each other
Dagnïc′ïna′n	When I return
Ge′go	Do not
Mawi′micikĕn	Weep for me

Analysis.—This melody is particularly graceful and pleasing. The tempo is not rigidly maintained. The metronome mark indicates the general tempo and the song is divided into measures by means of the accents. The words are not sufficiently distinct for transcription.

No. 167. "COME, LET US DRINK" (Catalogue no. 152)

Sung by GAGE′BINĔS′

VOICE ♩ = 53
Recorded without drum

WORDS

Umbe′	Come
Mïnïkwe′da	Let us drink

This is the song of a lovelorn youth who meets another and asks if he "has a bottle to cheer him up."

Analysis.—This melody is not unlike the preceding, except that it is set to a slower beat. The words can be recognized, but are too indistinct to transcribe.

Love Songs—Red Lake Reservation

MELODIC ANALYSIS

TONALITY

	Number of songs.	Catalogue numbers.
Major tonality	3	155, 157, 161
Minor tonality	2	151, 152
Total	5	

TONE MATERIAL

Fourth five-toned scale	1	157
Octave complete	1	151
Octave complete, except sixth	1	152
Other combinations of tones	2	155, 161
Total	5	

BEGINNINGS OF SONGS

Beginning on the twelfth	3	151, 152, 155
Beginning on the seventh	1	161
Beginning on the third	1	157
Total	5	

ENDINGS OF SONGS

Ending on the tonic	3	151, 152, 161
Ending on the fifth	1	155
Ending on the third	1	157
Total	5	

FIRST PROGRESSIONS

First progression upward	2	151, 157
First progression downward	3	152, 155, 161
Total	5	

ACCIDENTALS

Songs containing no accidentals	2	155, 157
Sixth raised a semitone	1	151
Second raised a semitone	1	152
Sixth lowered semitone	1	161
Total	5	

RHYTHMIC ANALYSIS

	Number of songs.	Catalogue numbers.
Beginning on accented portion of measure......................	4	151, 152, 155, 157
Beginning on unaccented portion of measure..................	1	161
Total...	5	
Songs recorded without drum...............................	5	

STRUCTURAL ANALYSIS

Harmonic...	None
Melodic..	5

MOCCASIN-GAME SONGS

No. 168   (Catalogue no. 133)

Sung by GI′WITA′BINĔS

VOICE ♩ = 92
DRUM ♩ = 116
(Drum-rhythm similar to No. 111)

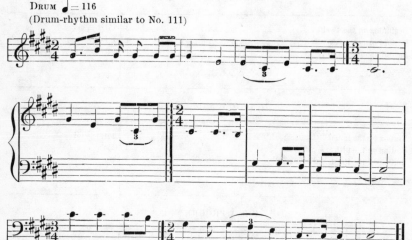

Analysis.—The singer said that he learned this song when he was a boy. The song was sung three times, the measure lengths and melody remaining the same, but the note values varying in the latter portion of the song.

The chief interest lies in the fact that there is no apparent relation between the pulse of the melody and the pulse of the drum, the melody being ♩=92 and the drum ♩=112, each being maintained very regularly. Each drum beat is preceded by the short unaccented stroke which characterizes the rhythm of the moccasin game.

No. 169   (Catalogue no. 142)

Sung by Gi'wita'binĕs

VOICE ♩ = 104

DRUM ♩ = 120

(Drum-rhythm similar to No. 143)

Analysis.—This song was sung six times, the pulse of the drum being maintained at ♩ = 120 while the voice is as steadily held at ♩ = 104. The note values and measure lengths are the same in all renditions. The tonality of the song is similar to the preceding except that the second of the scale is given less prominence, being used only as a passing tone.

No. 170   (Catalogue no. 144)

Sung by Gi'wita'binĕs

VOICE ♩ = 84

DRUM ♩ – 108

(Drum-rhythm similar to No. 143)

Analysis.—In this, as in numerous other instances, there is no mathematical proportion between the metric units of voice and drum, each expression being independent of the other.

No. 171   (Catalogue no. 148)

Sung by Gi'wita'binĕs

Voice ♩=72
Drum ♩=112
(Drum-rhythm similar to No. 143)

Analysis.—For transcription this was one of the most difficult songs in the entire series. It was sung three times, the essential points of the rhythm being identical throughout but the metric unit particularly hard to find. In this, as in similar instances, the metric unit, when found, can be readily traced throughout the record.

No. 172   (Catalogue no. 171)

Sung by WABEZIC'

Voice ♩=120
Recorded without drum

Analysis.—This song contains the tones of the second five-toned scale on E flat. Its interest lies in the prominence of D flat, giving the impression of a song containing only the minor triad with minor seventh added.[a]

The peculiar ending of this song gives it a slight resemblance to a negro melody.

No. 173   (Catalogue no. 174)

Sung by Gi'nawigi'cĭg

This song is in minor tonality, the first part comprising only the tones of the tonic chord and the last part containing the tones of the chords on the fourth and second of the scale. This suggests more harmonic possibilities than most of the songs.

---

[a] For a consideration of this tonality, see analysis of song no. 116, p. 130.

Voice ♩= 112
Drum ♩= 112
(Drum-rhythm similar to No. 143)

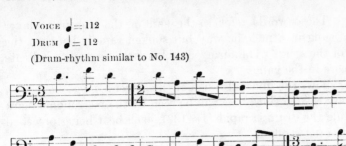

No. 174   (Catalogue no. 150)

Sung by WILLIAM PRENTISS

Voice ♩= 84
Drum ♩= 84
(Drum-rhythm similar to No. 143)

Analysis.—This melody is based on the tones of the second five-toned scale. It contains a subdivision of the count by which a short tone occurs on the accented portion of the count. This peculiarity has been found only in the songs collected at Red Lake.

No. 175. "HE GAVE US A DOUBLE CRACK"   (Catalogue no. 134)

Sung by GI′WITA′BINĚS

Voice ♩= 80
Drum ♩= 132
(Drum-rhythm similar to No. 111)

WORDS

Kinicono′kiwi′igonun′ .... I say, he gave us a double crack

Analysis.—These words refer to the skill of the opposing player and are not sung in a melodic way but spoken rapidly between the repetitions of the song. The term "double crack" is used to indicate a certain score in the game.

This song shows the unusual range of the singer's voice.

The melody is sung slowly, as will be seen by the metronome mark (♩ =80), while the drum is rapid (♩ =132), each beat being preceded by an unaccented stroke.

No. 176. "I AM STANDING TILL DAYLIGHT"   (Catalogue no. 143)

Sung by Gı′wıta′bıněs

VOICE ♩ = 126
DRUM ♩ = 132

(Drum-rhythm similar to No. 143)

Ke-ga-be-di-bĭk   wa-bun - ni - ka - pa - wi - yan

WORDS

Kagabédibĭk′......................... I who all night long
Wa′bunika′baniyan′................. Am standing up until daylight

Analysis.—In the six repetitions of this song the words occur only twice, and are used in two different portions of the melody, showing the freedom with which words may be omitted from or introduced into moccasin-game songs. The sharp interjected tones in the sixth and twelfth measures undoubtedly represent the exclamations given when a score is made.

In this song the metric unit of the voice is slower than that of the drum, a peculiarity of many songs which combine the element of restraint and control with the element of physical excitement.

Moccasin-game Songs—Red Lake Reservation

MELODIC ANALYSIS

TONALITY

	Number of songs.	Catalogue numbers.
Major tonality	None	
Minor tonality	9	133, 134, 142, 143, 144, 148, 15C, 171, 174

TONE MATERIAL

	Number of songs.	Catalogue numbers.
Second five-toned scale	6	133, 134, 142, 148, 150, 151
Octave complete except sixth	2	143, 144
Other combinations of tones	1	174
Total	9	

BEGINNINGS OF SONGS

	Number of songs.	Catalogue numbers.
Beginning on the twelfth	2	133, 142
Beginning on the fifth	3	143, 148, 171
Beginning on the octave	1	174
Beginning on the tonic a	2	144, 150
Beginning on the seventh	1	134
Total	9	

ENDINGS OF SONGS

	Number of songs.	Catalogue numbers.
Ending on tonic	9	

ACCIDENTALS

	Number of songs.	Catalogue numbers.
Songs containing no accidentals	9	

FIRST PROGRESSIONS

	Number of songs.	Catalogue numbers.
First progression upward	7	133, 142, 144, 148, 150, 171, 174
First progression downward	2	134, 143
Total	9	

RHYTHMIC ANALYSIS

	Number of songs.	Catalogue numbers.
Beginning on accented portion of measure	9	
Metric unit of voice and drum the same	2	150, 174
Metric unit of voice and drum different	6	133, 134, 142, 143, 144, 148
Recorded without drum	1	171
Total	9	

STRUCTURAL ANALYSIS

	Number of songs.	Catalogue numbers.
Harmonic	3	133, 142, 174
Melodic	6	134, 143, 144, 148, 150, 171
Total	9	

a The tonic is the lowest tone occurring in these songs.

WOMAN'S-DANCE SONGS

The woman's dance is the favorite social dance among the Chippewa at the present time. It is said to have been learned from the Sioux. Both men and women engage in it; an invitation to dance is accompanied by a gift, and the first invitation is usually given by a woman, the man returning it with a gift of equal value. The dancers form a circle, facing the drum and moving clock-wise with a shuffling step.

The drumbeat of this class of songs consists of an accented stroke preceded by an unaccented stroke about one-third its length. The songs show no general characteristics, but most of them are rather simple in melody and rhythm.

No. 177. "I HAVE BEEN WAITING"   (Catalogue no. 132)

Sung by GI'WITA'BINĔS

VOICE ♩ = 200

Recorded without drum

WORDS

Nin′imû′ce	My sweetheart
Mewicû′	A long time
Kibiïn′	I have been waiting for you
Gibiïc′ayûn′	To come over
Imaai′ayan′	Where I am

Analysis.—These words can be recognized on the phonograph record, but are too indistinct to be readily transcribed. The chief interest of the song lies in the range of the singer's voice and in the fact that the intonation is correct on both the highest and lowest notes. The song was sung twice and the general progression of the melody is duplicated accurately, though some of the note values vary.

No. 178. "COME, DANCE" (Catalogue no. 175)

Sung by GI′NAWIGI′CĬG

VOICE ♩ = 108
DRUM ♩ = 116

(Drum-rhythm similar to No. 111)

Um-be ni-nĭg

WORDS

| Umbe′ | Come |
| Ni′mĭg | Dance |

Analysis.—A decided syncopation in the last measures marks this song as different from the others. The words are spoken rapidly on a melodic tone, as though the dancer turned to some one sitting in the circle and urged him to dance, without interrupting his own song.

No. 179 (Catalogue no. 135)

Sung by GI′WITA′BINĔS

VOICE ♩ = 100
DRUM ♩ = 100

(Drum-rhythm similar to No. 111)

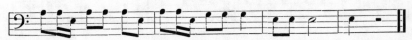

Analysis.—If this song were more exact in its repetitions, we might attach more importance to its beginning with the chord of A minor and ending with the chord of E minor.

No. 180   (Catalogue no. 141)

Sung by GĬ'WITA'BĬNĔS

VOICE ♩ = 132
DRUM ♩ = 132

(Drum-rhythm similar to No. 111)

No. 181   (Catalogue no. 153)

Sung by GAGE'BĬNES

VOICE ♩ = 108
DRUM ♩ = 120

(Drum-rhythm similar to No. 111)

Analysis.—This song has no words. A repetition was secured on the day following the first renditions. On comparison the renditions were found to be identical in rhythm and in the accuracy with which the accidental is sung. A slight difference occurs in the number of times which the first and last phrases are repeated. The rhythm is distinctive and is interestingly shown by "tapping it out" with a pencil.

No. 182   (Catalogue no. 154)

Sung by GAGE′BINĔS

Voice ♩ = 112

Drum ♩ = 120

(Drum-rhythm similar to No. 111)

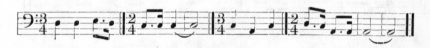

No. 183   (Catalogue no. 159)

Sung by JOHN MARK

Voice ♩ = 112

Drum ♩ = 112

(Drum-rhythm similar to No. 111)

This is the only song given by the singer; it shows a rhythm which is simple but very interesting. The only song offered by a singer is usually characterized by peculiarity of rhythm, indicating that the rhythm of a song is retained by a mind which does not accurately retain the melodic progressions.

No. 184   (Catalogue no. 177)

Sung by GI′NAWIGI′CĬG

Voice ♩ = 92

Drum ♩ = 116

(Drum-rhythm similar to No. 111)

No. 185. "WHERE ARE YOU?"   (Catalogue no. 86)

Sung by CAGAN'ASI

VOICE ♩ = 96
DRUM ♩ = 96
(Drum-rhythm similar to No. 111)

O - ki - tci - ta   to - ki - ya   *ho   kwi   ho*   *ho*

WORDS

Oki'tcita'........................... Leader of the warriors
Toki'ya........................... Where are you?

This is an old melody sung at a woman's dance given in special
honor of some warrior. In such a case two women would provide
the gifts and act as hostesses. At the opening of such a dance this
song would be sung by the men at the drum, calling for the warrior in whose honor the dance was given. As soon as the song
began the warrior would rise and begin to dance; then the two women
would rise, after which the guests would join the dance. When the
song was finished the warrior would relate his principal deed of valor;
then the women would distribute the gifts they had provided, it
being understood that they gave these presents in behalf of the
warrior.

Analysis.—The accidental in this song was accurately given in all
the renditions. A sixteenth note accented and followed by a dotted
eighth is a rhythmic peculiarity of this song.

Woman's-dance Songs—Red Lake Reservation

MELODIC ANALYSIS

TONALITY

	Number of songs.	Catalogue numbers.
Major tonality.....................................	3	86, 132, 159
Minor tonality.....................................	6	135, 141, 153, 154, 175, 177
Total.....................................	9	

MELODIC ANALYSIS—Continued.

TONES COMPRISED IN THE SONGS

	Number of songs.	Catalogue numbers.
Fourth five-toned scale	3	86, 132, 159
Second five-toned scale	1	141
Minor triad and fourth	1	154
Minor triad, fourth, and seventh	1	135
Octave complete except seventh	1	153
Other combinations of tones	2	175, 177
Total	9	

BEGINNINGS OF SONGS

Beginning on the eleventh	1	154
Beginning on the octave	2	153, 175
Beginning on the fifth	4	86, 132, 135, 141
Beginning on the third	1	177
Beginning on the second	1	159
Total	9	

ENDINGS OF SONGS

Ending on the tonic	6	86, 132, 141, 153, 154, 175
Ending on the fifth	2	135, 159
Ending on the third	1	177
Total	9	

FIRST PROGRESSIONS

First progressions upward	5	86, 153, 154, 159, 175
First progressions downward	4	132, 135, 141, 177
Total	9	

ACCIDENTALS

Songs containing no accidentals	8	
Sixth lowered a semitone	1	86
Total	9	

RHYTHMIC ANALYSIS

Songs beginning on accented portion of measure	8	
Songs beginning on unaccented portion of measure	1	86
Total	9	
Metric unit of voice and drum the same	4	86, 135, 141, 159
Metric unit of voice and drum different	4	153, 154, 175, 177
Recorded without the drum	1	132
Total	9	

STRUCTURAL ANALYSIS

	Number of songs.	Catalogue numbers.
Harmonic	None	
Melodic	9	

UNCLASSIFIED SONGS

No. 186. SONG REFERRING TO AN HISTORICAL INCIDENT (Catalogue no. 139)

Sung by GI'WITA'BINĚS

VOICE ♩ = 120
DRUM ♩ = 120
(Drum-rhythm similar to No. 111)

Nin - ga - gi - we - wi - ni - gog ma - ni - dog *we we we* nin -

ga - gi - we - wi - ni - gog ma - ni - dog

WORDS

Nin'gagiwe'winigog'................ They will take me home
Manidog'......................... The spirits

The free translation of the words as given by the singer was as follows: "The thunders will take me home whenever I mind to go home, my friends, and the wind it will take me home, too."

Narrative.—This song is based on an historical incident which was related on both the Red Lake and White Earth reservations.

The story as given at Red Lake was as follows:

Many, many years ago a Chippewa Indian named Djige'weckûn' ("traveling on the beach of the water") killed the trader's son and was taken to St. Paul for trial. At that time there was only one house in St. Paul.   The man was condemned to be hanged, but just as they were going to hang him a terrible storm arose.   The clouds were right over the tree where he was going to be hung.   Lightning struck the tree and the rain poured down so that everybody went home.   They did not try again to hang the Indian and he was allowed to go back to the reservation, where he was made a chief. He composed this song while he was a prisoner at St. Paul.

Analysis.—This song contains only the tones of the fourth five-toned scale on G flat, and ends on D flat, the dominant of the key.   The seventh of the scale, which is the essential tone of the dominant chord, is not present in the song and no portion of the song affiliates easily with the dominant chord as an accompaniment.   Indeed, the only chords suggested by the melody, or seeming to be desired by it, are the tonic and submediant, thus showing a feeling for the descent of the minor third.   The repetitions of this song filled an entire cylinder, giving ample time for noting its peculiarities.   The transcription is from a rendition about midway of the cylinder.

No. 187. Song of the Begging Dance   (Catalogue no. 149)

Sung by William Prentiss

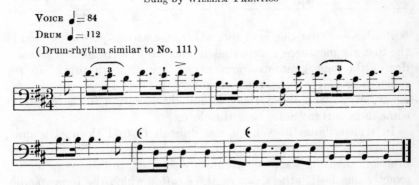

Analysis.—This is the begging song which was sung on the evening of July 4.   Its chief interest lies in the fact that the pulses of voice and drum are so dissimilar, each being steadily maintained.   The pulse of the voice is ♩=84; that of the drum ♩=112, preceded by an unaccented stroke.   The only correspondence is that three metronome beats at 84 are about equivalent to two beats at 112. If the song were in double time this would be an ordinary rhythm of "three against two," but the fact that the melody is in triple time makes this too complicated for analysis; one can only record the fact that these are the actual metronome measures of the pulses. (Compare analysis of song no. 1.)

The slight prolonging of the tones marked (• is the same in all the repetitions.   It is not sufficient to be indicated by a note value, but gives a peculiar effect of pleading.   This is one of the mannerisms of Indian singing which can not be accurately transcribed.

No. 188. Song of the Begging Dance   (Catalogue no. 170)

Sung by WABEZIC′

VOICE ♪ = 200
DRUM ♩ = 88

(Drum-rhythm similar to No. 111)

Analysis.—This song is of special interest as the phrase rhythm of the first six measures is repeated in measures 6–12 and the remainder of the song contains fragments of the same rhythm. In the repetitions of the song the rhythm of the first twelve measures is accurately repeated, but there is a slight variation in the length of some unimportant notes near the close.

In transcribing the song it was difficult to find the metric unit; however, this unit was finally found to be ♪ = 200. By this measurement the song was very accurately divided, certain tones having exactly one beat, others two or three, after which the tones readily grouped themselves into measures. The drum was next tested and found to be beating very regularly a triple time with an accented beat on the first and an unaccented on the third count of the triplet of eighth notes. The metronome showed the pulse of the drum to be ♩ = 88. The accent bell of the metronome was then set at a triple time and the indicator at 200 and the time space noted between the accents as given by the bell. This time space was almost exactly 88; therefore if the song were in triple time throughout, the drum and voice would coincide, but this synchronism is broken by the introduction of measures in double time while the drum continues to beat in triple time.

It is worthy of note that the A sharp in the fifth measure was always given correctly, but that the intonation on the fourth of the scale was flat, thus dragging down the third when reached.

The intonation of the octave was clear and correct.

No. 189. Song of Thanks for a Gift   (Catalogue no. 168)

Sung by Wabezic'

Voice ♩ = 72
Drum ♩ = 72

WORDS

Tci'wawicŏn'dûm.................. I am very grateful
En'dodawĭd'..................... For what he is doing for me

Analysis.—These words were not sung but were spoken between the repetitions of the song. The drum was struck only once in a measure and always followed the voice.

The long notes were sometimes held an extra count. This is unusual, as the long notes are usually found more uniform than the short notes in the repetitions.

The record is not entirely clear, but it is evident that the first part is major and the last part minor in tonality. The B flat is always taken firmly and accurately, the first E flat being slightly too high and the second one on true pitch. It is interesting to note that the change from major to minor is made on B flat instead of E flat.

No. 190. Song of Thanks for a Gift   (Catalogue no. 169)

Sung by Wabezic'

Voice ♪ = 160
Drum ♩. = 80
(Drum-rhythm similar to No. 111)

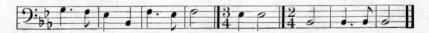

Analysis.—This song was sung four times, the rhythm being exact in the repetitions. The pulse of the voice is ♪=160 and is steadily maintained in both double and triple measures, while the drum as steadily beats a triple time at ♩. (dotted quarter note) =80, giving an accented beat on the first and an unaccented beat on the third count of a triplet of eighth notes, regardless of the voice. The song has no words and is similar to no. 189.

No. 191. Song of Thanks for a Pony   (Catalogue no. 136)

Sung by Gi′wita′binĕs

Voice ♩ = 76
Drum ♩ = 96
(Drum-rhythm similar to No. 111)

Analysis.—This song has an interesting rhythm, suggesting, though somewhat remotely, the galloping of an Indian pony. It is of minor tonality though lively in general character, showing that the rhythm of a song marks its character more strongly than does the tonality. The tones of the minor triad in ascending progression constitute an unusual opening for a song.

No. 192. Friendly Song (a)   (Catalogue no. 160)

Sung by Wabezic′

Voice ♩ = 80
Drum ♩ = 80

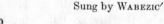

This is one of four "friendly songs," the others being nos. 193, 194, and 195. The singer said that they were used in the old times among the Pembina Chippewa, when a company of people went to a dance, to show that they came as friends. The singer had himself sung these songs in the old days. He said that some of the visiting Indians smoked their pipes and that back of them stood the men who sang these songs to assure the people to whom they had come that they were friendly. There were no words, but he said the people would know the song was meant to be friendly by the way in which it was sung; he said also that there was a "friendly way to beat the drum." It was stated further by the singer that this song was pure Chippewa and that no Sioux songs were used by the Pembina band.

Analysis.—Too much importance must not be attached to the fact that this song begins in the minor and merges into the major, for, although given accurately in the first rendition from which this is transcribed, the intonation is faulty in the other renditions. The rhythm in the last eight measures is always accurately repeated. The drum is in even beats of the same pulse as the melody but always struck slightly after the tone is sung. The chief interest of the song lies in the occasion of its use and in the accurate repetition of a peculiar rhythm in connection with a much less accurate repetition of the melody.

No. 193. FRIENDLY SONG (*b*)   (Catalogue no. 162)

Sung by WABEZIC'

VOICE ♩ = 92
DRUM ♩ = 92

I-we-di gi - cĭg - oñ   ni-*we*-ca - we-ni - mĭ - go   e

WORDS

Iwe'di.............................. Over there
Gicĭgoñ'........................... In the sky
Ni'cawe'nimigo'................... They have taken pity on me

This song is a march and is sung while the visiting Indians walk around the drum. It is used directly after song no. 192. The drum is in single beats to mark the time as the men march and has the same metric unit as the voice.

Analysis.—This song has a wild freedom about it and is very interesting. It was sung four times, the rhythm being repeated exactly but the melody varying slightly. The intonation is good and the song aggressively major in character. The descent of the minor third is conspicuous throughout this melody and there is no interval in the melody which is larger than a major third. It is also worthy of note that the second of the scale is treated as a passing tone, except in the third measure from the last, where it receives an accent.

No. 194. FRIENDLY SONG (c)   (Catalogue no. 163)

Sung by WABEZIC'

VOICE ♩ = 116
DRUM ♩ = 116

(Drum-rhythm similar to No. 111)

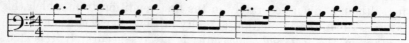

Ci - cĭg ni - mĭ-no-ta-gwûn

WORDS

Gi'cĭg.............................. The sky
Nimĭnota'gwûn..................... Loves to hear me

This song follows no. 194, the visiting Indians beginning to dance as they sing this.

Analysis.—Emphatically major in tonality, this song is characterized by the frequent descent of the minor third. There is no descending interval larger than the major third. Like the two preceding examples, this melody contains an indefinable element of freedom. The quadruple time is unusual, and the 5-4 rhythm unmistakable.

No. 195. FRIENDLY SONG (d)   (Catalogue no. 164)

Sung by WABEZIC'

This is the same kind of song as the preceding, and as the Indians would dance while singing it, the record was made with the same vibration of voice, adding to the difficulty of transcription.

The intonation in this song is uncertain, yet the prevailing descent of the minor third is unmistakable and the song contains no descending intervals larger than the major third. There are three complete records of the song and in each there is a feeling toward a major tonality in the first half and a minor in the last half, but the voice is too unsteady to permit analysis of this.

In one of the records there are two counts in the third measure followed by three in the fourth. This change is immaterial except as it shows that the singer felt it necessary to put five counts into these two measures. Throughout this song the drum is very perceptibly behind the voice.

This song is of value chiefly because of the frequent descent of the minor third and of the clearness with which the drum follows the voice.

No. 196. Song Referring to a Vision   (Catalogue no. 138)

Sung by Gi'wita'binĕs

WORDS

Wa'wia'weye'gancut'............... Round-hoofed
Gicawe'nimik'..................... Had pity on me

Analysis.—The singer said that he learned this song from a Mille Lac Chippewa many years ago. The record was played for an Indian at White Earth, and he recognized the song at once. The words refer to a vision of a round-hoofed animal which probably appeared to the singer in a dream.   The words are crowded into the first two measures of the music.   They can be recognized, but contain many interpolated syllables, and are too indistinct for transcription.

No. 197. SONG OF WE'NABO'JO   (Catalogue no. 272)

Sung by GA'TCITCIGI'CĬG

VOICE ♩= 208
DRUM ♩= 116
(Drum-rhythm similar to No. 111)

Gé - go - a - ĭn - a - a - bĭ - ke-gwûn   ge - go - ma - mic - kûc

gi - cĭg-wĕn   a   yu we he he   yu we he he   yu we he he

WORDS

Ke'goĭnabikegwûn'............... Don't look
Ge'gamamic'kwûc................. Or your eyes
Gi'cĭgwĕn'........................ Will always be red

This song is connected with a favorite folk-story in which We'nabo'jo invites the ducks to dance, telling them to keep their eyes shut, and then wrings their necks one after another.   The phonograph record is supposed to reproduce the event, even the cries of the ducks being given by the singer.   Before beginning the song the singer said: "I am arranging to have a dance, my little brothers and sisters." After the first rendition he said, "Dance, dance, dance faster, my little brothers and sisters, but don't open your eyes."   After the second he said, "How, how, take warning, my little brothers and sisters." This is mentioned to show the Indian custom of interspersing the renditions of the song with short speeches.

Analysis.—This is one of the few songs in 5–4 time.   It is plainly distinguishable from a triple measure followed by a double measure.   The metric unit is unusually rapid.   Repetitions of this song by other singers are found to be identical.

Unclassified Songs—Red Lake Reservation

MELODIC ANALYSIS

TONALITY

	Number of songs.	Catalogue numbers.
Major tonality..................................	4	139, 162, 163, 169
Minor tonality.................................	6	136, 138, 149, 164, 170, 272
Beginning minor and ending major..............	1	160
Beginning major and ending minor..............	1	168
Total...........	12	

Melodic Analysis—Continued.

TONE MATERIAL

	Number of songs.	Catalogue numbers.
Fourth five-toned scale..........................	3	139, 162, 169
Minor triad..............	1	272
Octave complete except sixth................	2	138, 164
Octave complete except seventh..............	1	163
Octave complete except sixth...............	1	164
Other combinations of tones................	4	136, 149, 160, 168
Total................................	12	

BEGINNINGS OF SONGS

	Number of songs.	Catalogue numbers.
Beginning on the fifth..........................	4	138, 149, 162, 163
Beginning on the third.........................	5	139, 160, 164, 168, 170
Beginning on the tonic a.......................	1	272
Beginning on the octave........................	1	169
Beginning on the fourth........................	1	136
Total.................................	12	

ENDINGS OF SONGS

	Number of songs.	Catalogue numbers.
Ending on the tonic.............................	8	136, 149, 160, 162, 163, 164, 168, 272
Ending on the fifth.............................	3	138, 139, 169
Ending on the third............................	1	170
Total.................................	12	

FIRST PROGRESSIONS

	Number of songs.	Catalogue numbers.
First progression upward.......................	5	136, 138, 169, 170, 272
First progression downward.....................	7	139, 149, 160, 162, 163, 164, 168
Total.................................	12	

ACCIDENTALS

	Number of songs.	
Songs containing accidentals	None	
Songs containing no accidentals	12	

Rhythmic Analysis

	Number of songs.	Catalogue numbers.
Beginning on unaccented portion of measure..................	3	139, 149, 170
Beginning on accented portion of measure.....................	9	136, 138, 160, 162, 163, 164, 165, 168, 272
Total.................................	12	
Metric unit of voice and drum the same......................	7	138, 139, 160, 162, 163, 164, 168
Metric unit of voice and drum different.....................	5	136, 149, 169, 170, 272
Total.................................	12	

a This song begins on the tonic, a portion of the melody being above the keynote and a portion below it.

STRUCTURAL ANALYSIS

	Number of songs.	Catalogue numbers.
Harmonic	2	162, 272
Melodic	10	136, 138, 139, 149, 160, 163, 164, 168, 169, 170
Total	12	

No. 198. DREAM SONG　　　(Catalogue no. 108)

Duplicate of no. 115 (Catalogue no. 209)

Sung by KI′OSE′WINI′NI

VOICE ♩ = 108
DRUM ♩ = 108

This rendition was by a younger singer and is less complete than no. 115, plainly showing the manner in which a song is slightly changed. This record was made more than a year previous to the other, and the duplication was accidental.

Two renditions of this song were secured from Ki'ose'wini'ni, one without the drum, and, after a lapse of several months, another with the drum. The rhythm of the song is identical, but the less important melody progressions vary slightly as the singer was inspired to elaborate somewhat. This transcription is from the first record and is believed to be more correct than the second.

No. 199. SONG OF THANKS FOR A PONY (Catalogue no. 137)

Duplicate of no. 152 (Catalogue no. 92)

Sung by GI'WITA'BINĚS

This duplication was made by a singer on the Red Lake reservation who was particularly free in his manner of singing. The original was made at Leech Lake. The song is evidently the same, the principal differences being due to the personality of the singer.

No. 200. LOVE SONG (Catalogue no. 145)

Duplicate of no. 138 (Catalogue no. 107)

Sung by GI'WITA'BINĚS

This and the two preceding songs are not included in the analysis of Red Lake songs, as they have been analyzed in a previous section.

Comparison of the two transcriptions will show the differences to be very slight, although the records were made on widely separated reservations.

INDEX

(For a list of the songs contained in this volume, see pages XI–XIX.)

211